REPORTS

Seven Days That Shook The World

The Collapse Of Soviet Communism

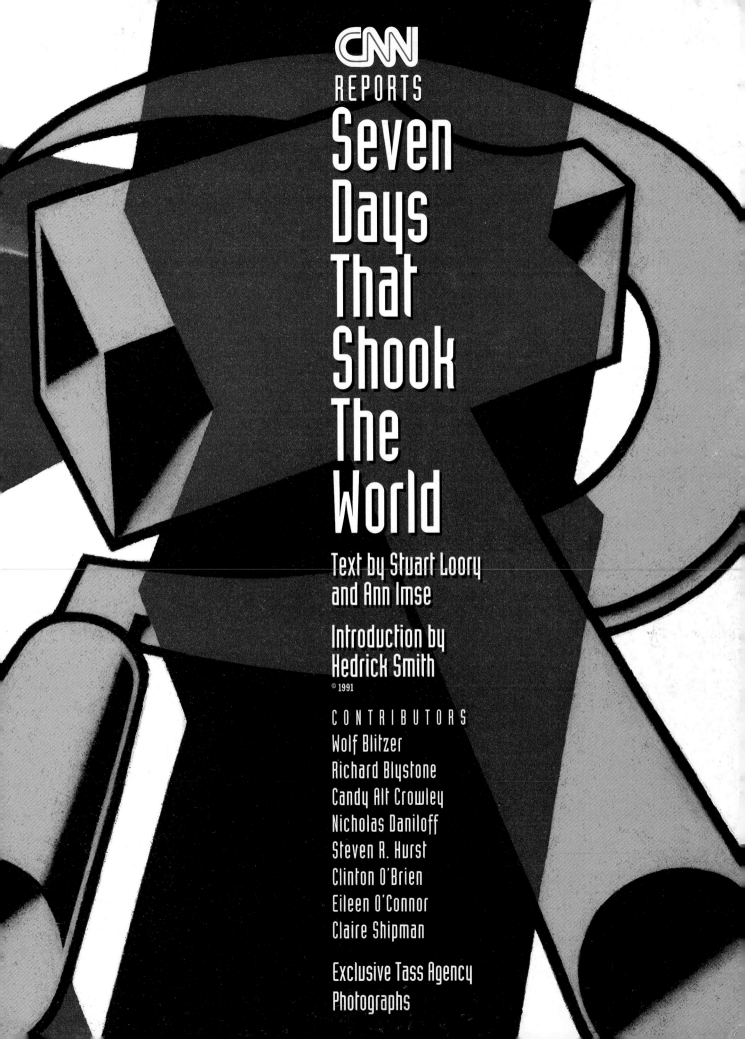

CNN
REPORTS

Seven Days That Shook The World

Text by Stuart Loory
and Ann Imse

Introduction by
Hedrick Smith

© 1991

CONTRIBUTORS

Wolf Blitzer

Richard Blystone

Candy Alt Crowley

Nicholas Daniloff

Steven R. Hurst

Clinton O'Brien

Eileen O'Connor

Claire Shipman

Exclusive Tass Agency
Photographs

SEVEN DAYS THAT SHOOK THE WORLD

Turner Publishing, Inc.

A SUBSIDIARY OF TURNER BROADCASTING SYSTEMS, INC.

ONE CNN CENTER, BOX 105366

ATLANTA, GEORGIA 30348-5366

FIRST EDITION

LIBRARY OF CONGRESS CATALOG CARD NUMBER

91-67690

10 9 8 7 6 5 4 3 2 1

ISBN 1-878685-11-2 (HARDCOVER)

ISBN 1-878685-12-0 (SOFTCOVER)

DISTRIBUTED BY ANDREWS AND MCMEEL

4900 MAIN STREET

KANSAS CITY, MISSOURI 64112

DESIGNED AND PRODUCED ON MACINTOSH COMPUTERS

USING QUARKEXPRESS 3.0 AND ALDUS FREEHAND 3.0.

COLOR SEPARATIONS BY GRAPHICS INTERNATIONAL, ATLANTA, GEORGIA

PRINTING BY R.R. DONNELLEY AND SONS, WILLARD, OHIO

FRONT COVER: Soldiers who turned their guns to the defense of the Russian Parliament Building stand atop their tanks in defiant solidarity with thousands of citizens protesting the coup on Monday evening, August 19, 1991.

BACK COVER: Moscow demonstrators torch a Soviet flag during protests against the August 1991 coup attempt. One year short of the diamond jubilee of the 1917 Bolshevik Revolution, Communist power falls to the forces of perestroika and glasnost.

R.E. Turner
Chairman of the Board
Turner Broadcasting System, Inc.

Tom Johnson
President, CNN

Staff for this book

AUTHORS:
Stuart H. Loory
Ann Imse

INTRODUCTION:
Hedrick Smith

CONTRIBUTORS:
Wolf Blitzer
Richard Blystone
Candy Alt Crowley
Nicholas Daniloff
Steven R. Hurst
Clinton O'Brien
Eileen O'Connor
Claire Shipman

Alan Schwartz
Editor-in-Chief

James W. Porges
Senior Editor

Larry Larson
Associate Editor

Marian G. Lord
Associate Editor

Michael J. Walsh
Director,
Design,
Photography,
& Production

Karen E. Robinson
Assistant Design &
Production Director

Carol Farrar Norton
Design/Assistant
Photography Editor

Barbara Griffin
Photography
Research Editor

Mary Beth Verhunce
Assistant
Photography
Research Editor

Ken Mowry
Informational
Graphics Designer

TABLE OF CONTENTS

Foreword by Tom Johnson

President, CNN

I was reluctant that Friday afternoon in August to go to Moscow. But if CNN was to get an interview with Soviet President Mikhail Gorbachev, a senior representative of the company would have to go in person to make the final pitch. A day and a half later, I was entering TASS headquarters.

A display of photographs in the window stopped me.

What images! Youngsters with painted faces similar to those making the antiwar protests of the 1960s and 70s in the United States. The menacing barrels of tank guns silhouetted against the Moscow skyline. Pictures of women at the barricades with signs saying "Soldiers, Don't Shoot Your Mothers" and of Boris Yeltsin atop a tank defiantly opposing the men who thought they had toppled Gorbachev.

Here was the photographic record of an astonishing week. Here was a book.

A few minutes later, I sat with Vitaly Ignatenko, the new head of TASS, the Soviet news agency, and he agreed. We decided on the spot to cooperate in publication of this book.

In 1917, John Reed, a young American journalist with Bolshevik sympathies, roamed the streets of Petrograd (which after almost three-quarters of a century as Leningrad is now again St. Petersburg) and recorded the events of the first Russian Revolution in *Ten Days That Shook the World*. Reed chronicled the beginning of an experiment that quickly turned sour, tragic, despotic, and, in the excesses of Josef Stalin, barbaric. Now CNN and TASS, in *Seven Days That Shook the World*, bring you the beginning of the conclusion of that story, the chronicle of the tumultuous end of the Soviet Communist experiment.

John Reed worked in a far simpler time. Broadcast journalism was then unknown. Reporters with nothing more complicated than notebooks and pencils covered stories. Today journalists equipped with computers, beepers, satellite telephones, flyaway earth stations, and camera crews bring viewers to the story instead of the story to the viewers. CNN has pioneered this kind of journalism in its eleven years. In the past two years, from Tienamen Square to the

Persian Gulf to the streets of Moscow, events — and their coverage — have moved in a rush.

We at CNN are dedicated to bringing our viewers in 123 countries the news as quickly and objectively as possible. We will continue to emphasize the live journalism that serves as a distant early warning of crisis in the modern world. We will not hesitate to step back and take a long look at history-in-the-making when the occasion calls for it. Our staff of professional men and women is uniquely qualified to do both jobs.

This book is a result of that combined effort.

Stuart H. Loory, a CNN vice-president, co-authored this book. He is a prize-winning journalist and author who in eleven years at CNN has served with distinction in many capacities. He established the CNN Moscow Bureau in 1983 and has been covering international relations and Soviet affairs for more than a quarter of a century. His co-author, Ann Imse, has just completed a three-year tour in Moscow for the Associated Press, reporting first hand the build-up to the August coup attempt, the coup, and the aftermath.

Other CNN staff members contributed insight, analysis, and personal experience to this project — most importantly Wolf Blitzer, defense correspondent; Richard Blystone, London correspondent; Candy Crowley, Washington correspondent; Steve Hurst, Moscow bureau chief; Eileen O'Connor, Moscow correspondent; and Claire Shipman, Moscow correspondent. The dozens of others who contributed to the success of this book are listed with thanks and with pride in the acknowledgments.

In addition, we are pleased to present an introduction by Hedrick Smith, the Pulitzer Prize-winning author of two classics on the Soviet Union, *The Russians* and *The New Russians*, as well as an essay by Nicholas Daniloff, a veteran journalist specializing in Russian affairs and author of *Two Lives, One Russia*.

Seven

INTRODUCTION BY HEDRICK SMITH

Shook

Days That

In the long sweep of time, there are rare and electric moments when history is suddenly thrust across an irrevocable divide—when with stunning swiftness events shake the foundations of a nation or an empire, forever transforming its political landscape, and the aftershocks radiate outward, altering the destiny of the entire world.

The World

The twentieth century has witnessed several such defining moments—the Bolshevik Revolution of 1917, the ascent of Adolf Hitler in 1933, the defeat of Nazi Germany and the onset of the Cold War in 1945, the breach of the Berlin Wall in 1989. Each was a turning point that affected the lives of hundreds of millions of people.

PREVIOUS PAGES: Night watch on the barricades: Thousands of volunteer citizens and soldiers form a human shield around the Russian "White House" where Yeltsin and his supporters defy the coup. **OPPOSITE:** A 14-ton symbol of terror — the statue of secret police founder Felix Dzerzhinsky — is toppled from its pedestal outside KGB headquarters late Thursday night, August 22.

A similar historical bolt of lightning struck Moscow during the third week of August 1991. That week marked the climax of the Second Russian Revolution, a peaceful political revolution launched in 1985 by Communist leader Mikhail Gorbachev but then swept far beyond his vision and his intentions by the powerful forces of democratic populism and nationalism that he had set free. To adapt John Reed's famous description of the Bolshevik Revolution, the third week in August 1991 was "Seven Days That Shook the World."

In that one volcanic week, an embryonic democracy faced down the crumbling despotism of the Soviet state and then demolished the command post of world communism,

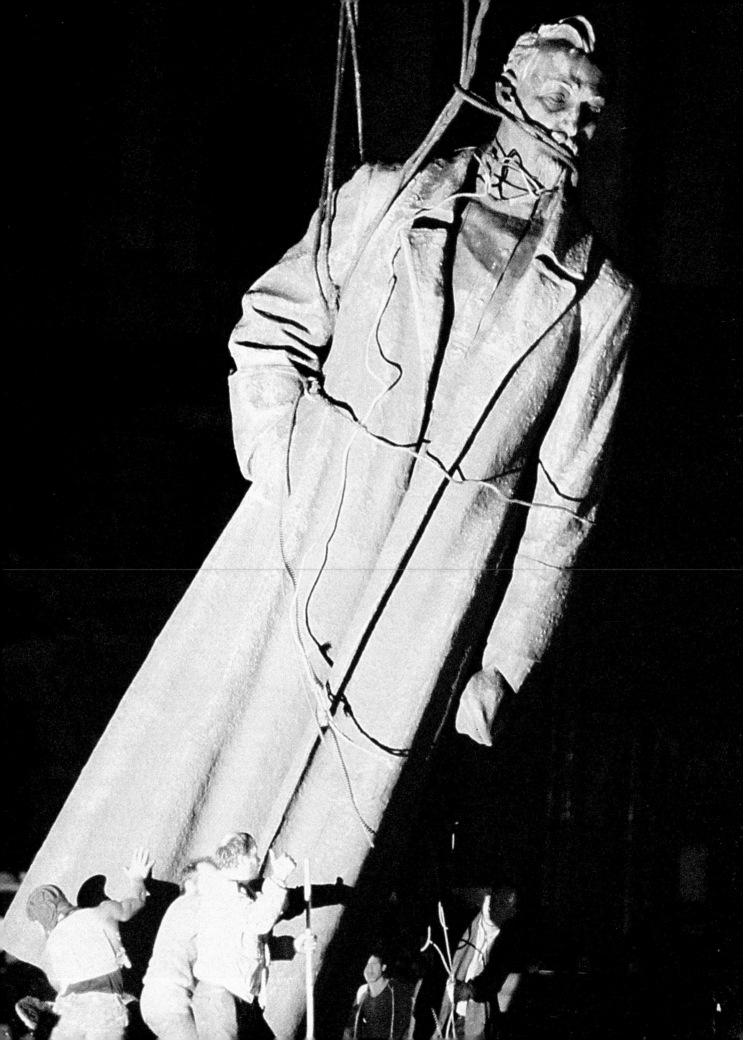

shattered the totalitarian state created by Lenin and Stalin, and broke apart the Russian Empire assembled by the czars. We in the rest of the world quickly felt the consequences.

Ironically, it was the defenders of the old order, the palace guard of the self-perpetuating Soviet power elite, who provoked the fateful confrontation. They brought about their own demise by launching a suicidal coup d'état.

History was turned on its head. In 1917, Bolshevism had seized power with a coup d'état riding a tide of popular discontent; in 1991, Bolshevism was thrown out of power by a coup that ran against the popular mood.

The coup in August 1991 was a desperate, last-ditch attempt by the reactionary apparatchiks of the Soviet state to save themselves by restoring authoritarian rule. They seized command and called out the tanks, convinced that an awesome show of force would intimidate the Russian people into the political submission taught to them through the centuries. The conspirators were out to strangle the spirit of democracy in Russian cities and the rising wave of secession sweeping from the Baltic republics to other regions.

But there immediately arose a bold opposition that demonstrated the magnitude of the changes that had already taken place in Russian society and in the psychology of the people. The hard-line coup had come too late. During six years of Gorbachev's perestroika, as the coup leaders and the world discovered, ordinary Russians had lost their fear and Soviet dictatorship had lost its teeth.

For the first time in Russian history, the Russian rank-and-file — especially young people and the new entrepreneurs – dared to put their lives on the line to defend democracy. And they won. They stymied the coup and defined a new destiny for their nation. Galvanized by the courageous defiance of Russian President Boris Yeltsin, reinforced by demonstrations in other cities, and protected by crucial mutinies within the armed forces and KGB, tens of thousands of Muscovites met the tanks at the barricades outside Yeltsin's White House, the parliament building of the Russian Republic. In less than seventy-two hours the faceless tyrants of Soviet communism retreated, unable to muster the will or the forces to bring the popular revolt to heel.

The daring of the democrats and the unraveling of the coup is a powerful and moving human story.

Seen from afar, this is the clash of the contending forces of democracy and despotism. Seen up close, it is a mosaic of vivid and touching personal epiphanies. In a system that had deliberately deprived individuals of the power of decision and personal responsibility, it was individual decisions that fueled the power of revolt and drained the coup of its strength.

It was Air Force General Yevgeny Shaposhnikov threatening to use his fighters against Army helicopters if an attack were launched against Yeltsin's stronghold; leaders of the most elite unit of the KGB refusing to obey orders for a commando assault; Valentin Lazutkin, a television executive, defying the coup's censors and putting pictures of Yeltsin and the civilian resistance on national television; a KGB colonel, sent to prevent such heresy, secretly raising a glass of vodka with Lazutkin, in toast to the rebellion. It was another KGB agent, on a subway, slipping a note to People's Deputy Oleg Kalugia with the warning that democratic deputies were about to be arrested that afternoon; the commander of troops at Gorbachev's Crimean dacha, alarmed by the President's house arrest, praying for the safety of Gorbachev and his family; Alexander Yakovlev, one of the liberal architects of perestroika, sleeping with a pistol under his pillow as protection, and later savoring his son's triumphant phone call that the coup plotters were in retreat. From the barricades, young Yakovlev joyfully bellowed, "Papa, they have shriveled!"

American Journalist John Reed traveled to Russia to report on the 1917 Bolshevik Revolution and wrote an eyewitness account called "Ten Days That Shook the World." He died in 1920 and is buried in the Kremlin.

A Cataclysm: The Death of an Empire

In their dizzying triumph, ordinary Russians could barely fathom the full significance of what they had wrought. For the collapse of the coup caused a tidal wave of change. By their suicidal stupidity and incompetence, the plotters hastened the destruction of all they had fought to protect. They accelerated trends of reform under way before the coup was launched. Their failure brought on the swift, final smashing of the old order.

"In three days, we made the march of a decade," jubilantly trumpeted Oleg Kalugia, a former KGB major general who had defected to the democratic reformers eighteen months earlier. "In a compressed capsule of time, we did what we could not have done in six years."

Gigantic statues were communism's icons. Before the end of that historic week in August, huge statues of Lenin and other Bolsheviks like Felix Dzerzhinsky, the first chief of the Soviet secret police, had been toppled by euphoric crowds from Moscow to Estonia; Gorbachev had quit the Communist Party and padlocked its headquarters; Yeltsin and Gorbachev had barred the once omnipotent Party's activities and nationalized its property. They had arrested the Old Guard plotters, fired an entire cabinet, launched purges of the Army and KGB. They had decapitated the central government.

The sudden power vacuum at the center of Moscow's 74-year-old Communist dynasty energized centrifugal forces and caused the almost instantaneous disintegration of the Soviet state. Long-subjugated peoples, who had

BELOW: Reacting to news of the "emergency," Muscovites mount an overnight vigil outside Yeltsin's "White House" — the Russian Parliment building. OVERLEAF PAGES 18-19: Russian revolutionaries gather for a conference with the Romanian Commission in 1917. OVERLEAF PAGES 20-21: Coup protestors form a human chain as a symbol of solidarity during the "Rally of Victors" on August 22, 1991.

never freely entered the Soviet Union or the Russian Empire, were suddenly liberated and empowered to decide their own destinies. Overnight, Moscow had to deal with them as equals. For three years they had seethed with nationalist fervor; now there was no army, no KGB, no Communist Party, no central government apparatus to hold them in check. In quick succession, the dominoes fell: the Baltic republics, the Ukraine, Moldavia, Byelorussia, Georgia, Armenia, and even the politically underdeveloped republics of central Asia, all declared their independence.

Trying to rescue slim vestiges of unity from the debris, Gorbachev and Yeltsin persuaded the Congress of People's Deputies, the federal legislature, to ratify the fait accompli — granting sweeping powers to the fifteen individual republics and rendering the central government all but impotent — in the hope that such massive concessions would entice the republics voluntarily to form a loose new confederation. But the first act of the transitional State Council was to recognize

Their tanks decorated with flowers, Army units mass in central Moscow and await orders to strike.
OVERLEAF: Demonstrators watch a military truck burn during violent clashes Tuesday night, August 20.

the independence of Latvia, Lithuania, and Estonia.

What had been called the Soviet Union was no more. What had been the epicenter of world communism lay in ruins. Communist China's aging leaders might bask in an economic boom, but they were left ideologically isolated and vulnerable in the years to come to domestic pressures for political change. Cuba's President Fidel Castro, long the beacon of Third World Communists, was set adrift by Gorbachev who cut off aid and moved to withdraw 11,000 Soviet troops. Yeltsin admitted openly that the Soviet experiment in communism had failed, and he lamented that Russia had been its laboratory.

"For us, all this was an earthquake," observed Eduard Sagalayev, one of Moscow's most experienced television producers. "It was like a natural catastrophe, a geological cataclysm which destroys the old earth we have known and creates an entirely new geography — new mountains, new rivers, new lakes, new valleys. Everything familiar is changed. In a natural calamity, there are victims — animals, people, nature itself; and this great process of our historical change will also entail tragedy for masses of people. It will not be possible to live through it peacefully, tranquilly. This is the end of a great power, the end of the Russian Empire, the end of a stage of our history that dates back long before 1917. But it brings progress: It is the movement of the people of Russia into the civilized world."

Why the Coup d'État Happened

The chain of events that produced that pivotal week of August 1991 began months and even years before. The decisive showdown did not come as a bolt out of the blue. History had been building to this climactic moment.

In a very real sense the seeds of conflict were sewn soon after Josef Stalin died in 1953. Stalin's successor — that ebullient, unpredictable, maverick Communist leader, Nikita Khrushchev — shook the pure faith of many Soviet Communists in February 1956 by unmasking Stalin as a bloodthirsty dictator who had coldly and unjustly sent great masses of loyal Communists to their deaths before firing squads or in the icy gulags of Siberia. In the late 1950s and early 1960s, Khrushchev had launched a period of ferment and experimentation that touched off political debate. As students and young adults, Gorbachev, Yeltsin, and their generation imbibed the spirit of anti-Stalinist reform and the freer ways of Khrushchev. They joined his army of protégés (and later became his political heirs), only to see their hopes for a more open and dynamic society snuffed out by the long static rule of Leonid Brezhnev.

But Khrushchev had opened the door; it was never again completely shut. Ideas of democracy were nurtured under Brezhnev by a tiny but daring band of political dissidents, whose spiritual leader was the late physicist Andrei Sakharov. Even among officialdom, beneath the surface conformity, several different tendencies developed inside the Soviet Communist Party – a sliver of reformers who wanted to carry on where Khrushchev had left off; a stony phalanx of neo-Stalinists bent on restoring iron rule; and echelons of leaders and opportunists, opposed to any real change because change threatened their creature comforts and their political baronies.

Brezhnev's death in November 1982 ushered in an interim period of seesaw between the tentative stirrings of early reform under Party leader Yuri Andropov (1983) and the stagnant rigidity of his successor, Konstantin Chernenko (1984).

After Gorbachev took over the reins in March 1985, he let in fresh breezes, but it was two years before he moved forcefully with what he called perestroika — the "reconstruction" of Soviet society. By early 1990, he was following a zig-zag course between reform and retrenchment. His political pendulum swung between a compulsion to destroy the top-heavy structure of the Stalinist state in order to modernize the Soviet economy and mobilize the energies and creativity of his people, and his conflicting instinct to preserve stability and national unity by clinging to familiar institutions of Party, state, and socialist economics.

The problem was that Gorbachev's policies of glasnost ("greater openness") and perestroika ("reconstruction") had unleashed two very powerful trends which he could not control: first, a populist revolution demanding genuine democratic change and removal of the Stalinist power structure; and second, a nationalist, anticolonial revolution in the minority republics demanding self-determination and threatening to break away from Russian rule. By mid-1989, Gorbachev found these two offspring of perestroika challenging him, pushing beyond what he had in mind. Gorbachev equivocated, then tried in various ways to reassert personal control, and later retreated into the arms of the Old Guard. He tried to play both the revolutionary and the ruler, both agent of change and protector of continuity.

The more Gorbachev's reforms gained their own momentum, the more he became paralyzed by his own ambivalence and the more he stoked the coals of confrontation between reform and reaction. He straddled

two rival and inimical systems of power: the populist power of democratic reformers elected as leaders of republics, national legislatures, and city councils, and inspired by Gorbachev's calls for political revolution; and the elitist power of the closed Party-state apparatus, determined to throttle democracy and sabotage any serious reforms. Ironically, by his inability to choose sides and fix a certain course, Gorbachev was the unintentional creator of the clash in August 1991.

In the final ten months before the failed coup of August, his political swings became more extreme. In his darkest period, the winter of 1990–91, Gorbachev aligned himself with the high command of the Army, KGB, and Interior Ministry for bloody military crackdowns in the Baltic republics and a political purge of central television. But that tactic failed — stymied by Yeltsin, the Baltic nationalists, striking coal miners, and mass demonstrations in Moscow and Leningrad. Once again, Gorbachev swung his pendulum the other way — into alliance with Yeltsin. He began drafting an agreement to reshape the structure of the Soviet Union to meet the demands of reformers and nationalists.

That move brought an ominous harbinger of August. The Old Guard leaders, infuriated by Gorbachev's tactics, tried to strip him of important powers in what was called "a constitutional coup." In June, Prime Minister Valentin Pavlov, Defense

Bodyguards protect Yeltsin during the crucial night of August 20-21. OPPOSITE: A masked member of the elite KGB Alpha unit, the same unit ordered to arrest Boris Yeltsin in the early hours of the coup.

Minister Dmitry Yazov, KGB Chief Vladimir Kryuchkov, and Interior Minister Boris Pugo proposed to the Supreme Soviet, the legislature, that some of Gorbachev's most crucial authority be legally turned over to Pavlov. At the last minute, Gorbachev woke up and scotched the cabal. He won the legislative vote, but strangely he did not punish his disloyal lieutenants.

In July, Gorbachev's long-time liberal adviser, Alexander Yakovlev, urged Gorbachev to fire his reactionary lieutenants, who were sabotaging reform and undermining him in the name of saving the country from chaos.

"I appeal to you — you have terrible people around you," Yakovlev told Gorbachev during one three-hour conversation. "Do something about this dirty circle."

"You exaggerate," Gorbachev replied.

Rather than break openly with the reactionaries, Gorbachev left them in office — strategically placed to attack him on another day. Indeed, the same four who had attempted "the constitutional coup" were the core conspirators of the real coup in August.

This time, Yakovlev actually predicted a coup was coming two days ahead of time. I asked him later if he had had advance evidence. No, he replied, just "the smell in the air."

The final detonator that ignited the coup was Gorbachev's agreement to join Yeltsin and nine other republic leaders on August 20 in signing a new union treaty that would move significant powers from the central government to the republics. The republics would gain primary control over the economy, over internal politics, and over the power to

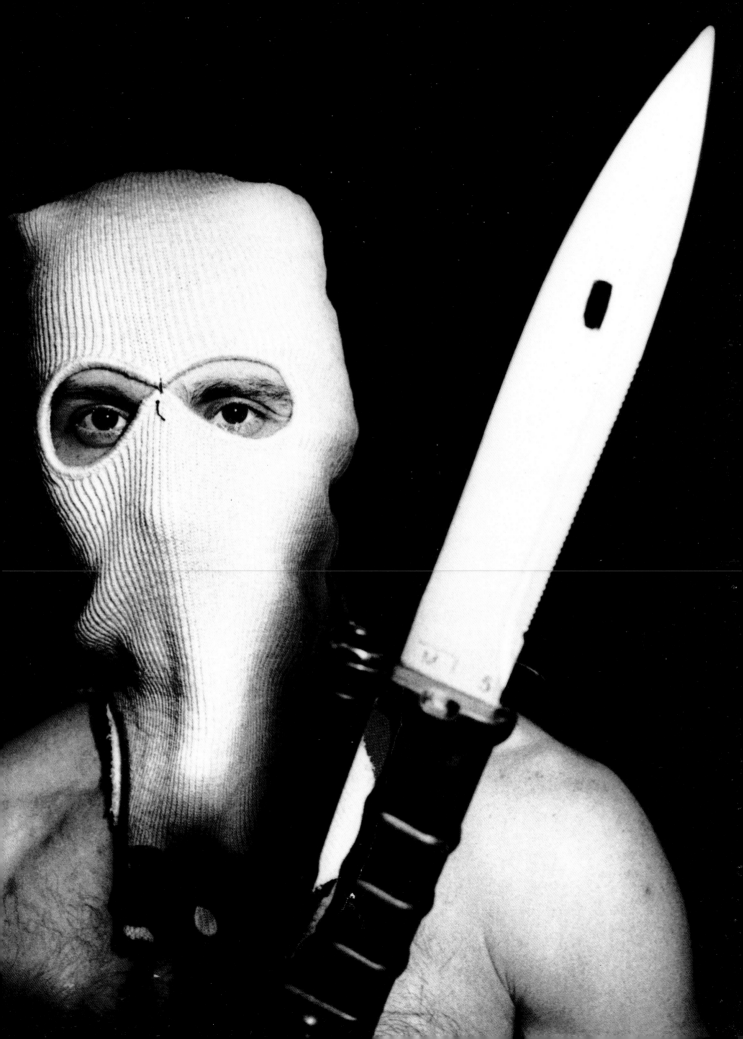

tax. And they would get the right to secede. The Kremlin and all its ministries and agencies would be grievously weakened. Gorbachev's lieutenants, the high command of the central government, clearly understood that this new treaty not only spelled the end of the Soviet Union, but also would be their political death warrant. Rather than let that happen, they staged a preemptive coup d'état to block the treaty and save their own necks.

The Coup and Why It Failed

In opposition to the "party of hope," as the democratic reformers called themselves, the eight-man Emergency Committee that staged the coup was "the party of fear."

Announcing their takeover to the Soviet people on August 19, the "gang of eight" painted a dark scenario. They played upon the mounting fears among the Soviet people that reform had run out of control, the economy was in chaos, democracy was synonymous with anarchy, the Soviet state was being ripped apart, and the country was on the brink of ethnic civil war.

"A mortal danger hangs over our great homeland!" they declared. "Taking advantage of the freedoms that have been granted, trampling on the shoots of democracy that have only just appeared, extremist forces emerged that adopted a course of destroying the Soviet Union, seeking the collapse of the state, and aiming to seize power at all costs.... Every citizen feels a growing uncertainty about tomorrow and deep alarm for his children's future."

Exaggerating the dangers came naturally to the coup plotters; after all, the crumbling Soviet state was their own pyramid of power. They were fearful of the future and anxious for the order of Stalinist times. To the masses troubled by the tumult of the Gorbachev years, the coup plotters offered themselves as protectors of order, stability, and national unity. They knew that Gorbachev's popularity had plummeted and assumed that the masses would be happy to see him pushed aside in favor of what Russians call "the iron fist." They were counting not only on tanks to intimidate the masses, but on the inbred reflexes of ordinary Russians to choose

single strong, charismatic leader; they had no Stalin, no Saddam Hussein, to make swift decisions and insist on loyal execution. As a committee of eight, they disagreed over strategy and tactics — most crucially on the issue of whether and when to resort to violence to achieve their ends. Moreover, the evidence suggests that while the inner conspirators had probably pondered a coup for months, they launched the actual plot too hastily, perhaps after getting a tip that Gorbachev was having crippling back pains on his Crimean vacation. It appears they began serious preparations only three or four days ahead, too little time to line up all the necessary forces. Only two or three hours before ordering tanks to roll, they were still trying to recruit key supporters. They never did obtain the political endorsement of the Communist Party leadership or of the conservative, anti-Gorbachev "Soyuz" faction of the parliament.

LEFT: At a news conference on Monday, members of the "dirty circle" claim Gorbachev is too ill to govern. BELOW: Gorbachev's son-in-law privately video tapes a statement by Gorbachev while he is still under house arrest in Foros. The tape is later shown on Soviet television. OVERLEAF: Protesters crowd a young soldier as they climb atop his tank on Monday, August 19.

order over the anarchic uncertainties of freedom.

After the coup, the tendency was to explain its failure primarily on grounds that its leaders were incompetent bunglers and drunkards, who neglected the most obvious steps to silence the opposition and to insure their own success. It is true that Gorbachev's lieutenants were as fatally inefficient in running the coup as they had been in running the government and the economy. They could issue blood-curdling decrees, order 250,000 pairs of handcuffs and 300,000 arrest forms, set up new detention camps outside of Moscow, and yet they could not carry out a successful coup d'état against virtually unarmed resistance. So much of their lives had been spent exalting central planning, that they confused paper-plans with action in the real world.

The coup plotters were hampered, too, by the lack of a

But to explain their failure as primarily a product of sheer incompetence is to accept a half-truth that misses far deeper and more significant revelations about the plotters, about the opposition, and about the nature and depth of the transformation in Soviet society since 1985.

Fundamentally, the coup of August 1991 failed because its leaders were pathetically ignorant of their own society. They were so insulated from the popular mood by yes-men and the lying and sycophancy endemic to the Soviet bureaucracy that they did not comprehend the magnitude of the sea-change that had already taken place during perestroika.

The failure of the coup

leaders was not a failure of petty omissions, but a failure of grand miscalculations. They bleated continuously about the chaos caused by Gorbachev's budding democracy, but they did not understand the power of that democracy: the simple but critical fact that pro-reform leaders like Boris Yeltsin, Leningrad Mayor Anatoly Sobchak, and the Baltic presidents had forged a genuine connection with the masses that would rally hundreds of thousands of people. Even more stunning, the coup leaders did not understand that their own power had become an empty shell, that their troops no longer felt the fear of Stalin's icy discipline or the pull of Communist ideology or the simple duty to obey orders. The marshals and generals in command of the coup — baby-faced KGB Chief Kryuchkov (sarcastically nicknamed "the Cherub" by his underlings); the lumbering, cautious Defense Minister Yazov; and the conspiratorial Interior Minister Pugo — did not anticipate the rebellion within their own ranks from the colonels and majors and captains who refused to follow their orders. For it is an old Russian trait, captured in folk wisdom, for Russians to "think one thing, say another, and do a third." In short, disguise their real feelings and actions from superiors. It was not simply that orders lost their force as they descended through the ranks, but the mentality of the generation of Old Guard generals in their sixties was at odds with the mentality of many majors and colonels in their forties, and a world apart from most draftee privates and corporals in their late teens and early twenties.

Analyzing the coup commanders, General Yevgeny Shaposhnikov, the 49-year-old Air Force commander who sided with Yeltsin, remarked tellingly: "These were a generation of officers born in the 1920s. They emerged during the reactionary time of Stalin. When perestroika began at the top, they supported it. But when it continued at the grass-roots level, they failed to under-

stand it. This explains the actions that they took and the disaster that they suffered — because they were out of touch with realities in the armed forces and in society."

Their second grand miscalculation was to insist on the facade of legality for their seizure of power and then limit their actions accordingly. Vice-President Gennady Yanayev, the weak-willed front-man for the coup, cited Article 127(7) as the legal basis for seizing power; he asserted that Gorbachev was so ill that he had to be temporarily replaced. Almost no one bought the big lie about Gorbachev's being incapacitated. But the plotters felt they needed the appearance of constitutional legitimacy for two primary reasons. One was to gain acceptance abroad in order to forestall international support for the opposition and to maintain the vital flow of aid and trade to the Soviet Union. The second, evidently, was to be able to go back to Gorbachev once they had firmly established their control and to present him with a fait accompli and thereby secure his blessing and cooperation for a new authoritarian regime.

Remarks by Yanayev and Prime Minister Pavlov, hinting at disagreements among the coup plotters, suggest that the civilians wanted to avoid violence and refused to support bloody suppressions. At one point, well into the coup, Yanayev summoned Leonid Kravchenko, the chief of state television, to prepare a television statement vowing there would be no bloodshed.

"We will not take the White House by force," Yanayev told Kravchenko. "There will be no arrests."

Defense Minister Dmitry Yazov wheeled on Yanayev and snapped derisively, "It's not you who decides, Genna."

"Did you hear Yeltsin's decree that we are criminals and they will arrest us?" chimed in the KGB's Kryuchkov. "And you are going to tell them there will be no arrests? You can't do that!"

Even so, all had accepted the legalistic strategy at the outset and that handicapped the conspirators in the crucial early hours of the coup. The Soviet KGB and the military had ample experience in overthrowing governments and in bloody crackdowns, from Hungary in 1956 to Czechoslovakia in 1968 to General Wojciech Jaruzelski's declaration of martial law in Poland in 1981.

The night before martial law was announced in Poland, it was said, the Polish army and police, operating with KGB advice and intelligence, arrested up to five thousand key figures of Solidarity and Poland's political opposition. But in the Soviet coup of August 1991, no such mass arrests were carried out during the critical night of August 18–19. So long as the coup plotters hoped to maintain the pretense of legality, they could not arrest Yeltsin. Since Yeltsin was the popularly elected president of Russia, his arrest would have been an immediate admission to the world that the coup was a naked seizure of power. Only toward the end of the first day, after a press conference where it was evident that the claim of legality would not wash, was the way cleared for open suppression.

By then, the chance for a lightning swoop to round up opposition leaders had disappeared. Crowds were already in the streets of Moscow coalescing around Yeltsin, a born rebel with an instinct for the jugular and a keen sense of timing. He had quickly fashioned the defiant and unforgettable symbol of resistance — his sturdy figure planted astride a tank, his arm aloft, calling for troops to mutiny and civilians to go on strike to block the "reactionary, anticonstitutional coup." At that moment — at noon, Monday, August 19 — the crowd numbered fewer than one thousand people and Yeltsin seemed uncertain whether the soldiers would try to grab him. Nonetheless, he savaged the coup plotters, and support mushroomed. Russians had been taught how to respond to a military crackdown by the brave Baltic nationalists in January 1991. On television, they had seen unarmed Lithuanians and Latvians surround their parliament buildings, throwing up crude barricades to block tanks and opposing troops with their bare hands. Now, Russians applied the Baltic lesson.

Television may not lie but it often exaggerates and magnifies, in this case giving the impression of a massive popular rebellion. Actually, the crowds outside Yeltsin's White House probably never exceeded 150,000 — not very large for a national capital of nine million people, when Prague, Leipzig, and Yerevan had produced demonstrations of 500,000 or more.

On Tuesday night, August 20, when Yeltsin's stronghold braced for an assault, only about 30,000 people braved danger and a cold rain. The core protesters were the young sons and daughters of the elite and a sprinkling of young Russian Orthodox priests, all too young to have haunting personal memories of past repressions. With them were some private entrepreneurs who understood that the coup's success would kill chances for market economics. But the great mass of Muscovites, especially middle-aged Russians conditioned by past repression, sat on the fence, watching, waiting, passive, living their normal routines during the three critical days when the fate of the coup was decided.

Nonetheless, instant mass communications, both Soviet and international, carried reports of resistance and fanned the fires of rebellion. Moscow's prodemocracy Echo Radio was shut down by KGB squads only to return to the air again and again. The pro-Yeltsin Russian Television and Radio Network, immediately taken off the air by the coup, made videotapes and shipped them to twenty major cities through airline pilots and sympathetic travelers. It even managed one burst of broadcasts to the Soviet Far East and Eastern Siberia. Amateur radio operators showed up at Yeltsin's headquarters Tuesday to set up a short-range radio link to the Moscow region, extended the next day when transmitters brought from Voronezh, 280 miles from Moscow, were smuggled into the White House. In keeping with their claim of legality, the coup conspirators allowed Western news media to operate; Gorbachev and millions of Soviet citizens followed every breaking development from broadcasts of the BBC, Voice of America, and CNN. Editors of liberal newspapers banned by the coup combined to produce one underground paper, printed secretly on the presses of the pro-free enterprise weekly, *Kommersant*. Faxes and copying machines spread the message of resistance by reproducing leaflets that were plastered all over the Moscow subway system.

Learning from Baltic defiance, unarmed Russians defend their own parliament building on Monday, August 19. OVERLEAF: On Tuesday, August 20, a mass rally fills Palace Square in Leningrad. As rebellion spreads, doubts grow about military loyalty, and coup plotters find it increasingly difficult to maintain control.

Rebellion spread quickly, making it impossible for the conspirators to gain full control by cracking down in one place. Leningrad became the second center of the resistance; 200,000 people demonstrated in the square outside the Winter Palace where the Bolshevik Revolution had toppled the last czar. Other mass demonstrations took place from Sverdlovsk in the Ural Mountains, to Murmansk in the far north, to Kishinev, the Moldavian capital located near Rumania. By one count, roughly one-third (53) of the provincial governments in the Russian Republic declared their support for Yeltsin, and only four declared their loyalty to the coup plotters. By the second day, not only was the coup opposed by republican governments in Russia and the Baltics, but in Kirgizia, Kazakhstan, Moldavia, and by part of the Ukrainian government. The spread of rebellion, though less visible on global television than the confrontation in Moscow, was crucial. The coup plotters would need many military units to quash rebellion in different centers, and the military's loyalty and reliability was quickly thrown into question.

Military mutinies and defections were at least as important to the failure of the coup as the popular resistance. Clearly, one of the major miscalculations of the coup plotters was their failure to recognize that much of the Army was infected with the same democratic spirit as the masses, especially among the draftees who manned the tanks. The fraternizing and protests of the civilians played on those common bonds and disarmed the young troops. Near Yeltsin's headquarters, women slung a huge banner appealing to the troops: "Don't Shoot Your Mothers."

Beyond that, Yeltsin had great popularity among the military. In his election as president of Russia in June, only two months before the coup, Yeltsin had polled perhaps half of the military vote, and higher proportions among younger soldiers and junior officers. Seemingly blind to this fact, the coup's high command made the stunning mistake of occupying Moscow with the Kantomirovsky Tank Division and the Tula Paratroop Division, units based near Moscow in regions where Yeltsin had done heavy politicking. Not surprisingly,

The parents of Dmitri Komar grieve at the coffin of their son. He was one of three civilians killed in Moscow on Tuesday night, August 20, before the ultimately suicidal coup collapsed from within.

some of the first small tank units to swing over to Yeltsin came from the Kantomirovsky Division; one of the first high-level commanders to meet secretly with Yeltsin was Major General Alexander Lebed, commander of the Tula paratroopers. The national paratroop commander, General Pavel Grachev, was also opposed to the coup.

Another advantage to Yeltsin was his tie with the Air Force. Shrewdly, he had chosen an Air Force ace of the Afghan war, Colonel Alexander Rutskoi, as his vice-presidential running mate. Rutskoi used his military contacts to unravel the coup from inside. Among the high officers who quickly opposed the dispatch of troops into Moscow was the Air Force commander, General (now Marshal) Yevgeny Shaposhnikov. More than once, Shaposhnikov stuck his neck out, urging Marshal Yazov to pull Army units out of Moscow and to quit the "gang of eight." During a tense argument on the night of August 20, when Yazov and the KGB were considering an assault that would use helicopters as well as tanks, Shaposhnikov threatened to scramble Air Force fighters against the helicopters.

The assault on the White House never took place, not only because of Air Force opposition and defections in the Army, but also because the KGB's crack commando units, the Alpha Group and the Beta Group, mutinied. Orders were given several times and refused each time by the troop commanders. In post-coup interviews, the KGB elite commandos said they were motivated by pro-democracy sentiments and a reluctance to trigger the massive bloodshed that an assault would have entailed. In addition, any smart KGB officer knew that the KGB was a feared and hated institution among the military as well as among the general population. With some Army units lined up on Yeltsin's side, a KGB-led attack on Yeltsin would have risked a wider conflict between the KGB and uncommitted Army units.

And so, without the ability to use their own crack

units to crush a determined and growing opposition, the coup plotters had to back down. Their misguided and ultimately suicidal plot collapsed from within.

What Comes after the Successful Revolt

With the collapse of the August coup, Russia has passed into a new era – a new stage of reform driven by a new leader.

Gorbachev, the architect of perestroika and once the prime agent of change, has become a transitional figure, a front-man for policies decided by others, a broker among republic leaders who hold real power. Between 1985 and 1990, Gorbachev established himself as one of the seminal figures of the Twentieth Century: He freed Eastern Europe from the Communist yoke; he permitted the reunification of Germany and signed the first agreements for nuclear arms reductions and the withdrawal of Soviet forces from Europe; at home, he broke the power monopoly of the Soviet Communist Party and provided the breeding ground of a political opposition. He generated vital institutional changes – free speech, a freer press, elections, legislatures, the emergence of new leaders and new political movements, and the stunning notion that society should be ruled by law and not by arbitrary force from on high. In fact, these were the very changes which rescued Gorbachev from the putsch. But his zig-zagging and ambivalence had undercut his popularity. So when the reactionary conspiracy struck him down, the democratic reformers and the throngs in the streets rose up – not to save Gorbachev but to save themselves; not to perpetuate perestroika but to launch a more ambitious democracy; not rallying to Gorbachev's banner, but to that of a new leader.

Boris Yeltsin, the renegade ex-Communist who had made himself the sworn enemy of the Party apparat since his ouster from the Politburo in 1987, was the man of the hour. As the popular hero who had led the popular revolt, Yeltsin eclipsed Gorbachev not only in popularity but in real power. Long before the coup, Yeltsin had earned what Gorbachev had squandered by his political hesitation and ambivalence – mass popular support. Yeltsin had won legitimacy at the ballot box: three election victories in three successive years, culminating in June 1991 with his victory as the first popularly elected national leader in one thousand years of Russian history. What is more, Yeltsin projected what Gorbachev had lost — a strong sense of direction. In place of Gorbachev's hesitation, he had an action agenda: privatizing the economy, rooting the ubiquitous networks of the Communist Party out of Russian society, dismantling the apparatus of the centralized Soviet state, and shifting real power to the republics. But while Yeltsin had proven himself as the rebel leader, he had yet to prove himself as a leader who could govern the huge land of Russia and deal with other national leaders on an equal footing.

For the successful uprising against the August coup opened the way to peril as well as promise. The people who put down the August coup soon discovered that destroying the Communist grip on the Kremlin did not insure democracy in a society where the institutions and habits of democracy were so fragile. Russia, the Ukraine, and the new independent Baltic states might proclaim and protect a free press and move toward a multiparty system, but in Central Asian republics like Tadzhikistan and Uzbekistan, former Communist Party bosses simply changed labels and began setting up new one-party dictatorships; a similar trend emerged in Georgia under the anti-Communist nationalist Zviad Gamsakhurdia.

The handicaps facing sincere reformers were huge. Smashing the old central government dispersed power to the republics, but that raised the risk of ethnic conflict. Indeed, right after the coup collapsed, Yeltsin aroused new fears of Russian dominance. He touched raw nerves in the Ukraine and Kazakhstan by threatening to make territorial claims against those republics, each of which has large ethnic Russian minorities, if the two republics refused to join Russia in a new confederation. Nursultan Nazarbayev, the Kazakh leader, warned of the danger

Soviet citizens ride defiently atop the first armored vehicle that attempts to enter Red Square. OVERLEAF: Fist raised, Boris Yeltsin becomes the central icon of the Second Russian Revolution.

of inter-republic warfare, and Yeltsin's colleagues quickly pulled him back from ethnic brinkmanship. Gorbachev helped calm the waters.

The plunging economy posed another awesome obstacle. Neither the old central plan nor the incentives of market economics insured enough production to feed ordinary people adequately and guarantee them a decent standard of living. The rapid unraveling of the old Soviet empire raised the new danger of economic rivalries, in which the larger, stronger republics would beggar their neighbors and make economic reform all but impossible. Yeltsin, Gorbachev, and others strove valiantly to retain some bare framework of economic cooperation that would provide the base for eventual improvements.

But in every walk of life the successful rebellion against the August coup had monumentally transformed the structure and environment of the political landscape, making the entire enterprise of reform more unpredictable than ever. Yet even if there were new problems, there were also unmistakable gains. The paralyzing burden of a central government opposed to democracy, national self-determination, and market

economics had been swept away. The centurions of the old order had been put in jail or thrown on the defensive. Even facing great hardships, ordinary people felt relief from the black threat of repression, and democratic reformers sensed new opportunities. Yeltsin — like Gorbachev in 1985 — proclaimed that all which had gone before was inadequate. Like the earlier Gorbachev, too, Yeltsin plunged boldly into the uncharted territory of yet-to-be-defined reforms, confident that positive change would generate its own momentum. Bold and undaunted, he thrust his nation and his people into a new stage of history without looking back.

Whatever the uncertainties, the political earthquake of August 1991 has given democracy in Russia both a human face for the rest of the world to see as well as a better chance to succeed than ever before in the millennium of Russian history. The door to new experimentation is open wide, if new leaders are capable of grasping the opportunity.

© 1991–HEDRICK SMITH. *Hedrick Smith is author of* The New Russians, *which has been updated since the August coup.*

Soviet Union at a Glance

Although the Soviet Union is being torn apart by the collapse of the Communist Party and rising nationalist patriotism, economic survival may hinge on cooperative agreements between the newly independent republics.

LITHUANIA
Dominated for the last 400 years by Poland and then Russia. Industrialized, with heavy engineering, shipbuilding, and building materials. Produces two-thirds of world's amber. Mostly urban. Population-3.7 million. Lithuanian-80%, Russian-9%. Production-1.4% of Soviet economy.

LATVIA
Historically dominated by Scandinavians, Swedes, Russians. Riga is the capital and major port. Manufactures railroad cars, paper, and woolen goods. Has cattle, grain, and forest resources. Population-2.7 million. Latvian-54%, Russian-33%. Production-1.1% of Soviet economy.

ESTONIA
Briefly free following World War I after being taken from Sweden in 1721 by Peter the Great. Smallest of the Baltic troika, exporter of dairy products. Provides shale to power Leningrad. Population-1.6 million. Estonian-65%, Russian-30%. Production-0.6% of Soviet economy.

GEORGIA
Fought over by various factions since the Mongols invaded in the late 1100s. Declared independence in 1918 but held by Soviet force. Produces grain, fruit, vegetables, and 95% of nation's tea. Population-5.4 million. Georgian-69%, Armenian-9%, Russian-7%.

TADZHIKISTAN
Originally part of Persian Empire. Captured after 1917 Revolution in war with central Asians. Became a republic in 1929. Rich deposits of coal, also oil. Population-5.1 million. Tadzhik-59%, Russian-10%. Production-0.8% of Soviet economy.

Legend
- Mobile-based ICBMs
- Silo-based ICBMs
- Strategic bomber bases
- Plutonium-producing nuclear reactor
- Early warning radar
- Oil
- Coal
- Industrial center
- Agriculture

Map labels
Arctic Ocean
NORWAY
SWEDEN
FINLAND
GERMANY
LITHUANIA LATVIA ESTONIA
Tallinn
Leningrad
RUSSIA
Riga
Vilnius
POLAND
Minsk
BYELORUSSIA
Moscow
CZECHOSLOVAKIA
HUNGARY
Kiev
ROMANIA
MOLDAVIA
Kishinev
UKRAINE
BULGARIA
GEORGIA
Caspian Sea
Aral Sea
Tbilisi
TURKEY
ARMENIA
AZERBAIJAN
Yerevan
Baku
UZBEKISTAN
IRAQ
TURKMENISTAN
Ashkhabad
IRAN

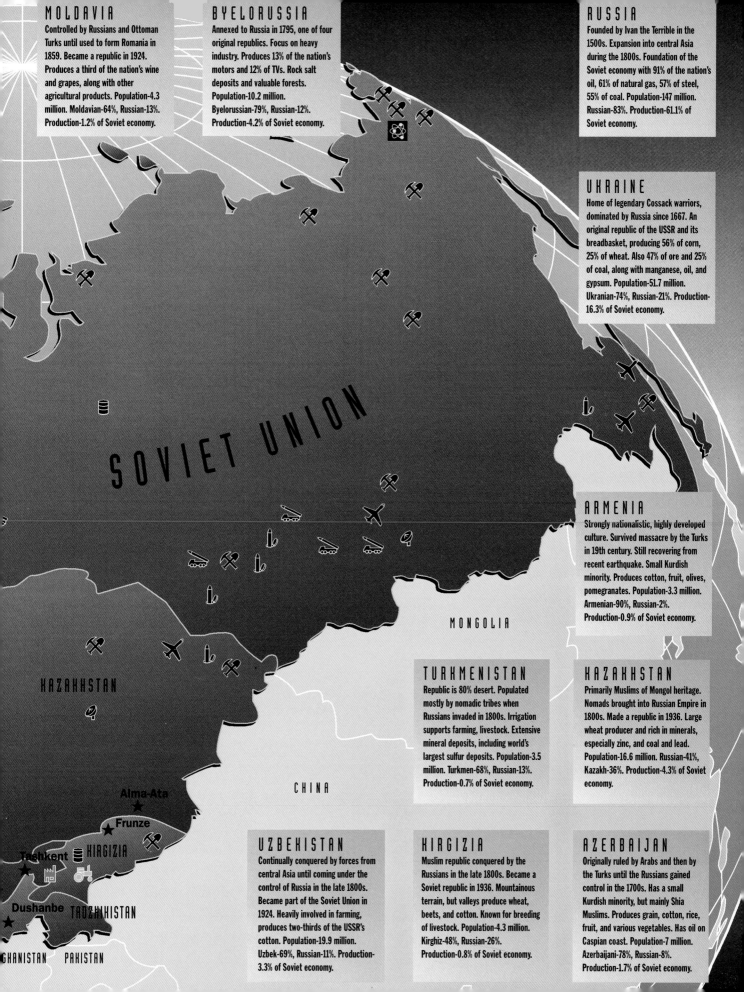

MOLDAVIA
Controlled by Russians and Ottoman Turks until used to form Romania in 1859. Became a republic in 1924. Produces a third of the nation's wine and grapes, along with other agricultural products. Population-4.3 million. Moldavian-64%, Russian-13%. Production-1.2% of Soviet economy.

BYELORUSSIA
Annexed to Russia in 1795, one of four original republics. Focus on heavy industry. Produces 13% of the nation's motors and 12% of TVs. Rock salt deposits and valuable forests. Population-10.2 million. Byelorussian-79%, Russian-12%. Production-4.2% of Soviet economy.

RUSSIA
Founded by Ivan the Terrible in the 1500s. Expansion into central Asia during the 1800s. Foundation of the Soviet economy with 91% of the nation's oil, 61% of natural gas, 57% of steel, 55% of coal. Population-147 million. Russian-83%. Production-61.1% of Soviet economy.

UKRAINE
Home of legendary Cossack warriors, dominated by Russia since 1667. An original republic of the USSR and its breadbasket, producing 56% of corn, 25% of wheat. Also 47% of ore and 25% of coal, along with manganese, oil, and gypsum. Population-51.7 million. Ukranian-74%, Russian-21%. Production-16.3% of Soviet economy.

ARMENIA
Strongly nationalistic, highly developed culture. Survived massacre by the Turks in 19th century. Still recovering from recent earthquake. Small Kurdish minority. Produces cotton, fruit, olives, pomegranates. Population-3.3 million. Armenian-90%, Russian-2%. Production-0.9% of Soviet economy.

TURKMENISTAN
Republic is 80% desert. Populated mostly by nomadic tribes when Russians invaded in 1800s. Irrigation supports farming, livestock. Extensive mineral deposits, including world's largest sulfur deposits. Population-3.5 million. Turkmen-68%, Russian-13%. Production-0.7% of Soviet economy.

KAZAKHSTAN
Primarily Muslims of Mongol heritage. Nomads brought into Russian Empire in 1800s. Made a republic in 1936. Large wheat producer and rich in minerals, especially zinc, and coal and lead. Population-16.6 million. Russian-41%, Kazakh-36%. Production-4.3% of Soviet economy.

UZBEKISTAN
Continually conquered by forces from central Asia until coming under the control of Russia in the late 1800s. Became part of the Soviet Union in 1924. Heavily involved in farming, produces two-thirds of the USSR's cotton. Population-19.9 million. Uzbek-69%, Russian-11%. Production-3.3% of Soviet economy.

KIRGIZIA
Muslim republic conquered by the Russians in the late 1800s. Became a Soviet republic in 1936. Mountainous terrain, but valleys produce wheat, beets, and cotton. Known for breeding of livestock. Population-4.3 million. Kirghiz-48%, Russian-26%. Production-0.8% of Soviet economy.

AZERBAIJAN
Originally ruled by Arabs and then by the Turks until the Russians gained control in the 1700s. Has a small Kurdish minority, but mainly Shia Muslims. Produces grain, cotton, rice, fruit, and various vegetables. Has oil on Caspian coast. Population-7 million. Azerbaijani-78%, Russian-8%. Production-1.7% of Soviet economy.

SOVIET UNION

MONGOLIA

CHINA

KAZAKHSTAN

Alma-Ata

Frunze

Tashkent   KIRGIZIA

Dushanbe   TADZHIKISTAN

GHANISTAN   PAKISTAN

Day 1

TAKEOVER

Late in the afternoon of Sunday, August 18, 1991, two heavy black ZIL limousines wheeled off the Sevastopol-Yalta highway in the heart of the Crimean "Communist Riviera," accompanied by four smaller black Volga escort cars.

They passed a "no-entry" sign and continued down a side road to a heavily protected gate—the entrance to Soviet President Mikhail S. Gorbachev's vacation dacha at Foros on the Black Sea. The mission of their occupants: to restore Communist domination to the USSR.

The motorcade rolled up to the gate at 4:50 p.m.,

Day

1

8/18/91 SUNDAY

4:50 pm
Valery Boldin, Oleg Baklanov, General Valentin Varrenikov, Oleg Shenin, General Generalov, arrive at Gorbachev's Foros dacha to inform the President of his ouster. All communications between the dacha and the outside are cut.

7:30 pm
The coup plotters leave Foros for Moscow following Gorbachev's refusal to step down as President of the Soviet Union.

11:30 pm
Vladimir Kryuchkov, head of the KGB, convenes a meeting of coup conspirators at the Kremlin to consolidate control and plan the announcement of the State of Emergency.

and when the KGB border guards received orders to let it pass immediately, their 25-year-old commander, Lt. Dmitry Guroshko, did not give the matter a second thought. He had been told to expect Gen. Vyacheslav Generalov, deputy head of the KGB 9th Directorate, which guarded Soviet leaders, who would accompany the President back to Moscow to preside over the signing of the Union Treaty intended to preserve the collapsing Soviet Union.

Immediately after the cars sped through the gate, Guroshko, working in a concrete guard house between the two fences at the service entrance to the compound, noticed that the security guard at the inner fence had been doubled. But even this did not seem out of order.

"There was no fuss, no trouble," the young lieutenant said later. "I thought it was some kind of reinforcement."

At the same time communications inside the compound, between the compound and the border-guard headquarters in nearby Foros, and between the dacha and the rest of

the world were cut. Guroshko took this as coincidence. "I asked the security man at the gate what had happened to communications," he said, "and he didn't answer. At first I thought something was wrong at the telephone station at Foros. We set up walkie-talkie communications over the militia [police] radios to keep in touch with our people patrolling and with our headquarters. We did not realize that anything was wrong."

Unbeknownst to the border guards those two ZILs contained the men who would inform Gorbachev of his ouster: Valery Boldin, Gorbachev's chief of staff; Oleg Baklanov, first deputy chairman of the country's Defense Council; Gen. Valentin Varrenikov, deputy defense minister; Oleg Shenin, a Communist Party Central Committee Secretary; and the expected General Generalov. Awaiting the plotters inside the compound were Lt. Gen. Yuri Plekhanov, chief of the KGB 9th Directorate, and Maj. Gen. Vladimir Medvedev, longtime chief of the presidential bodyguard.

As the cars came down the driveway, Olga

Lanina, 34, Gorbachev's personal secretary, finished her work for the day and prepared to leave the compound and return to the resort down the road where she and her husband (a KGB driver of a ZIL limousine in the presidential motorcade) and Anatoly Chernyayev, Gorbachev's chief international policy adviser and the only senior staff member with him, were staying. Without explanation, the security guards told her she could not leave the house. She knew there was trouble. For one thing, she saw Plekhanov and Medvedev leaning against a parapet whispering to each other furtively.★ For another, Lanina recounted, "I had a bad feeling when I saw Boldin. There wasn't anything normal about

★ Medvedev was ever present at Gorbachev's side, traveling with him wherever he went. In Moscow, he stood personal guard at his office doorway. He performed the same functions for Gorbachev's predecessors going back to Leonid Brezhnev. It is not clear if he was involved in the plot. He was dismissed from his job but was not arrested or charged.

him coming there." The presidential chief of staff always stayed behind in Moscow to handle problems while the President was away.

By now it was after 5 p.m. Chernyayev tried to phone Yuli Kvitsinsky, first deputy foreign minister, in Moscow, to see if he knew what was happening. "I picked up our duty phone and I thought 'hell.' It was dead."

Gorbachev, informed of the motorcade, immediately sensed something was wrong. He had not expected such a big delegation and he wanted to know why they had come.

"I picked up the telephone but it wasn't working. I picked up a second, a third, a fourth, but none of them worked," he later told a news conference. "They were all cut off. I picked up an internal phone. But everything was cut off. I then realized that this mission was not the sort of mission with which we ordinarily had to deal.

"I didn't need additional information. I saw that this was a very serious situation. I

OPPOSITE: In December 1990, homeless Soviet citizens construct a tent city in the shadow of the Kremlin and St. Basil's Cathedral to protest their economic grievances against the state. BELOW: The President's personal bodyguard, left, Vladimir Medvedev, with the Gorbachevs.

thought that they were going to try to blackmail me or force me or compel me to do something. Anything was possible."

He later told the Russian parliament, "At that time I knew it was a question of life and death. My family in hearing me all said, 'we'll either live together as we've been living or we'll die together.'"

Gorbachev's wife, Raisa Maximovna, was at his side and tried the phones as well. Two months later she recalled:

"Mikhail Sergeyevich has eight or ten telephone operators and all the phones were silent. I picked up the receiver and checked it out and all the phones were silent, even that of the commander-in-chief. We have this telephone everywhere — in our country house, in our flat, our apartment—everywhere. It's under a kind of lid and we do not even remove dust from this phone because we are not supposed to remove the lid. He picked up the receiver on that phone and there was silence there. We knew that was all, that there was nothing else we could do."

The President thought first of his family. He called them together and informed them of the visitors. He later said, "I told [my wife and daughter] they would either blackmail me or there would be attempts to arrest me or take me somewhere [but] that I would not step back, not under any pressure, blackmail or threats. I would neither change nor take up new positions.

"The family told me they would go through this to the end," the President said. Mrs. Gorbachev told a Soviet newspaper later that the decision was not easy. "We know our history and its tragic episodes," she said, alluding to the Communists' murder of the czar and his entire family after they were deposed.

"I paced the room and thought," the President said. "Not about myself, but about my family, my granddaughters. Then I

decided: In this situation, it is impossible to value my own skin."

By now the delegation was already sitting in Gorbachev's office, awaiting the confrontation, not a difficult feat considering the complicity of General Plekhanov, head of the presidential security detail.

Gorbachev later described the scene this way:

"They didn't stand on ceremony. With Chief of Staff Boldin at the head, they gave me an ultimatum, to transfer power to the vice-president."

Whether or not Gorbachev knew that this was going to happen is debatable. A telephone log kept by the KGB communications system, which controlled the presidential switchboard, indicated he had four telephone contacts with KGB Chief Vladimir Kryuchkov that morning. The secret log showed that Gorbachev called Kryuchkov twice on the "combat communications system" starting at 7 a.m., just after medical treatment for a painful lower-back problem.★

Gorbachev was furious as he opened the meeting in his office. "Who sent you? What committee?" he demanded.

"The State Committee for the State of Emergency in the country," one of the visitors responded.

"Who created it? I didn't create it. The Supreme Soviet didn't create it," Gorbachev said.

The plotters ignored the comment, continuing: "The situation is nearing catastrophe. . . We should take measures, a state of

---

★ The President also spoke with Vice-President Gennady Yanayev; Oleg Shenin, a member of the Communist Party Politburo; Prime Minister Valentin Pavlov; and Deputy Prime Minster Vladimir Sherbakov. He spoke several times with Kryuchkov. Why he had these conversations is not known. The entire log indicated a round-robin of calls among the men plotting the overthrow with Gorbachev. The nature of the calls remains unknown.

Soviet citizens express their lack of confidence in Gorbachev and his policies in a pre-coup demonstration. OVERLEAF: At this state-run store near Moscow, women stand in line to buy meat as the economic situation continues to worsen.

emergency. . . we shouldn't daydream any-more."

Gorbachev replied: "I was always an opponent of such measures, not only because of moral and political reasons, but because in the history of our country they have always led to the deaths of hundreds, thousands, and millions. . . And we need to get away from that and refuse it forever.

"You and those who sent you are adventurers. I don't care what will happen to you, but you'll destroy the country, everything we are doing.

"Only those who want to commit suicide can now suggest a totalitarian regime in the country. You will kill yourselves. Go to hell, shitheads."

The plotters were dogged: "Resign."

"You won't get that from me. Tell that to the people who sent you here," Gorbachev reiterated.

The President urged the plotters to think ahead, to realize the public would not accept any new dictator. He urged continuation of his policies of consensus-building, cooperation with the Western nations, and intensification of his reforms.

"You will face defeat," he continued, "but I am scared for the people and all we have done in these years."

Gorbachev offered to call an urgent session of parliament and, if it agreed, to declare a state of emergency.

In describing the meeting later, he said, "But you know, this was a conversation with deaf mutes. Their cycle was in motion; it was clear that we couldn't have any more conversations."

Perhaps, in retrospect, Gorbachev could have seen the trouble brewing. Two days before, one of his closest friends and advisers Alexander Yakovlev had resigned from the Communist Party with the warning that a right-wing coup was in the offing.

He was right.

Defense Minister Dmitry Yazov later told prosecutors, according to *Der Spiegel*, the conspirators had been meeting for months in various places to discuss how Gorbachev was backing away from the Communist Party. Typically, the group included KGB Chief Kryuchkov, Gorbachev's Chief of Staff Boldin, the Defense Council Deputy Chief Baklanov, and Yazov. They were unhappy because the Communist Party was falling apart, the economy was collapsing, and Gorbachev kept traveling to other countries without telling them what he was doing there, Yazov said. Particularly at the G-7 meeting of the seven major industrialized countries in July, where news reports said Gorbachev laid out Soviet economic reform plans, the group had no idea what Gorbachev was saying, Yazov said.

"We were not prepared to become more dependent on the United States, politically, economically, and even militarily," Yazov said. "The people's standard of living was dropping, the economy was collapsing, ethnic conflicts and conflicts between republics were worsening…he betrayed the army." Gorbachev kept taking on more international debt, but did not accomplish anything with it, Yazov complained. The hard-liners argued against pursuing international aid, but Gorbachev pursued it anyway.

"Gradually, the idea ripened that Gorbachev had exhausted himself as a statesman," Yazov said.

Then the date of August 20 was set for signing the Union Treaty, which,Yazov explained, they saw as an organized attempt to destroy the Soviet Union and replace it with a loose confederation of sovereign states.

"We knew the state would disintegrate," Yazov said, and the group concluded that the treaty had to be stopped.

Late on Saturday afternoon, August 17,

KGB Chief Kryuchkov called him for an urgent meeting at a military base on the south edge of Moscow, Yazov said. Boldin's cronies, Shenin and Baklanov, showed up as well, and someone suggested traveling to see Gorbachev in hopes of preventing the signing of the Union Treaty.

"There was no conspiracy or plan," Yazov insisted to prosecutors.

An internal KGB investigation said, however, that Kryuchkov had been plotting the coup since November 1990. Kryuchkov "was fixated on methods of force," said the report's author, Anatoly Aleinikov. Kryuchkov wanted to oust Gorbachev to stop the development of democracy and the decline in the KGB's fearsome power. With the help of a few trusted KGB aides, he drew up detailed plans for the coup, including lists of people to be detained, phones to be tapped, people to be followed. But he apparently did not tell all of the others who became part of the Emergency Committee that they were being drawn into an elaborate plot.

Boldin, too, was pursuing his own agenda in the Kremlin. As the President's chief of staff, he controlled hiring and firing, and used that power to bring Communist Party officials into key government jobs where they could continue to control the country, even as Gorbachev was trying to loosen the Party's stranglehold on power.

Despite Yazov's insistence that he personally never intended Gorbachev's permanent ouster, he was not surprised that Shenin, Baklanov, and Boldin flew to Foros with Army Land Forces commander Varrenikov and the head of Gorbachev's security force, Plekhanov. "Plekhanov knew the entire security system," Yazov said. "I already knew that Kryuchkov had authorized him to change the guard."

The group's goal was to persuade Gorbachev to drop the Union Treaty and declare a state of emergency, suspending democracy and returning to the harsh dictatorial rule of the past to prevent the country from collapsing — or to resign so that Vice-

Despite a high profile in the international arena, including his participation with President Bush in the Moscow summit meeting in July 1991, Gorbachev's popularity continued its downward spiral at home. OVERLEAF: Gorbachev's shift towards the conservative hard-liners was seriously questioned during the 28th Communist Party Congress in July 1990.

President Gennady Yanayev could do it. If they failed, Yazov admitted, they were prepared "to take decisive measures."

For months, Gorbachev's popularity rating had been in a nosedive. The public that once adulated him for his proclamations of glasnost and perestroika now reviled him for causing a serious economic slump, for allowing prices to rise, for trying to curb vodka consumption, for allowing speculators to grow rich at the expense of the common people, and for unpredictable swings in his policies. In short, he could do little right in the eyes of Soviet citizens, no matter what their political views.

He intended the Union Treaty, agreed to by presidents of nine of the Soviet Union's fifteen republics, to give his domestic image a lift as well as put the country on a more solid political footing. He was again moving toward cooperation with the liberal political forces in the country, allying himself against the conservatives, mostly members of the hopelessly tattered Communist Party he still nominally led.

Internationally, however, he was buoyed by two recent successes. Three weeks before, the 60-year-old Soviet President had completed a summit meeting with U.S. President George Bush in Moscow where the two leaders signed the START Treaty to reduce nuclear weapons. A month before he had upstaged the leaders of the world's wealthiest nations at the annual G-7 Summit meeting in London and had talked his way into an associate membership in the International Monetary Fund. His message: Not only was Soviet economic agony his domestic problem but, in an interdependent world, it was a problem for all the great powers.

The Union Treaty scheduled to be signed in forty-eight hours would accomplish a cherished part of his vision of holding together the empire that had survived and grown from the medieval time of Ivan the Terrible to the

Gorbachev's opulent dacha in Foros. Gorbachev and his family were on their annual vacation when the coup plotters sealed the compound and placed them under house arrest.

modern days of Leonid Brezhnev. This domestic success would help him to regain his position at home and that, in turn, would increase his stature with the other world leaders. But the treaty frightened the Party leaders who were now mounting a coup. They feared for their rank and privileges in a country where the Communist Party no longer exercised absolute power and was increasingly on the defensive.

While Gorbachev and the plotters met, his wife, his son-in-law Dr. Anatoly Virgansky, and his daughter Irina, all stood anxiously outside the meeting room. "We were trying to be close to Mikhail Sergeyevich," Mrs. Gorbachev said. "We knew something terrible had started....We didn't have any plans. We just had this desire to be close to him."

Gorbachev's personal security staff and other underlings waited elsewhere around the house and grounds, trying to figure out what was going on. Boris Golentsov, one of the deputy chiefs of the presidential bodyguard, did not understand why his boss, General Medvedev, was leaving. He was always with the President. Golentsov and a fellow bodyguard realized that something was wrong when General Generalov, the deputy chief of the presidential security force, approached them and said there would be no treaty signing as planned. Instead, he said, "Mikhail Sergeyevich will be arrested when he goes to sign the treaty in the Grand Kremlin Palace. He's going to stand trial and there will be an international scandal. For this not to happen, he needs to stay here for awhile. And he's been asked to resign. It will be announced tomorrow."

Generalov then told the men he had brought five guards loyal to the coup plotters, armed with Kalashnikov automatic rifles, to take up key positions in the compound. He explained that the five would augment the KGB security guard already in place, insuring

that Gorbachev and any loyalists did not leave the compound.★

When the meeting in Gorbachev's office broke up, the delegation from Moscow filed out past Mrs. Gorbachev and the rest of the family. Baklanov, one of the plotters and a member of Gorbachev's staff, offered his hand. Defiantly, she refused it.

"What is going on? What have you brought?" Mrs. Gorbachev asked him.

Baklanov paused. Finally he said cryptically, "Enforced circumstances." He and Shenin turned and left.

Gorbachev emerged from his office, waving a paper on which he had written the names of the members of the Emergency Committee, Mrs. Gorbachev said. Parliamentary Chairman Anatoly Lukianov's name was on it — but there was a question mark next to his name.

The plotters, getting no satisfaction from Gorbachev, were on their way by 7:30 p.m. General Varrenikov flew directly to Kiev to try to win support for the coup from Leonid Kravchuk, president of the Ukraine. The rest returned to Moscow.

For months now Gorbachev had attempted to straddle the divide between the reformers and the conservatives who held power. He was a product of the very Communist Party rule that the conservatives were determined to maintain. The ambivalence of his position

★ The security at the compound was a bureaucratic nightmare. There were four rings of security around the compound that Sunday. The first was a set of electronic monitors outside the perimeter. Then there were two chain-link fences — one inside the other. The KGB uniformed border guard patrolled in-between. These troops were always unarmed. The inner ring of KGB uniformed security troops was armed and responsible for clearing workers at the service entrance and visitors at the main gate. The final ring was the presidential bodyguard, the men who traveled with Gorbachev, who were constantly at his side. Normally, visitors were allowed only if approved in advance. On that Sunday, Kryuchkov alone commanded all the various protective forces in a coordinated way.

Gorbachev's Summer Home

Odessa

Karkinitskiy Zaliv

Chernomorskoye
Mys Tarkhankut
Yevpatoriya

Black Sea

CRIMEA

● Simferopol

Sevastopol Yalta

Foros

Mys Sarych

80 km

Main house
Opulent three-story dacha that includes family living quarters, study, and offices. Location of Gorbachev's confrontation with plotters and subsequent house arrest.

Recreational building
Houses indoor swimming pool overlooking the sea and other recreational facilities.

Escalator to beach
Enclosed escalator runs from the house to the beachfront.

Guest house
Has accommodations for thirty people.

Security zone
KGB border guards patrol along path between two chain-link fences. Gorbachev's personal bodyguards patrol the interior of the compound. Sensors, including cameras and motion detectors, are located along the perimeter of the compound to detect anyone approaching.

Dock

Kitchen

Staff quarters
Living quarters for guards, servants, support personnel. Includes main dining hall for staff.

Main entrance
Located between double chain-link fences, guard house contains security and communications equipment. Guards patrol along path between fences.

Service entrance

Maintenance facilities for compound
Includes garage for vehicle maintenance and main communication building.

Marine guards
KGB navy coastal patrol boats with armed marine troops

was exemplified by his vacation home. He denounced the high-living excesses of Communist Party leaders during his consolidation of power in the 1980s, but he built this pleasure dome for himself on the southern Crimean coast at the same time, apparently using KGB management to supervise the construction and Party funds to finance it. The site was deep in the heart of the ruling elite's summer playground where palace-like dachas, sanatoria, hotels, pensions, campsites, and hostels catered to visitors of various levels in the hierarchy. The late Communist leader Leonid Brezhnev had a dacha down the road nearer to Yalta, but it did not suffice for the Gorbachevs.

The huge family residence dominates the compound. The house is three stories with a steep, orange-tile roof and a kind of enclosed widow's walk at the peak. Balconies run along the top two floors. An enclosed hundred-yard-long escalator runs from the house to the beachfront. There is a separate recreation building—including an enclosed swimming pool—that resembles a church; a building housing kitchen facilities; a movie theater; a guest house that can accommodate more than thirty people; a small dacha for the family doctors; and, separated from the rest, a three-story hotel-like structure to house the family's personal staff as well as the security people. Next to it are two industrial-type buildings housing the garage and workshops. On the roof of one is a satellite dish. The entire private resort is designed to cater to the Gorbachevs' apparent penchant for beach-walking, swimming, and film viewing, all woven into a routine for the President that also included his work.

The village of Foros itself, three miles east of the dacha, is a collection of vacation facilities, mostly for military people. It is set on a steep hillside between the coastal highway and the sea. The area is so crowded with

high-ranking officials that the 9th Directorate of the KGB has a regional headquarters in Miskhor, another resort town in the Yalta area, to maintain protection services.

Depending on which of two official exchange rates are used, the cost of the Gorbachevs' compound could easily have been in the $20-million range, spent at a time when the Soviet economy was entering a severe tailspin and the government was going into debt. Crimeans who watched the construction severely criticized Gorbachev for what they considered an excess.★

The meeting just completed shattered the tranquility of the day. Gorbachev had spent several days in severe pain from an ailment variously described as lumbago, a slipped disc, or radiculitis. The ailment had struck him early in the week while he was on a walk, and the pain was so severe that he had to be carried home.

That Sunday morning, a doctor specially brought from elsewhere in the country had given him relief through a series of injections and manual therapy. The doctor met Gorbachev at 6 a.m. and the President told him: "Do what you want. Take out the nerve, a vertebra, or even the whole leg, but I must be in Moscow on August 19."

The treatment, composed of massage and injections of antibiotics and anesthetics, worked. For the first time in days Gorbachev was able to sit up, stand, and recline without great pain.★★

★ In the days after the coup when officials such as Anatoly Chernyayev, Gorbachev's personal international affairs adviser, talked to reporters about the events in Foros, none of them candidly described the luxury of the compound.
★★ The story of Gorbachev's illness was first revealed by Aleksei Adzhubei in the newspaper *Izvestia*. Adzhubei is the son-in-law of the late Nikita Khrushchev, a predecessor of Gorbachev who was removed from office on October 15, 1964, in a coup d'état carried out by his underlings while he was on vacation in his Crimean dacha.

He had telephoned leaders throughout the country and made all the arrangements for the Union Treaty signing. With Chernyayev's help he was finishing drafts of two important documents. One was the speech he would deliver at the signing ceremony, and the other was an article outlining his ideas on the future of the Soviet Union. He was writing about the possibility of a right-wing coup d'état as one of the options facing the country, Chernyayev said later.

Finally, he had managed to spend some quality time with his family. August was vacation month in the Soviet Union, and that was no different for the leader than for anyone else. The private time with Raisa Maximovna, his wife of 38 years; their daughter Irina, 34; her husband, Dr. Virgansky; and granddaughters, Oksana, 11, and Anastasia, 4, in previous times had been sacred. He had built a close family and wanted to keep it that

way even in these difficult times.

Col. Pyotr Kharlamov, 47, commander of all Crimean Border Guards, received reports at his headquarters in Foros of strange doings at the presidential compound while relaxing with his family that afternoon. Though an officer in a KGB unit, he also considered himself a democrat and was, in fact, a non-communist member of the Leningrad city council, commuting to meetings there.

Kharlamov thought about the communications break, not only in the compound telephones but in the six-channel radio telephone setup operated by the KGB. "There was little chance that could be coincidental," he thought. Then he heard of the reinforcement of the security guards.

"Judging by the facts, I had strong fears that the Gorbachev family was in danger," Kharlamov said. The thought made him ill.

Mrs. Kharlamov, informed by her hus-

Gorbachev confers with long-time friend and Chairman of the Soviet legislature, Anatoly Lukianov, while standing at Lenin's tomb during the Revolution Day parade in 1990. The legislature would later strip Lukianov of his parliamentary immunity so he could stand trial for his role in the coup.

Many of the coup plotters were elevated to their positions by Gorbachev himself and were often among those closest to him at state occasions such as this one in April 1990.

band of the situation, suggested a remedy — prayer.

"I am an atheist," Kharlamov said later, but when my wife suggested we go to church, I immediately agreed. The Kharlamovs — colonel, wife, and two sons — went to an ancient church built on a rocky promontory high above Foros.

"My wife bought four candles and gave me one. She and the children lit theirs for the Gorbachev family. As a military man, I prayed that there would be no civil war in the country."

Then he returned to his headquarters to plan the defense of Mikhail Gorbachev. He spent all night at his desk.

At the dacha, Gorbachev had also begun

analyzing the situation. Apparently he knew that the plotters would justify their actions by reporting him ill. Though a virtual prisoner, he decided to do what he could to show good health, knowing that at least his guards could see him and that the word would get out.

So, despite the meeting with the plotters, he went through the evening vacation routine. The family went down to the beach and were seen walking by the border guards and also by marines stationed aboard two picket ships protecting the compound from seaborne danger. Then they went to the movie theater and watched a film.

Although Mikhail Gorbachev was under constraints, almost deposed, he did nothing to signal it that Sunday night, leaving some of the people responsible for protecting him mightily confused.

Meanwhile, Gorbachev's aide Anatoly Chernyayev found General Generalov, who had been left in charge of Gorbachev's jailers, and asked, "What's going on?"

Generalov replied that the garages had been locked and placed under guard, and the security forces beefed up.

"But we have the signing ceremony," Chernyayev protested.

"There will be no signing ceremony," Generalov replied.

Chernyayev then suggested it was time for him to go back to his own vacation quarters off-compound for dinner.

"Don't be a fool," Generalov told him. "No one is going to leave this place."

Later, Chernyayev walked out to the sentry post at the gate. A new guard was there. "Who are you?" the soldier demanded.

"I am an aide to the President," Chernyayev replied.

"Where are you going?" the soldier said.

"What's the matter?" Chernyayev responded.

"You cannot pass," the guard snarled. "Now get back to your kennel!"

While the Gorbachevs acted as if nothing was wrong, Colonel Kharlamov tried to solve the protection problem. He had to figure out how to use his unarmed force to protect the President. But against whom? There were at least three possibilities:

• The plotters themselves might try to harm Gorbachev.

• An extremist group might try to storm the compound, taking advantage of uncertain times.

• The Yeltsin faction might conceivably set up a provocation that would result in Gorbachev's death.

With survival politics in the Soviet Union, nothing is simple.

Those in the Foros compound awoke Monday morning to learn from the radio that their leader was ill and, as a result, the Emergency Committee had been formed and power transferred to it. All the border guards as well as the marines at sea knew that the report was nonsense. As one of the border guards put it:

"The thing is this: We had seen him the night before walking on the beach and going to the cinema. We knew he was not sick. We knew something was wrong."

By 9 a.m., the Soviet Union was trying to come to terms with the putsch from the scant information on radio and television. In Foros, Colonel Kharlamov had decided what he would do. He issued an order to his troops saying that their primary mission was to

A pre-coup gathering of "three great friends," Pugo, Yazov, and Kryuchkov, is caricatured in the Soviet magazine "Stolitsa" (Capital). These three would later play major roles in the coup attempt.

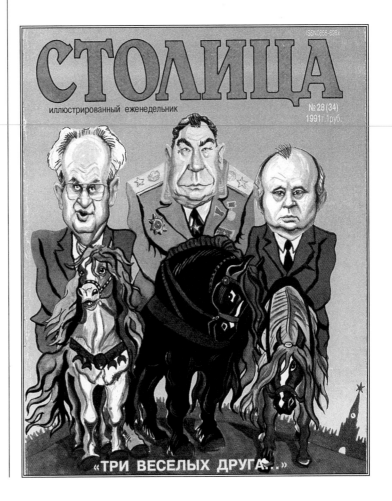

protect the President and his family at the dacha — with their bare hands, if necessary — as well as the Constitution of the USSR. Moreover, units would not accept any papers or orders from the extra-ordinary State Emergency Committee.

Captain 1st Class Victor Afereyev, head of the KGB marine unit charged with protecting the President from the sea, reached the same decision. Afereyev and Kharlamov had a close working relationship, and together they worked out a plan to try to bring the armed seaborne marines to shore to defend Gorbachev if possible. The task would have been difficult. The picket boats had drafts too deep to dock at the compound.

The two commanders were only too willing to lead their units into heroic actions, but their capabilities were limited.★

Inside the compound that Monday, captors and captives were all mixed up. The thirty-two loyal members of Gorbachev's bodyguard, now headed by Boris Golentsov, continued to live in the large hotel-like building about a hundred yards away from the Gorbachevs' house. They shared the building with the KGB security guard that prevented the President and his supporters from leaving. The two groups avoided trouble even though both were armed. Gorbachev's bodyguard kept their weapons in the guest house near the dacha, and the security troops never did anything to try to disarm them. All of the workers on the compound, loyal to Gorbachev or not, ate in the same dining room.

The President's family did not know to what extent their physical safety was threatened. Whom or what could they trust now? The Gorbachevs, for example, decided not to order any food brought in but to live on what was already on hand in the dacha, the better to avoid poisoning.

"The worst part was not knowing anything. Nothing was clear," said Dr. Virgansky. "It was only after about twenty-four hours that we knew the personal bodyguards would fight for us."

Because Gorbachev decided to maintain an air of normality during his house arrest, he was seen walking the grounds near the beach at least once a day on Monday, August 19, and Tuesday, August 20.

Life at the dacha settled into a routine. Gorbachev said his granddaughter Anastasia took the situation best of all. "She didn't understand anything. She was running around, asking everyone to take her to the beach. . . and we had to take her. The last day the guards asked us to stop, because anything could happen, anything at all."

Only a four-year-old could not be worried about the situation. A country that spanned eleven time zones, with a population of 290 million people, was splitting into many pieces, and the man who struggled to hold it together had now been told his services were no longer needed. A country that had a better record of changing leadership through violence, terror, and death than through democratic or peaceful means was now demonstrating how difficult it was to break established patterns.

The USSR was in agony with its first family incommunicado in fear and uncertainty. A few days later the President would say:

"Seventy-two hours of total isolation and struggle. I think everything was done to psychologically break the President down. It is difficult to talk about it."

May 1991. Gorbachev's growing dilemma: Walking the tightrope between hard-line demands for stricter control and the republics' growing insistence on freedom and reforms.

★ Later, to the consternation of the two military men, Gorbachev would claim that he was surrounded by border guards and marines at sea who were armed and in league with the plotters. Col. Kharlamov said: "The President was given disinformation by people on his staff and I have the documents to prove it." By mid-September the border guards had been removed from the KGB but they had not yet been placed anywhere else. Col. Kharlamov was worried that his unit would not find a home and that he himself might be punished without justification.

Day 2

BATTLE LINES

The Kremlin, a name synonymous with intrigue,
is a 78-acre complex of buildings inside a 1.5-mile
crenelated brick wall built by Italian masters in the
fifteenth century. There are medieval churches
with gold-leafed onion domes, the Great Kremlin
Palace built for the czars in the nineteenth century,
office buildings used by the Bolsheviks after they
took over the country in 1917, monuments and
museums, and—inside the ancient
Troitsky Gate—the starkly modern
Palace of Congresses, the last great
edifice built inside the wall.

Just hours after the takeover,
the self-proclaimed Emergency
Committee orders tank units to
surround the Russian Parliament
Building, which would become
the rallying point for the anti-
coup forces.

Day

2

8/19/91 MONDAY

6:06 am
Soviet news agency TASS reports that Vice-President Gennady Yanayev has taken over the duties of USSR President due to Mikhail Gorbachev's "inability" to perform his duties for health reasons.

7:00 am
Decree by Emergency Committee closes opposition press and suspends all political parties other than the Communist Party.

8:00 am
Armored personnel carriers are seen moving several miles north of Red Square toward the Kremlin.

Here in 1961, Nikita Khrushchev predicted the ultimate victory of communism over capitalism. Three years later, he was ousted by a junta of his closest underlings. His reforms had threatened their positions and had brought economic hardship and political uncertainty to the country.

On the evening of Sunday, August 18, 1991, a small group of the men closest to Soviet President Mikhail Gorbachev met in the Kremlin to make final plans to announce his replacement. They thought they had already accomplished his ouster in the same way that Khrushchev's underlings had successfully deposed him in October 1964. The meeting was convened by Vladimir Kryuchkov, chief of the KGB.

Midnight approached. The delegation that had gone to Foros to press Gorbachev into signing a document of abdication in favor of a USSR State Committee for the State of Emergency had returned to Moscow, unsuccessful in its mission.

Kryuchkov keynoted the session with a fierce pep talk filled with disinformation. His view of the political landscape featured threats to the Soviet establishment everywhere. The internal democratic movement was a plot of the Bush Administration to overthrow the government. Western banks were working to destabilize the Soviet economy. Democracy was subversion. Protest was a breakdown in law and order.

The democrats were, he said, planning a coup. He told the meeting that "special forces" of the democratic movement were planning to get together, presumably the next day, at several downtown Moscow locations including Pushkin Square, the Manezh, Red Square, and the Ukraine Hotel. He showed the group lists the KGB had allegedly obtained of officials targeted for execution by the democrats including all of the plotters in the room.

As KGB chairman, Kryuchkov held power in the Soviet Union in the 1990s similar to that wielded by the late FBI Director J. Edgar Hoover in the United States in the 1950s and 60s. The KGB collected information from millions of informers and some Soviet officials suggested Kryuchkov used this information to blackmail his fellow bureaucrats.

Among those summoned to the meeting was Foreign Minister Alexander Bessmertnykh, an accomplished diplomat who replaced Eduard Shevardnadze in the top job at the Foreign Ministry earlier in the year. Bessmertnykh was on vacation in Byelorussia when he received the order to return to Moscow on a military airplane. At Chkalovsk Air Force Base near Moscow, an aide met him to brief him on the latest news internationally. The aide could find no indication in any cable traffic of a world crisis that needed such extraordinary attention.

It was after midnight now, and from his limousine, Bessmertnykh called the Kremlin to find out if the meeting was still scheduled. Because there appeared to be no emergency, he thought it might be postponed until morning.

The meeting was still on. "Come immediately," he was told.

Still dressed in jeans, he arrived in the Kremlin and was taken to a large conference room in the Council of Ministers Building, the headquarters of the Gorbachev government. Bessmertnykh described the scene:

"There was a long table covered in green and the meeting was already in session. It had been going on for several hours. People were coming in and out. A lot of things were happening. I looked around and saw the top people — almost everyone from the ruling circle except Gorbachev himself. I saw General Plekhanov [chief of the KGB's security guard] and Boldin [Gorbachev's chief of

staff]. All the right people.

"My immediate feeling was that this was a meeting convened by Gorbachev himself. The regular people in the regular place. The President's closest associates."

Kryuchkov took him into a smaller room.

Bessmertnykh later reconstructed their private conversation in an appearance on ABC's "Nightline," and other interviews. Kryuchkov opened with a description of the situation in the country from the plotters' viewpoint, saying:

"The situation in the country is terrible… It's a crisis. It's dangerous. People are disappointed. Something should be done, and we decided to do something through emergency measures. We have established a committee,

an emergency committee, and we would like you to be a part of it."

Bessmertnykh questioned the authority under which the committee was organized: "Is that committee arranged by instructions of the President?"

"No," Kryuchkov answered. "He's incapable of functioning now. He's lying flat in a dacha."

Bessmertnykh asked for a medical report on Gorbachev's health and was told it was not available.

"The decision came to me very quickly," he said. "I do not like emergency situations. All of my training as a diplomat leads me to try to avoid them. By nature I resent them."

A folder with a list of the names of the pro-

Unsure of why they have been sent, young troops and their armored personnel carriers take up positions in the center of Moscow.

8:15 am
Twenty-three members of the Russian Federation's Council of Ministers adopt a handwritten statement condemning the Emergency Committee for carrying out an illegal "right-wing coup" and call for a general strike.

9:00 am
Paratroopers take possession of Lithuanian television and radio facilities in Kaunas.

10:00 am
Russian Federation Supreme Soviet leadership convenes a meeting headed by Boris Yeltsin. The group adopts a statement of ten demands, including the release of Gorbachev.

10:30 am
Statement by coup leaders to the Soviet people claims that "the country has become ungovernable."

11:00 am
Soviet troops and tanks take up positions near the Russian Parliament Building.

posed state-of-emergency committee lay on a table. Bessmertnykh's name was on it.

He recalled: "And that was when I took out my pen, picked up the paper, and crossed my name off the list. I said, 'Mr. Kryuchkov, I'm not going to be part of that committee and I categorically reject any participation in that.'"

The two then rejoined the larger meeting. Kryuchkov told the other plotters of Bessmertnykh's refusal to join.

One of the plotters was cynically rueful: "We needed a liberal on the committee."

Bessmertnykh says he remained at the meeting to argue against the takeover, saying: "What you are doing will bring a terrible blow to the Soviet Union and its foreign policy. It will be isolated. There will be sanctions. There will be embargoes. There will be no grain. There will be no food. That will be the situation, especially if blood is spilled and especially if something happens in the Baltic republics."

His warning was sloughed off. One conspirator said: "Well, the Western countries don't help us anyway."

Bessmertnykh left the meeting after an hour and went to his Moscow apartment. Even though he disagreed with the methods of the plotters, he said later he still thought the men might be acting legally, that Gorbachev might really be stricken.

"I was very much concerned. I knew there was an emergency situation. I was worried about Gorbachev personally, that he might really be sick. I had just seen him at the summit meeting and he looked very fit. I could not understand. I waited until the morning to hear the medical reports.

Leonid Kravchenko, president of the USSR State Television and Radio Company and once a close ally of Gorbachev's, was relieved of his job for failing to oppose the coup.

"When the medical reports did not come in the morning, I felt something cool inside me. I was worried."

According to Prime Minister Valentin Pavlov, one of the conspirators, the original plan called for a convening of the Supreme Soviet to have that body and Vice-President Gennady Yanayev, one of the plotters, sign proclamations declaring the incapacity of Gorbachev and the state of emergency.

But the plotters discarded that plan in favor of a middle-of-the-night takeover of information hubs and the state of emergency declaration in the committee's name, all backed up by the movement of troops and armored vehicles into the city.

As the Kremlin meeting continued, a phone rang in the suburban dacha of Leonid Kravchenko, president of the USSR State Television and Radio Company, and roused him from a deep sleep. A KGB staff car arrived within a few minutes. Reluctantly, grumpily, he got in and, at 2 a.m., he was sitting in the Communist Party Central Committee office of Yuri Manayenkov in downtown Moscow. Manayenkov, a high-ranking Party secretary, told Kravchenko a state of emergency for the country would probably go into effect in two hours and he should begin preparing Soviet television and radio to make the announcement.

Kravchenko had been installed by Gorbachev less than a year earlier as head of Soviet television with orders to bring that unruly organization under control. Its staff members had taken glasnost seriously. Its

journalists had begun to probe the dark cran-
nies of Soviet institutions, exposing all of the
weaknesses of the system, too often leveling
criticism on Gorbachev and his regime.

By November 1990, Gorbachev had had
enough. He cast his lot firmly with the conservatives. Kravchenko, who had been
moved from the number-two job at Soviet
television to become director-general of
TASS, the official news agency, was moved
back to television to become chairman of the
huge and important enterprise. Izvestia had
interviewed him and headlined the article:
"My Job Is to Serve the President."

Kravchenko's concept of state television
was that it serve as a mouthpiece for the
President. And serve the presidency he did.

He canceled hard-hitting programs and muz-
zled journalists. Many workers in the state
television system, who had learned recently
to think that their job was to serve their viewers, spoke up for their beliefs, criticizing
Kravchenko. He said later he received many
death threats and, as a result, the KGB 9th
Directorate — security detail for the Party
elite — had assigned a full-time bodyguard to
him and his wife.

Kravchenko said that he told Manayenkov
he should be talking to TASS as well. "I took
out my phone book and called Gennady
Shishkin [TASS deputy chief], asking him to
come over. It never occurred to me I was
doing something wrong. I thought I was just
showing professional solidarity with a friend.

**Russian President Boris
Yeltsin makes his first and
most important speech atop
a tank outside the Russian
Parliament Building.**

11:17 am
An Emergency Committee decree read on Soviet television demands all guns be turned over to the KGB. The committee promises price rollbacks and increased food supplies.

11:50 am
Yeltsin mounts a tank outside the White House and proclaims all decisions and instructions of the Emergency Committee are unlawful.

1:00 pm
Columns of armor continue to roll into Moscow. Ten tanks of the Taman Division move to the Russian White House in support of Yeltsin.

1:25 pm
Russian television taken off the air.

2:00 pm
Large crowds assemble in front of the Russian Federation Building. Troops seal off Red Square, forcing demonstrators out of the area.

Thirty or forty minutes later he was there, and we were told to report at 5 a.m. to the office of Shenin [a Politburo member] to get the documents."

The two left together, Shishkin to go to his office and Kravchenko to return to his apartment. Kravchenko volunteered to save Shishkin another trip by picking up the documents for both organizations at 5 a.m. and delivering one set to TASS.

"That was just regular behavior to help a colleague. It had nothing to do with coup plotting," Kravchenko insisted.

Shishkin began a chain reaction of phone calls through his organization. Alexander Merkushev, chief editor of TASS's English language service, received his wake-up at 3 a.m. and was ordered to assemble a staff and report to work immediately. Merkushev and his assistants, awaiting their instructions, argued over what the important story might be. They knew only that they would be ordered to transmit a package of several state documents.

"After a couple of cups of coffee we realized that the date was August 19, the eve of the signing of the Union Treaty. We thought the Communist Party had a secret meeting on Sunday and decided to remove Gorbachev as its general secretary. Nothing less, we argued, would have warranted piping all hands on deck in the early hours of the day."

When Kravchenko showed up at TASS on schedule, there was a polite memo attached to his package of proclamations, acts, announcements, statements — all programmed to be doled out during the next several hours.

"We request," the memo said, "that the materials be transmitted in the following order: 1. Edict by Vice-President Gennady Yanayev. 2. Statement by Chairman of the USSR Supreme Soviet Anatoly Lukianov.

3. Acting President Gennady Yanayev's Address to Heads of State and Governments and the U. N. General Assembly."

Radio and TASS were ordered to start transmitting the items simultaneously at 6 a.m. The first appeared on the wire at 6:06 a.m.:

GORBACHEV - REMOVAL
URGENT — YANAYEV: GORBACHEV UNABLE TO
PERFORM DUTIES
19/8 TASS A-11
MOSCOW AUGUST 19 TASS — VICE-PRESIDENT
GENNADY YANAYEV HAS TAKEN OVER THE DUTIES OF
USSR PRESIDENT FROM AUGUST 19, 1991, IN
KEEPING WITH ARTICLE 127, CLAUSE 7, OF THE
SOVIET CONSTITUTION DUE TO MIKHAIL
GORBACHEV'S INABILITY TO PERFORM HIS DUTIES
FOR HEALTH REASONS, SAYS A DECREE BY VICE-
PRESIDENT YANAYEV CIRCULATED HERE TODAY.
ITEM ENDS 190620 AOU 91

Immediately afterwards the text of an announcement by Vice-President Yanayev, Prime Minister Pavlov, and Oleg Baklanov, first deputy chairman of the USSR Defense Council, moved on the wire. It was the official decree backing up the TASS urgent item. The subsequent documents made the state-of-emergency declaration specific. Newspapers were shut down, television curtailed. Central government rule was proclaimed for all the republics. The Emergency Committee promised a "merciless war on the criminal world," solutions to the food and housing problems, and a rollback on the spring price rises.

The action was clearly intended to turn the clock back to a time before the Gorbachev regime when the Communist Party reigned supreme.

The text was dated August 18 and

In a short but impassioned speech, Yeltsin calls for a general strike and defiance of the new "emergency" government.

3:00 pm
Moscow is jammed with traffic, crowds, tanks, and troops.

3:30 pm
Emergency Committee orders Yeltsin to "clean out his office" within the hour and demands the evacuation of the entire Russian Republic Building.

5:00 pm
Yeltsin calls on all armed forces and KGB personnel in Russia to obey his orders.

5:03 pm
Acting President Yanayev issues a decree placing Moscow under a state of emergency due to demonstrations and rallies against the coup. Taxis, buses, and private vehicles barred from entering the city center.

6:00 pm
In a news conference, Yanayev explains that Gorbachev is "incapacitated."

claimed the state of emergency was necessary to overcome life-threatening political and ethnic crises and confrontations; to maintain territorial integrity, freedom, and independence of the motherland; and to preserve the union. The announcement proclaimed the state of emergency starting from 4 a.m., August 19, for a period of six months, citing constitutional authority.

Most importantly, it established the USSR State Committee on the State of Emergency, creating a new authoritarian government for the entire country just before Gorbachev was to sign the treaty that stripped the central government and the Communist Party hierarchy of its power.

The Emergency Committee members included KGB Chief Kryuchkov, Interior Minister Boris Pugo, Defense Minister Dmitry Yazov, and Defense Council Vice-Chairman Baklanov. Together they controlled all of the armed forces in the country. Additionally Prime Minister Pavlov and Vice-President Yanayev offered the committee civilian legitimacy, if not wisdom. Finally, there were two relative unknowns, Vasily Starodubtsev, chairman of the Farmers Union, and Alexander Tizyakov, president of the Association of State Enterprises. They were apparently selected at the very last minute, intended to show that the committee had a broad economic base.

"Even though democracy was only a baby," Alexander Merkushev of TASS wrote later, "we had somehow got used to its durability, and the announcements by the self-appointed Emergency Committee seemed surreal, totally out of this world."

If the material was surreal, so was the scene at what was once the single most tightly controlled propaganda outfit in all the world. For decades TASS had been the international mouthpiece of the Moscow-controlled move-

ment to spread communism throughout the world. Deputy Director Shishkin, running the agency in the absence of the vacationing Director-General Lev Spiridonov, suddenly began allowing subordinates to make decisions he would normally make on what stories should be distributed on the wire. The subordinates even considered running stories pointing out that the plotters were violating the laws they were acting under.

Some correspondents defied orders to send positive items about the coup and saw their stories run on the wire as written. "There were no military censors hanging over our heads," said Merkushev.

TASS foreign correspondents called from abroad, asking if the announcements were a hoax.

It was no hoax. Tanks, armored personnel carriers, and other military vehicles were clattering toward the center of Moscow. By first light of dawn, it appeared the plotters had set in motion a totalitarian machine that would roll toward restoration of the kind of domination that had kept the Soviet empire in thrall for almost three-quarters of a century.★

But the plotters were not strong enough to drive the machine. They requested TASS to run the material; they discussed a Supreme Soviet meeting to declare the state of emergency; they hesitated instead of arresting potential opponents immediately. They apparently expected stronger support from the people. In 1964, there was no uproar when a previous generation of high-ranking officials ousted Nikita Khrushchev, allegedly for health reasons, dressing their action in the quasi-legal cloak of Communist Party Central Committee approval. Now Gorbachev was far

---

★ "We had two armored divisions in a city of ten million and we counted on that to scare everyone — that was naive," Yazov said afterwards. The conspirators just assumed that everyone would keep quiet and submit.

more disliked than Khrushchev had been.

The men who engineered the coup made the mistake of thinking there were only two choices in the country — either themselves or Gorbachev. The plotters neglected the possibility that there were non-Gorbachev supporters who were also democrats or that there were democrats who would support Gorbachev despite his predisposition to side with conservatives when he thought balance was needed.

"It is a characteristic of our politicians not to know what's going on in our country," Valentin Lazutkin, first deputy chairman of Soviet television, would remark later in a comment on the way the plotters behaved. They did not realize that the Soviet people had developed a will of their own, that they could no longer be commanded, that they had to believe in their leaders.

Boris Yeltsin heard the news at his summer dacha in Arkhangelskoye, a suburban village west of Moscow. He decided in the first hours of the crisis to move boldly, assuming an attitude that would propel him from an ambivalent and sometime demagogic challenger of Gorbachev into his rescuer and the most powerful man in the Soviet Union.

But first he arranged protection for himself. If General Grachev, commander of all Soviet paratroop forces, is correct, Yeltsin called at 6:30 a.m. Grachev told the Russian president that Defense Minister Yazov had ordered him the previous night to bring his division, without artillery, to Moscow.

"Don't worry. I will provide you with security no matter what happens," Grachev told Yeltsin. The general said he would provide defense even against an attack ordered by the USSR defense minister. Throughout the day, Grachev maintained contact with Yazov, although he said that from very early in the morning he was following Yeltsin's and

not Yazov's orders.★

Next Yeltsin convened a meeting at 7 a.m. with Russian Prime Minister Ivan Silayev, Moscow Mayor Gavril Popov, Leningrad Mayor Anatoly Sobchak, and key advisors.

In search of information, Yeltsin's team members called Gorbachev's offices in the Kremlin and at Communist Party Central Committee headquarters in Moscow. No one could come to the phone. Everyone was busy. They tried the Crimean dacha but

Vladimir Kryuchkov, KGB chief and mastermind of the plot, justified the coup by claiming that the internal democratic movement in the USSR was a plot by the Bush Administration to overthrow the Soviet government. OVERLEAF: Coup protesters in Moscow's Manezh Square demand information from an Army officer about the military's intentions.

★ Yazov was the puzzle of the coup. A career military officer, conservative but honorable, few of his colleagues could imagine him betraying his friend and president, Gorbachev, or sending his army against his own people. Gorbachev said after the coup he thought the plotters must be using Yazov's name. Yazov could not issue the final order to attack the White House and kill thousands of Soviet citizens. His deputies could only explain his participation in the coup by his age: born in 1923, he was raised in the harsh dictatorial rule of Stalin and instilled with a loyalty not only to his motherland but also to the Communist Party. He told colleagues and prosecutors he never considered Gorbachev's life in danger. "I won't be a Pinochet," he told one aide, during the coup, referring to former Chilean President Augusto Pinochet, who came to power in a coup that killed his predecessor, Salvador Allende.

could not get the call through. Newspaper editors reported they had all received copies of the Emergency Committee's decrees.

All the signs pointed to a coup d'état.

Why Yeltsin was not immediately arrested by KGB Alpha Group anti-terrorist troops, who before dawn surrounded his dacha, became one of the mysteries of the coup. Maj. Gen. Viktor Karpukhin, Alpha Group commander, later told the newspaper *Sovietsky Sport*, that he was ordered to arrest Yeltsin that morning but refused to do so. The post-coup commission appointed to investigate the KGB took testimony indicating an order had been issued to arrest Yeltsin when he returned from a trip to Kazakhstan the day before. The commission discovered the order had been ignored.

"I was aware of every step made by Yeltsin," Karpukhin said. "We could have arrested him at any time without making the slightest noise." Karpukhin told the paper

that he realized from the beginning that Gorbachev was not ill and that he decided not to obey orders but to delay by pretending to be taking action.

A story circulated that troops sent to arrest Yeltsin missed him by forty minutes — first at his dacha, then at his in-town apartment, and finally at the Kremlin where he was denied access to his office under orders from the committee. Silayev later said that the story was apocryphal, that Yeltsin and the rest of the group went directly from the dacha to his office in the White House, in effect

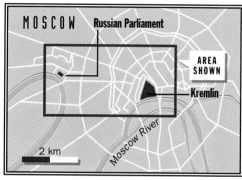

- **Tanks and troops**
- **Tanks and troops defected to Yeltsin**
- **Barricades**
- **Clash between troops and protesters**

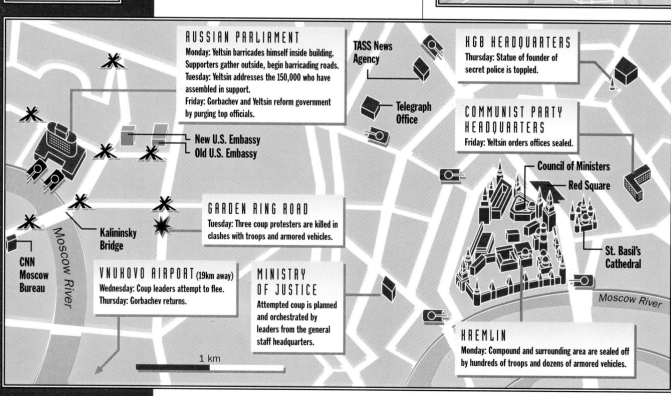

RUSSIAN PARLIAMENT
Monday: Yeltsin barricades himself inside building. Supporters gather outside, begin barricading roads.
Tuesday: Yeltsin addresses the 150,000 who have assembled in support.
Friday: Gorbachev and Yeltsin reform government by purging top officials.

TASS News Agency

Telegraph Office

KGB HEADQUARTERS
Thursday: Statue of founder of secret police is toppled.

COMMUNIST PARTY HEADQUARTERS
Friday: Yeltsin orders offices sealed.

New U.S. Embassy
Old U.S. Embassy

Council of Ministers
Red Square

GARDEN RING ROAD
Tuesday: Three coup protesters are killed in clashes with troops and armored vehicles.

Kalininsky Bridge

St. Basil's Cathedral

Moscow River

CNN Moscow Bureau

Moscow River

VNUKOVO AIRPORT (19km away)
Wednesday: Coup leaders attempt to flee.
Thursday: Gorbachev returns.

MINISTRY OF JUSTICE
Attempted coup is planned and orchestrated by leaders from the general staff headquarters.

KREMLIN
Monday: Compound and surrounding area are sealed off by hundreds of troops and dozens of armored vehicles.

1 km

achieving sanctuary against everything but an all-out attack.★

Valentin Sergeyev, a minister without portfolio in Yeltsin's government, was shaving in his Moscow apartment and listening to the radio at 6 a.m. He heard the familiar national anthem and then the first announcement of the state of emergency. Within ten minutes he was on his way to the White House.★★

Sergeyev said that by 8:15 a.m. twenty-three ministers of the Russian Federation's Council of Ministers had adopted a hand-written statement of denunciation, condemning the Emergency Committee for carrying out an illegal "right-wing coup." The statement, signed by President Yeltsin, Vice-President Alexander Rutskoi, Prime Minister Silayev, and Supreme Soviet Speaker Ruslan Khazbulatov, called for an immediate general strike. It was duplicated and posted on walls and bulletin boards all over Moscow.★★★

★ Some democratic leaders were arrested or narrowly escaped capture. Telman Gdlyan, a prosecutor who was accused of misconduct for pursuing corruption cases all the way to the Communist Party leadership, was arrested and taken to a detention center in a military base. Only three people were held there, though it had been prepared with sixty beds, an indication that many more arrests were planned but did not take place. After the coup, investigators found 300,000 blank arrest warrants had been printed and 250,000 pairs of handcuffs had been delivered to Moscow.
★★ Yeltsin's headquarters is a 19-story building on the Moscow River known by at least three names: the Russian Parliament, the Russian Federation Building, and the White House. This last became the name indelibly stamped on it during the coup. Built during the Brezhnev era, the structure is a tribute to the wasteful lavishness of Party bureaucrats. On the fifth floor, for example, an enormous ornamental conference room has crystal chandeliers, pastel murals depicting life in an idealized society, and a single long white table that seats a hundred people.
★★★ At 5:30 p.m., Monday, Yeltsin authorized Deputy Prime Minister Oleg Lobov to establish an underground Russian government if Yeltsin and the others were captured. He sent them to his hometown of Sverdlovsk, where he knew there was a back-up administration center hidden seventy kilometers out in the forest in case of war. Yeltsin's friends from Sverdlovsk quickly had the center's fax and teletype machines sending Russian calls to oppose the coup across the country. Local riot police deployed as guards.

At his apartment, retired KGB Maj. Gen. Oleg Kalugin, once that organization's station chief in Washington, also heard the news and, shortly after 8 a.m., also sped off to the White House. He was followed by two black Volgas full of former colleagues from the KGB's Department of Surveillance. Kalugin was a renegade. A year before he had publicly spoken out in protest of the KGB's repressive tactics, for the way it still spied on the Soviet people. As a result, Gorbachev ordered his pension revoked, and he was stripped of his medals and other honors. He was, however, a deputy of the Supreme Soviet and he used that forum effectively to continue to speak out.

Kalugin's skills as an analyst, honed over decades of intelligence work, led him to conclude early that the coup was doomed. Here is his later description of the situation three hours after the coup was announced:

"Several deputies showed up. We met in the White House and decided to call for a meeting of a larger group on the 20th. They were mostly younger deputies. I was the oldest one there. I said the coup was an adventure that would flop in two or three days. There had been no shooting, no arrests. Something had obviously gone wrong. Why weren't they out arresting people at 4 o'clock in the morning? The more delay of action there was, the less likely it was to succeed."

Across town, at the Ostankino Television Center, Valentin Lazutkin, first deputy chairman of the State Television and Radio Company, arrived for work a little after 9 a.m. fresh from a vacation. He had not listened to the radio or watched television. He knew nothing of the coup yet. His first tips were the armored vehicles outside the building and fifty soldiers in the big lobby of the building who were checking identity cards carefully. Lazutkin was detained briefly

Midnight
The crowd stages a
night vigil outside the
Russian White House.
The public is still uncertain
of Gorbachev's true
whereabouts.

while the soldiers puzzled over his card. They had never before seen one for an official of cabinet rank and did not know what to make of it. Lazutkin at that moment knew nothing of the State of Emergency. He was still in vacation mode.

By that time Moscow Radio had for several hours been broadcasting a mixture of lugubrious classical music and the official announcements of the new government. Television had been reduced to one channel running such old favorites as "Swan Lake," classical concerts, and balalaika ensembles along with the announcements. The format was of the kind generally reserved by Communist Party propagandists only for an announcement that a leader had died. The intent is to calm an anxious populace during a time of potential shock. When a beloved or feared leader has died, the treatment can be soothing. When used to accompany the Emergency Committee announcements, the music only reinforced the uncertainty and brought back memories of the old days when the Communist Party was the supreme ruler.

The White House meeting of Yeltsin's cabinet members was only one of many gath-

erings in the capital in the coup's early hours as all sides planned their first moves in the battle for control of an empire.

At 6 a.m., Dmitry Yazov, defense minister and Emergency Committee member, convened a ten-minute meeting of his top commanders and explained the military's role in the state of emergency. He said troops were on alert throughout the country. It would be the job of the military to maintain order and protect military installations. He added: "Don't let yourselves be provoked. Please, don't do foolish things. There will be people who will throw themselves under the tanks on purpose and I don't want bloodshed. The rest you will know from radio reports."

Air Force chief General Yevgeny Shaposhnikov said that statement made him think that Yazov never intended to order the use of force against civilians. "Yazov's short speech was far from enthusiastic, and his mood seemed depressed," Shaposhnikov said. "He allowed no questions."

In the Kremlin, Vadim Bakatin, a member of Gorbachev's National Security Council, arrived at work confused. He had not heard the full text of the announcement but wondered, if the President was ill, why all the talk about changing policies. "Either health or perestroika?" he mused. "A statement on behalf of the Soviet leadership? What leadership?"

Bakatin first wrote a letter of protest to Vice-President Yanayev, the nominal head of the Emergency Committee, and then went to see him. He found the vice-president excited, pacing back and forth, smoking nervously, his face swollen and bags under his eyes after a sleepless night. Bakatin asked what was happening. Yanayev answered vaguely that he had been visited by officials who had met with Gorbachev in the Crimea and had plans to put him on trial.

"I don't know myself what's going on," Yanayev said, "They came and tried to persuade me for two hours. I didn't agree, but they finally persuaded me."

Bakatin resigned his position in protest — a decision he would rescind the next day.

For the rest of the coup, the Council of Ministers Building in the Kremlin was occupied by two opposing camps. Yanayev occupied a large office on the second floor. Veniamin Yarin, a loyal Gorbachev staff man, worked just down the hall. Bakatin worked right above Yanayev on the third floor. Yevgeny Primakov, another Gorbachev adviser, occupied an office in another wing. It was only one of many places around the country

where the opposing sides would maintain contact with each other.

At the White House, the Russian Federation Supreme Soviet leadership convened at 10 a.m. to discuss the situation and to decide on a course of action. Yeltsin had just arrived in the building. The group adopted a statement of ten demands of the Emergency Committee. Item one demanded the release of Gorbachev. Other items demanded that a doctor be allowed to visit Gorbachev, that communications be restored for him and for Yeltsin, that newspapers be allowed to publish, that Silayev and others be allowed to visit Gorbachev in the Crimea, and that all

LEFT AND ABOVE Muscovites confront troops and attempt to persuade them to abandon their positions and rally behind Yeltsin. **OVERLEAF:** Coup demonstrators dig up cobblestones to construct barricades around Yeltsin and the Parliament building.

junta orders be abrogated.

Prime Minister Silayev, Vice-President Rutskoi, and Khazbulatov were delegated to represent the Russian Republic's leadership and deliver the edicts to the plotters in the Kremlin.

Yeltsin held a brief press conference inside the building to make his first personal statement of condemnation and to read the statement just adopted. He denounced the plotters for carrying out a coup, becoming the first official to make that charge publicly.

Meanwhile at another important meeting, Kravchenko laid out the coup coverage instructions to the top officials at Soviet television. The meeting recessed while Kravchenko took a call on the Kremlin phone system — the so-called *vertushka* instituted by Lenin in the early days of Soviet power to communicate quickly from one department to another.★

During the recess Lazutkin went to his office and used a government phone himself to try to get some guidance on the true state of affairs. First he tried Vitaly Ignatenko, Gorbachev's press secretary. Ignatenko was on vacation. Next he called Alexander Dzasokhov, a Communist Party Politburo member and friend. Like Bakatin in the Kremlin, Lazutkin wanted to know what was happening and his friend responded mysteriously: "I am trying to figure out what is happening myself. Be ready. Be careful."

Dzasokhov hung up abruptly. Lazutkin

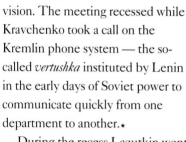

Foreign Minister Alexander Bessmertnykh reportedly refused to join the Emergency Committee, but he later lost his job for not showing stronger opposition to the coup.

★ The term *vertushka* originally referred only to the system in the Kremlin itself. But over the years, as government and Communist Party leadership dispersed, the term was expanded to cover the entire private phone system of the top leadership. Lenin controlled those communications so carefully that the vertushka switchboard was in an anteroom of his office.

took his response as a sign that the coup plotters might not be in complete control. If they had been, Dzasokhov would have warned him to get on the team.

At 4 p.m. Foreign Minister Bessmertnykh convened a meeting of his deputies at his office in the gingerbread skyscraper housing the Ministry of Foreign Affairs. It was not far from the White House, but there had been no contact between officials in the two buildings all day. At the time he did not know Yeltsin had issued a call for opposition to the coup. He did not hear about that until he returned home in the evening.

Bessmertnykh described that Monday: "It was a strange, cool, unclear, somewhat frightening day. Almost everyone believed something legal had taken place. But, still, the situation was dangerous. I was worried not only for Gorbachev and the country but for myself. After all, I could have been arrested after I refused to join the committee. I asked my wife please not to go out and not to take our grandson out."

Bessmertnykh's brain trust met in that atmosphere to study their options. They could all resign to emphasize a protest by the ministry of the actions of the Emergency Committee. That would make their position clear and remove legitimacy from the committee. Or, alternatively, they could remain in place and try to protect the nation's relations with other countries — particularly the United States.

"We had worked hard for many years to improve those relations and we didn't want them to be hurt now. We wanted to protect the policy, the new thinking, and the Foreign Ministry," Bessmertnykh said later.

The majority agreed to remain on the job. Bessmertnykh said, "We decided, just the small group of us, to do everything to protect the foreign policy....If you are sent to protect something precious, you've got to do it, not run away just because it is politically advisable."

Bessmertnykh was to be criticized later for not speaking out soon enough against the coup and for not giving direct enough orders to his diplomats around the world to register objection. Actually, he said, he sent two cables to ambassadors. The first, on Monday, instructed all Soviet diplomatic missions to follow only the policies of the Soviet presidency, the Council of Ministers, and the Supreme Soviet. It omitted any mention of the Emergency Committee. The second cable, the following day, instructed ambassadors to take orders only from the Foreign Ministry and not from any other governmental organization.★

In many places around the vast country the Emergency Committee was moving to establish control. It took paratroopers thirty-five minutes to take possession of the Lithuanian television and radio facilities in Kaunas, the republic's second largest city. (On January 13, troops had occupied television facilities in Vilnius, Lithuania's capital, but then there had been a pitched battle in which fifteen citizens and one KGB Alpha Unit officer were killed.) The operation was finished by 9 a.m., and Lithuania's President Vytautas Landsbergis took to the air to protest. Later in the day, the television center in Riga, the capital of Latvia, was occupied. The port of Tallinn, the capital of Estonia, was closed.

In Moscow, tanks, armored personnel carriers, and other vehicles were on their way into the city and had taken up positions in Red Square, near the City Hall, central tele-

vision, and the White House. There were reports of troop movements outside Leningrad. Airline ticket offices were closed down to keep the citizenry from moving around. Domestic flights were cancelled.

When the state of emergency went into effect, all the newspapers and magazines were shut down officially, and later only nine of Moscow's publications were allowed back on the streets. The authorities began to arrest some pesky but relatively minor figures, like former Army Col. Vitaly Urazhtsev, now chairman of *Shchit* (Shield), the democratic union of servicemen. He was taken into custody near the Russian Federation Building.

Reports trickled to Moscow from the provinces indicating that politicians were beginning to take sides — going with Yeltsin into opposition or lining up with the Emergency Committee. There was no pattern in the beginning. As the days went on, however, the vast majority of regions in the Soviet Union would side against the plotters.

Boris Yeltsin's Rubicon was just down the front steps of the office building from which he governed. He crossed it at high noon on that Monday, before the brooding gray skies of the day turned dark and it started to rain.

Kalugin was there: "The White House at that time was in complete disarray. They did not know what to do. They were trying to find out what was really happening. At 11 a.m., Yeltsin had a short press conference. At about noon Yeltsin, [General Konstantin]

After Yeltsin's speech, Russian Defense Minister Konstantin Kobets would vow that, "Not a hand will be raised against the people or the duly elected president of Russia."

★ Bessmertnykh's role would become controversial as will be discussed later. But this telegram in effect gave diplomats authority to follow the dictates of Prime Minister Pavlov, Supreme Soviet Speaker Lukianov, and, most importantly, acting President Yanayev, all of whom were also members of the Emergency Committee.

Kobets [Russian Republic defense minister], and I went outside and approached a tank. Yeltsin was nervous and shaken. He did not know what would happen as he climbed on the tank. He did not know how the soldiers would react. And a lot depended on their reaction. The tank commander hid his head and averted his eyes. There was no microphone. Yeltsin began speaking:

" 'Citizens of Russia...the legally elected President of the country was removed from power...we are dealing with a rightist, reactionary, anticonstitutional coup...Accordingly we proclaim all decisions and instructions of this committee to be unlawful...We appeal to citizens of Russia to give fitting rebuff to the putschists and demand a return of the country to normal constitutional development....' " ★

Kalugin continued: "There were only about fifty or one hundred people there when Yeltsin began, but the crowd started to build. The real dramatic speech was given by Kobets. He is a military man, and when he climbed up on the tank, the crowd began shouting, 'Down with the general! Down with the general!' Someone in the crowd shouted 'What kind of general is he? He wears a uniform but he has no troops.' Kobets was unknown to the crowd and wore the insignia of a signal corpsman. His appearance did not inspire faith."

Kalugin added: "Kobets said very few words but they were important. 'Soldiers and officers, I am the defense minister of Russia. Not a hand will be raised against the people or the duly elected president of Russia.' "

By now the crowd had grown to about fif-

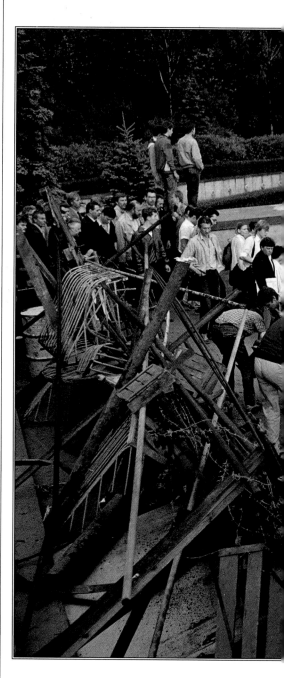

teen hundred, and they applauded immediately. The general had made a strong psychological impact on the crowd and, more importantly on the troops. A major said: "We are not going to shoot the president of Russia." Yeltsin repeated the line to a delighted crowd.

One hour later ten tanks belonging to the Taman Division turned their guns away from

---

★ Yeltsin's performance recalled the famous scene seventy-four years earlier when Vladimir Lenin returned to Petrograd in 1917 and, outside the Finland Station, similarly mounted an armored car to proclaim the so-called April Theses calling for the transformation of the bourgeois revolution already under way into the proletarian revolution to be led by the Communist Party.

the White House toward the direction from which attacking troops would be coming. They would defend the Yeltsin government against any attack by troops loyal to the plotters. Yeltsin had landed the first blow in the battle to turn the coup around. Elsewhere in Moscow crowds of demonstrators were gathering — particularly at the Mossoviet (the City Hall) on Tverskaya Street and in front of

the Manezh, the former czarist riding stables just under the Kremlin Wall and near the entrance to Red Square. Hearing of the military concentration at the White House, the crowd started marching there to help defend the Yeltsin government.

As he started back into the White House with Yeltsin, Kalugin was approached by one of

the KGB agents following him and warned that his car, in the path of the advancing demonstrators, might be endangered. He started down the street with the intent of moving the vehicle. He was too late. The parade overtook him and he was recognized.

"General, lead us to the White House," someone in the crowd shouted.

"So I led the crowd of several thousand people," the smiling, pixieish former master spy said. "They were all excited, all young people. They were chanting 'Yeltsin! Yeltsin!'

"At the White House I was delegated to go in and get Yeltsin out to speak. So I went inside. He was closeted with aides. I could not see him, but I did see Rutskoi and told him, 'You or Yeltsin must come outside.' There was a long delay. It started raining and the crowd dispersed before another speaker appeared."

Kalugin was still concerned — for the safety of his car and for his own freedom. So, his KGB tails in tow, he went to retrieve his car and move it from the increasingly dangerous area near the White House. He decided the safest place was as close as he could get to the headquarters of the enemy.

He drove to the Communist Party Central Committee headquarters in Old Square to see a friend. He parked the car, left the surveillance people to watch it, and walked into the headquarters which, physically, is a structural maze matching the bureaucratic blind alleys of the Party.

With help from his friend, he left the building through another entrance, eluded his followers, and went off to a meeting of democratic deputies at the nearby Rossiya Hotel. The two cars full of KGB agents watched his car in the parking lot of the Central Committee and he was a free man.

In addition to the nine officially sanctioned papers, some publications continued without authorization. Anticipating permanent shutdown, several papers got together and formed what was called "The Common Paper." It was printed secretly and distributed all three days that the Emergency Committee remained in some semblance of control. One of the papers in the consortium was *Komsomolskaya Pravda*, the official publication of the Young Communist League, now an outspoken critic of repression.

At 2 p.m., a KGB colonel identified only as A. Kichinkhin walked into the newspaper's offices and handed over an open letter addressed to soldiers and agents of the KGB and Interior Ministry. Kichinkhin said he was resigning from the KGB because he "was not willing to take part in the repressions and violent acts carried out by the security services on behalf of Kryuchkov." He asked his colleagues to follow suit.

As the first afternoon progressed, Marshal Yazov, the defense minister, knew the time for military action to neutralize Yeltsin was drawing near. He convened a meeting in his office to discuss plans for storming the White House. Among those present were Maj. Gen. Victor Karpukhin, commander of the KGB's elite Alpha Unit, the highly trained detachment of anti-terrorist experts, and Gen. Alexander Lebed, commander of a paratroop division.

Earlier in the day, Lebed had promised support to Yeltsin, according to some reports. His boss, Maj. Gen. Pavel Grachev, had also promised the Russian president protection early in the morning. Now Lebed and Karpukhin conferred with one of the key members of the Emergency Committee, apparently to plan an assault on the White House. Lebed and Karpukhin both reported to Yazov that they had spent time during the day studying the problem of storming the White House. They had both visited the

"No to the military coup d'état" proclaims a protester's sign on busy Kalinin Avenue near the Kremlin.

scene and studied video taken there.

General Grachev, the commander of all paratroopers, argued against an attack: "There are too many people there," he said. "There will be bloodshed."

General Varrenikov, deputy defense minister, was hawkish: "Don't try to frighten us."

Karpukhin later told the newspaper Sovietsky Sport and also the KGB investigating commission that he informed his superiors that, given the thousands of people already assembled at the White House, an attack would cause unacceptable casualties. Perhaps no order was given by the Defense Ministry, but at 8 p.m., Monday, KGB Chief Kryuchkov decided he would take unilateral responsibility for an attack. On his command, First Deputy KGB Chief Geny Ageyev issued a verbal order to Karpukhin to prepare the Alpha Group to attack the White House at 3 a.m., Tuesday.

Karpukhin told the investigating commission he transmitted the order but never intended actually to attack. His two deputies, Mikhail Golovatov and Sergei Goncharov, claim Karpukhin was serious in transmitting the order and that they, after consulting with their junior officers, refused to carry it out. Whatever the truth, the Alpha Group remained at its secret base outside Moscow for the whole time of the coup and never came into town.

The crowd outside the White House was growing. By the early evening hours it was several thousand strong and reports from across the country, though mixed, were beginning to indicate a wave of support

Gennady Yanayev, the front man for the coup, during the Emergency Committee's first press conference. His trembling hands and transparent lies about Gorbachev's health drew ridicule rather than respect from the international press corps.

for the Yeltsin-led opposition. The supporters began assembling the beginnings of the impressive barricades that would go up during the coup. Throughout the country coal miners were starting to strike. The plotters were losing control.

At his dacha on the Crimean Peninsula a thousand miles south of Moscow, President Mikhail Gorbachev had little information with which to assess the situation and few staff to help him. The only two aides with him were Anatoly Chernyayev, his foreign affairs adviser, and Olga Lanina, his personal secretary. Present also were his family and the family physicians. Since late Sunday afternoon, they had settled into a strange kind of house arrest. Both the personal guard loyal to Gorbachev and the security guard that had imprisoned him continued to live in the same quarters. The Gorbachev loyalists were free to come and go as they pleased and were allowed to keep their arms.

Gorbachev was able to follow the news to some extent on the radio during the day. At first he listened to Soviet broadcasts which contained only the official announcements. Later an antenna was rigged in the compound to receive international short-wave broadcasts from the BBC, Voice of America, and Radio Liberty, among others. As reports came in over and over again that the Emergency Committee had acted because he was sick, those with Gorbachev began to worry that he might be executed to do away with the evidence that he was well.

The fear was intense. Gorbachev spoke in whispers in his dacha, thinking that the KGB had wiretapped and bugged the building — a particularly humiliating possibility, thought Chernyayev. The security agency had had plenty of opportunity to do so. It supervised the building of the compound, equipped it, and guarded it. And now the nation's leader

came to the realization that even he was not immune to the pervasive psychological terror suffered by the general populace.

Gorbachev spent Monday drafting demands for the restoration of communications and for a plane to take him back to Moscow. General Generalov, in charge of the President's captors, told the President he would send the request to Moscow by airplane, because he had no other communications with the capital.

The conspirators did not realize that Gorbachev's son-in-law, Anatoly Virgansky, had a videocamera with him on vacation. Late that night, Gorbachev and Virgansky closed the curtains and began to make a tape they thought might well become the President's last statement and political testament.

"There has been a grave deception which has led to an unconstitutional coup d'état,"

Gorbachev declared. "Everything announced by Comrade Yanayev and then made public in the documents of this committee — all of this is an outright lie." He went on to describe how his communications had been cut off, how everyone was under house arrest, how the plotters had arrived and he had refused to submit to their demand for a state of emergency.

Gorbachev read his statement and then wrote out another denouncing the coup and demanding that the Soviet parliament take over running the country from the Emergency Committee. He wrote it partially in longhand so people could recognize his handwriting. His doctor wrote a statement attesting to Gorbachev's good health. They videotaped everything, and then made four identical copies to be smuggled out of the compound by four different routes in the

Despite attempts to silence it, the glasnost-inspired Soviet press continues to report the growing coup protest centered around the Parliament Building.

hope that one would reach the outside world.

Asked later if the tapes were meant to be used as evidence if the worst happened, Mrs. Gorbachev told a Soviet journalist, "Yes, that's exactly what we intended."

Though the captors had cut the antenna feeding television sets in the dacha, the President's guards were able to cobble together another antenna, and television service was restored in plenty of time for the captives to see the coup begin to come apart.

Yanayev issued a decree at 5 p.m., Monday, specifically placing Moscow under a state of emergency because of "rallies, street marches, demonstrations, and instances of instigation to riots." Citing the Soviet constitution as his authority to protect the security of Moscow's citizens, Yanayev issued the emergency proclamation, and named Col. Gen. N. V. Kalinin as commander of troops in the Moscow military and empowered him to use force if necessary.

A half-hour later a news conference started in the Foreign Ministry Press Center. Yanayev, flanked by several of the Emergency Committee members, was the principal speaker. His hands trembled noticeably. Yanayev opened with a prepared statement:

"The situation has gone out of control in the USSR and we are facing a situation of multi-rule [meaning a breakup of the USSR]. This is a cause of popular discontent. Normal life under these circumstances is impossible

We have no other alternative but to take resolute action in order to stop the country from sliding down to disaster. We are determined without further delay to restore law and order, to stop the bloodshed, and to wage relentless war on the criminal underworld...."

He then accepted questions from reporters. If Yanayev thought he was being chivalrous in declaring, "Yes please, ladies

Unaware of the significance of the moment, two young boys stand unafraid atop a tank.

first," and then calling on Carroll Bogert of Newsweek, to ask the first question, his etiquette was not rewarded. In Russian, the American reporter asked: "Where is Mikhail Sergeyevich Gorbachev? What is he sick with? Specifically, concretely, what disease does he have?"

"Mikhail Gorbachev is now on vacation; he's undergoing treatment in the south of our country. He is very tired after these many years and he will need some time to get better. It is our hope that Mikhail Gorbachev, as soon as he feels better, will again take up his office. At any rate the policy that was initiated back in 1985 by Mikhail Gorbachev will be continued by all those present here."

The reporters sensed the timidity among the plotters. The next question: "The Emergency Committee...has stated...it will try to address the food problem. Do you have any specific measures in mind? What are your resources?"

The Emergency Committee had no program in mind. Yanayev said: "I think tomorrow we will adopt a document that will provide for emergency actions and measures to salvage the crops already brought in. Secondly we will try to use the whole potential of the country to make up an inventory of everything we have in this country...."

In other words, the committee would commission another of the endless studies that preceded decision-making in a planned economy. Another reporter asked about the legitimacy of the committee: "Are you aware that you committed a military coup last night? ...And a second question: How long will [newspaper registration] take?...And will political censorship be reintroduced?"

Yanayev answered defensively, "We will expedite the newspaper registration process. As for your statement that tonight there was a...there was a military coup, I beg to disagree...because we are basing ourselves on constitutional provisions."

One reporter wanted to know if Gorbachev was involved in the coup, asking: "Did you discuss with the President your takeover before doing it? Did he agree? Why is there no bulletin on his health? And the second question, did you ask for any suggestion or any advice through General Pinochet?"

The reporters broke into applause for their colleague. For several months there had been talk of the possibility that the Soviet leadership might try to apply a so-called Pinochet Solution in which the USSR, like Chile of the 1970s, would be returned to strongman rule but with a free economy.

Yanayev ducked the Pinochet part of the question, saying: "I believe that in due course the medical bulletin on the President's state of health will be issued. As for your statement that we have snatched power, ousted from office President Gorbachev — because President Gorbachev is temporarily incapacitated, and is unable to continue in office... the vice-president of the Supreme Soviet takes over."

Finally one reporter asked for a promise from the committee that it would not harm Gorbachev: "Can you provide a guarantee or can you give us your word of honor in front of members of the mass media that Mikhail Gorbachev will continue to feel better?"

Yanayev made the promise: "Let me tell you that nothing threatens Mr. Gorbachev. He is in a safe place....I hope that my friend, President Gorbachev, will return to his office and we will work together."

It was all over in twenty-five minutes, and now the Emergency Committee had an emergency of its own. Exposed as a group without a plan, uncertain of itself, clear only in its determination to turn back the calendar to a time when central authorities in Moscow ruled by fiat and fear without a free press or free speech to hector them — this was not an

Yeltsin makes his second speech from a balcony at the Russian Parliament Building. He encourages coup protesters to continue their support and ordered the Army and KGB to obey him in Russia

Emergency Committee that could strike fear into the hearts of the press, either Soviet or international.

In the streets, a small but important number of ordinary citizens were also showing their contempt for the committee. Now it was clear that the glasnost-inspired press was not knuckling under despite the suspension of most of the capital's newspapers and the repression of television. Only central government public officials — as opposed to those in Yeltsin's Russian government — remained wary. Soviet officials had a lot at stake personally, and they also had the longest memories of how dangerous a coup could be. But after the press conference, the almost solid front of caution began to crumble.

Valentin Lazutkin, the first deputy chairman of Soviet television and the man running the system from day-to-day, watched the press conference on a closed-circuit feedback at the Ostankino television center. This coup is not going to succeed, he realized. And that recognition underpinned key decisions he would make in the next few hours.

At 6 p.m., the Council of Ministers met in the Kremlin under the chairmanship of Prime Minister Valentin Pavlov, one of the Emergency Committee members. It took Pavlov three hours to get a vote of support for the state of emergency, but in the end only two of the ministers indicated any loyalty to the President even though every one of these officials was hand-picked by Gorbachev.

One participant argued that the plotters were not being tough enough in controlling anti-coup demonstrations.

"I am against tanks. Let the people stroll around a little bit," Pavlov replied.

Pavlov's fellow conspirators were taking action, but not to move tanks. While his meeting was under way, Interior Minister Boris Pugo, another conspirator, placed a call from his Kremlin office to Lazutkin at Soviet television.

"At 2015 [8:15 p.m.]," Pugo said, "we expect an interview with [Anatoly] Sobchak, [mayor of Leningrad] on Leningrad television. Don't let it go through, either in Leningrad or throughout the rest of the country."

Lazutkin promised to call Leningrad.

When Pugo's call came in, he was in a planning meeting for the upcoming main evening news program, *Vremya*. In the room was a KGB colonel sent to monitor the goings-on and, if necessary, censor the material. With two aides, Lazutkin went into an outer office, leaving the colonel behind to keep check on the program planners. Lazutkin ordered a secretary to place the call to Leningrad but to make sure that the call did not go through until 8:30 p.m.

Although Leningrad television had been taken off the air in Moscow it was still being shown in Leningrad and throughout much of the rest of the Soviet Union. Because of the timing of Lazutkin's call, Sobchak appeared on the air throughout most of Russia that night calling for defiance of the Emergency Committee. In a broadcast seen in seventeen cities throughout the country (stretching from the Baltic Republics to Perm in the Ural Mountains and to some parts of central Asia) Sobchak said:

"Once again there is an attempt to block our people's path to freedom, democracy, and true independence. Today a band of irresponsible politicians from the top ranks of the Communist Party and former government officials have announced a state of emergency in contradiction to the law."

In Leningrad earlier in the day, Sobchak and his deputy mayor, Admiral Vyacheslav Sherbakov, a former submarine skipper, called on Col. Gen. Alexander Samsonov, the military district commander, and asked him not to move troops into the city. Samsonov was responsible for enforcing the emergency locally. Mayor Sobchak, who was a lawyer, told Samsonov that he was working with "a collection of state criminals" and left him to wrestle with his conscience. At midnight, the general agreed not to deploy troops in the city. By then, Yeltsin

had replaced him as military commander with Deputy Mayor Sherbakov.

Lazutkin was concerned that Soviet television, throughout the day, had not obtained a single interview with any of the Emergency Committee members, and now he had to format the main evening news program. He devoted the first half-hour of the program to the official announcements of the day. They were read by a somber anchor just as they had been received by Kravchenko sixteen hours before and as they had been repeated endlessly throughout the day on television and radio. Also in that half-hour was a report from Kiev on a comment by Ukrainian President Leonid Kravchuk that did not offer complete support to the Emergency Committee but did not criticize it either. And then there were reports from the Baltic states, including one brief account of a man-in-the-street interview that was critical of the State of Emergency.

By the time Lazutkin's meeting ended, Sobchak had already been on the air and Lazutkin's call went through to Leningrad. He spoke with Victor Shenin at the local station. "It was very important that I actually called Leningrad," Lazutkin said later. "We were under control. They [the KGB] were listening to our phone calls. The colonel from the KGB was already stationed in my office and was following me everywhere."

Now Lazutkin went to an editing room where Vladimir Medvedev, the only correspondent from his organization who had been on the street in front of the White House, was putting together his report. Lazutkin reviewed Medvedev's script and looked at the as yet unedited video portions of the report. He made only two suggestions: one, to cut a long section the reporter was devoting to quoting Yeltsin (he thought that it would give the KGB monitors too much time to decide to take the program off the air), and, two, that he change his signoff. Medvedev took the first suggestion and ignored the second.

"The colonel was in the room," Lazutkin said and he understood everything. But he didn't make a telephone call and he did not order any action himself, even though he had a direct order to show only support for the Emergency Committee."

The piece ran for two-and-a-half minutes. It started with Yeltsin standing on the tank issuing his demand that Gorbachev be allowed to address the nation. Then it showed the crowds in front of the White House receiving decrees from the Yeltsin government and building barricades. Medvedev reported that people were coming from all over, that no calls for volunteers were needed, and that many planned to spend the entire night. This segment was followed by a similar one-minute report from Leningrad. Minutes later Lazutkin's phone rang. It was Boris Pugo, the interior minister and a coup leader. His anger came through the telephone in a rush:

"You have disobeyed two orders. Sobchak should not have been on the air from Leningrad and the *Vremya* story on Moscow was treacherous. You have given instructions to the people on where to go and what to do. You will answer for this."

Lazutkin told Pugo he was ready to answer.

The next call came from Yuri Prokofiev, the Communist Party boss in Moscow, who said: "You have shamed the working man of Moscow. You have to be punished. Who was in charge?"

Lazutkin again took responsibility.

And then Dzasokhov, the Politburo member with whom Lazutkin had conferred earlier, called: "Do you remember our conversation this morning? I beg you. Do anything to avoid bloodshed. But hold on."

Dzasokhov had not given his approval to the report, but he had not criticized it either. Lazutkin took that as tacit approval for a policy of telling both sides of the story on central television.

Next he received a call from acting President Yanayev who was really looking for Kravchenko. Yanayev did not mention the controversial report in the news program. Finally Lazutkin asked if he had seen it.

"I saw it," Yanayev sad, "It was a good balanced report. It showed everything from different points of view."

"But they said I would be punished for it," Lazutkin said.

Yanayev replied: "Who are they? From the Central Committee? Fuck 'em."

The log jam was broken. In the next days, Soviet television would be relatively evenhanded in its presentation.

While all this was going on, Oleg Kalugin had made his way from the Central Committee headquarters to the nearby Rossiya Hotel, one of the largest in the world. There he was to meet with a group of deputies to continue their planning session for a Supreme Soviet meeting. When the meeting ended, he wanted to return to the White House but he was afraid of arrest. His colleagues suggested ordering an ambulance and putting him in it to avoid detection. He refused and decided to spend the night in the hotel.

"I found a two-room suite," he said, "and knocked on the door. There were Americans inside. I told them 'This is martial law. Please vacate this room and go into the other.' They rushed out of the room and I spent the night there, knowing I would be safe in a room registered to Americans."

The next morning Kalugin went back to Central Committee headquarters to retrieve his car and drove home to his apartment to check on his wife. The KGB agents were still waiting at his car and they followed him home. He later went back to the White House, this time taking the metro.

"One of the surveillance people following me approached from the rear in the subway," he said, "and said 'Stay quiet. Don't turn around. You and your friends will be arrested either tonight or tomorrow. Pick up the paper I have in my hand but don't look around. There is a name and a telephone number. Memorize them and destroy the paper.'"

The name and phone number were the agent's own. He wanted to hear from Kalugin when the crisis was over to express solidarity with the anti-plot cause.

"I went to the White House and stayed there until the end," said Kalugin.

At the television center, the KGB colonel assigned to monitor the operations and keep them loyal to the Emergency Committee went to see Lazutkin in his office at the end of the day.

"He said he had been watching everything all day long and he understood everything we were doing," Lazutkin recalled. "His name was Vladimir. He said, 'Valentin Valentinovich, I am from a military background. My father lost his hand in the Great Patriotic War. I was in the war. I am not a politician. But I have seen what you have done and I am ready to share your fate.'

"We drank a hundred grams of vodka together," Lazutkin said.

As Monday came to a close, the crowd in front of the White House swelled to tens of thousands. Many had been drawn there by the *Vremya* report, including Lazutkin's own son, Sergei, a 23-year-old student who had seen the report on his father's news program and had been inspired to stand up for Russia. The barricades were growing. A camaraderie was developing among the people who stood

around the bonfires warming themselves and sharing cigarettes and snacks, in many cases with the soldiers who might be ordered at any time to attack and disperse them.

The protests in the streets may have been decisive. But there was also a revolution underway within the KGB that made maintenance of discipline impossible. For example:

• The KGB 9th Directorate's border guard unit in the Crimea had decided to protect Gorbachev, if necessary, with bare hands, defying orders to imprison him.★

• The Alpha Group under the 1st Directorate refused even to prepare to attack the White House.

• The agent who alerted Kalugin to his impending arrest was from the 7th Directorate (internal surveillance) that had millions of loyal informers on its payroll.

• The censor at Soviet television who refused to carry out his orders was from the 2nd Directorate (counter-intelligence), a department previously known for its unquestioning obedience.

• Also there was the open letter of protest from the KGB's Colonel Kichinkhin to *Komsomolskaya Pravda* in which he asked his fellow agents to join the democratic movement.

Increasingly, Vladimir Kryuchkov, KGB chief and key plotter, was leader of an organization that was no longer following with the accustomed unanimity. Like the rest of Soviet society, the KGB was crumbling. Without obedience of KGB troops, the coup could not possibly succeed.

★ General Achalov called a meeting in the Defense Ministry where KGB General Viktor Karpukhin, commander of the anti-terrorist Alpha Group, was ordered to lead the storming of the White House with 15,000 troops. Karpukhin said he told his subordinates, "This is crazy. We won't do it." He said he tried to meet with Kryuchkov, but was refused. But Karpukhin was fired after the coup, because the deputy commanders of the Alpha Group testified that Karpukhin ordered the attack and they refused to obey him.

Facing an uncertain night, a prodemocracy demonstrator stands silhouetted in the Moscow dusk.

Day 3

BARRICADES

In the small hours of Tuesday morning, Muscovites could feel the fear. On the main thoroughfares, the rumble and roar of armor made sleep impossible. The few cars out in the early hours had to dart between columns of tanks.

Fear brought nightmares solidly based on Soviet history. Older people, especially, remembered when night was a terrifying time that could bring police knocking on the door to take a loved one away, never to be seen again. A poll taken later that day would find that three-quarters of Muscovites

A young tank driver considers an anti-coup leaflet that calls for the soldiers to ignore emergency government orders and to join in the defense of Yeltsin and the Russian Parliament Building.

Day 3

TUESDAY 8/20/91

1:00 am
Soviet troops open fire on a van in the Latvian capital of Riga killing the driver, Raimonds Salminsh, and injuring a passenger. Soldiers also seized Latvian radio.

7:30 am
Defense Minister Yazov considers the Tula Division unit near the White House unreliable and orders it to withdraw.

11:30 am
50,000 people rally in support of Yeltsin in Kishinev, Moldavia.

12:30 pm
200,000 people crowd in front of the Winter Palace in Leningrad in response to Mayor Anatoly Sobchak's call for a mass demonstration against the coup.

surveyed said they expected mass repressions soon.

At the White House, the seat of Boris Yeltsin's government, thousands of defenders who had seen the Red Army's violent crackdown in Lithuania in January continued to fortify the barricades begun the day before. The Lithuanians had turned the headquarters of their independent government into a fortress only after Soviet troops attacked their television station and killed fifteen civilians.

Around their White House, the Russians built a fortress wall of buses, concrete sewer pipe, park benches, fencing, a playground jungle gym, steel reinforcing bars, concrete panels, and whatever else could be thrown into the mix. They even used an electrical generator sent by central government television to broadcast the next day's session of the Russian Federation's Supreme Soviet.

Red roses dangled from the muzzle of one of the tanks guarding the building, and teens in camouflage shirts borrowed from the soldiers sat on the hatches, strumming guitars while the crews tried to sleep inside.

One twenty-year-old sergeant said he hoped other tank units would defect and there would be no fighting. He added that his parents were proud of him for switching sides. "I answer for myself," he said.

Inside the White House, well-known Soviet journalists took turns at a microphone to speak to the crowd of defenders. Meanwhile a complete radio service was going into operation to broadcast to most of the country. It had begun the day before with a ham radio operator transmitting to other hams, urging them to spread the news of Russian President Boris Yeltsin's defiance. Then radio engineers in Voronezh, a provincial city three hundred miles southwest of Moscow, loaded transmitting equipment into a truck and drove to Moscow. That allowed the Russian government to leapfrog its trans-

missions out of Moscow. They were picked up by local stations and relayed across the eleven time zones of the huge country.

The Emergency Committee — the anti-Gorbachev plotters — had banned Russian radio from the airwaves and had taken over its facilities. But White House staffers and volunteers were putting out the word by fax and telephone as well as through make-shift transmitters. In the office of Prime Minister Ivan Silayev half of the phones still worked.

At 6 a.m., Marshal Dmitry Yazov, defense minister and a member of the Emergency Committee, met with his commanders. The ten tanks of the Taman division that had defected to Yeltsin on Monday and turned their guns on the rest of the military units in front of the White House caused "a considerable stir and confusion" at Army headquarters. The Leningrad Navy base and a paratrooper academy in Ryazan, a few hours southeast of Moscow by road, also declared allegiance to Yeltsin. In the Far East, a submarine captain put to sea flying the Russian flag and told his sailors not to obey the Emergency Committee. Garrisons on the military-dominated Sakhalin Island and Kamchatka Peninsula in the Pacific Ocean pledged allegiance to Russia and Yeltsin. Troops in Moldavia balked at taking pro-coup orders.

The reports from across the country told the story of a Red Army divided and foreshadowed a bloody civil war if the conflict between Yeltsin and the conspirators broke into gunfire. "What have we gotten into?" Yazov asked, cursing at every report.

Maj. Victor Lopatin, deputy chairman of the Russian Republic Defense Committee, talked with officers who attended Yazov's meeting and later told the Los Angeles Times, "From Yazov's point of view, his army was falling apart as a result of the coup,

and with that, the coup would fail…. He could look ahead and see defeat."

But Yazov did not give up. He changed deployments. At 7:30 a.m., the Tula Division paratroops brought to the White House the night before by General Lebed began withdrawing. The defenders, who had decorated the division's armor with Russian flags and flowers the night before, were delighted, thinking that perhaps the confrontation was finished. They were wrong. In reality, Yazov ordered the withdrawal because he considered the troops unreliable, according to Col. Viktor Samoilov, a Yeltsin supporter from the Russian Defense Committee.

Less than half an hour later, a KGB major from a unit positioned inside the Kremlin arrived at the White House. Colonel Samoilov argued against obeying the conspirators. Finally, the Major said, "I can

A Tula Division tank is decorated with flowers by coup protesters shortly before being withdrawn from the confrontation by Defense Minister Dimitry Yazov. Yazov believed this division would prove "unreliable" if an attack were ordered.

5:00 pm
Boris Yeltsin speaks with British Prime Minister John Major by telephone. Yeltsin asks Major to demand Gorbachev be examined by a doctor and allowed to speak with Western leaders.

5:30 pm
Crowd at the White House estimated at 150,000.

7:00 pm
Tanks and armored personnel carriers move within a mile of the White House.

9:00 pm
Acting President Yanayev promises Yeltsin that troops will not attack. The Moscow military commandant announces a curfew starting at 11 pm.

guarantee that the 3rd Battalion of KGB Special Forces won't shoot. And if we are ordered to storm the White House, we won't do it."

The day before, defections were announced joyfully by the White House, but it was soon discovered that the announcements only allowed Yazov to take countermeasures. By Tuesday, Samoilov said Russian legislators and officials had learned their lesson and conducted their lobbying efforts quietly, suggesting to Soviet officers that they could obey their orders to take positions around the city. "Just don't shoot," Samoilov said. One after another, officers and soldiers agreed. But there was no way to know who was telling the truth, Samoilov added.

Samoilov's boss, Gen. Konstantin Kobets, put his personal efforts into trying to convince Moscow garrison commander, Gen. Nikolai Kalinin, and armed forces chief of staff, Gen. Mikhail Moiseyev, not to attack. He telephoned them constantly, especially his old friend from the military academy, Kalinin. "Kolya, Think!," General Kobets said over and over.

Early in the morning an embarrassed officer of the Taman Division visited the White House. He politely begged the return of the ten tanks which had defected from his division. "We understand you as a colleague," Samoilov told him sympathetically, and said the tanks could withdraw. Five of the ten did so later that morning. "We didn't want a confrontation," Samoilov explained. "We wanted to prevent bloodshed."

A chilly rain made Moscow feel more like autumn than mid-August; it was a gray and depressing morning. The national television news had infuriated the conspirators by reporting Yeltsin's strike call the night before. In Moscow, the message was plastered all over the metro stations. This was the morn-

ing to test the mass response.

Millions considered Yeltsin's strike appeal — and ignored it. There were only isolated pockets of support. Most important were the nation's coal miners. The printers at *Izvestia*, the government newspaper, also walked out. But more typical were workers like Andrei Borodin, a 23-year-old Muscovite, who said,

"I will wait to see what happens," or the young man replacing radiators in an apartment house, who laughed off his ability to influence events. "We're just workers. We can't change the weather," he said.

At Moscow's Watch Factory Number 1, the entire staff of 7,000 showed up for work. In Suzdal, three hours from Moscow, newspaper editor Vladimir Potapov reacted to news of the coup simply by removing the portrait of Gorbachev from his wall. He thought a bit more and removed the picture of Lenin as well, he told The New York Times later. The people of the ancient settlement of Suzdal voted 70 percent for Yeltsin in June but they did nothing to help when he and the

**10:00 pm
Interior Minister and
Emergency Committee
member Boris Pugo
disbands the Moscow
police because he suspects
them of being sympathetic
to Yeltsin.**

reformers needed them. That was a pattern in many places.

The first bloodshed of the coup occurred in Riga, Latvia. Soldiers opened fire on a van that moved too close to the main Riga railway station. They killed Raimonds Salminsh, 30, a bus driver, and injured another person. Soldiers also seized Latvian radio. They surrounded the television tower and the Riga headquarters of the Latvian People's Front, the mass movement that had led the tiny republic's fight for democracy and then independence. In neighboring Estonia, troops peacefully occupied the television tower in Tallinn.

In Uzbekistan, in central Asia, where most of Gorbachev's democratic changes had never been allowed to take root, President Islam Karimov, also the republic's Communist Party chief, had leaders of the movement opposing him arrested.

From other regions, too, there were reports heartening to the anti-Gorbachev forces. In Rostov-on-Don, the local KGB, military, and police commanders formed an emergency committee to take over the city, starting with the local press and television.

In Tatarstan, an autonomous republic within Russia trying to break away from Russian control, President Mintimer Shamiev supported the coup. Police with rubber truncheons broke up a demonstration against the coup, and the manager of the Communist-controlled

Leningrad's mayor, Anatoly Sobchak, calls for a mass meeting in Palace Square to protest the seizure of the government by the Emergency Committee. **OPPOSITE:** In Leningrad, 200,000 citizens rally in Isak Square to protest decisions by the coup leaders.

printing plant pulled Yeltsin's statements from the front page of the local newspaper as it was going to press.

Reports of support for the Emergency Committee in Moscow and Russia, however, appeared to be isolated. White House officials had good news from around the republic. Yeltsin's people telephoned officials in one-third of the oblasts — administrative areas — in Russia, and found that fifty-three supported Yeltsin and only four supported the Emergency Committee.

In Leningrad, Mayor Anatoly Sobchak organized a mass rally at the Winter Palace. "We wanted 100,000 people in the street to tell the plotters what they would face here, and we got nearly 200,000," Sobchak said later to the Los Angeles Times. Thousands of workers from the Kirov factory, a tank manufacturer that had switched to making tractors because of Gorbachev's arms cuts, marched to the demonstration.

"To see how people were awakening, beginning to respect themselves, almost made me cry," machinist Alexander Kondrashov told The New York Times. "They knew what could happen; they knew where this might lead. They felt that they were people, human beings. They stopped being afraid."

The Leningrad newspapers *Smena* and *Nevskoe Vremya* were on the streets as usual Tuesday. *Smena* bannered its front page, "Nobel Peace Prize to Whoever Arrests

"Nobel Peace Prize to Whoever Arrests Yanayev." Leningrad television continued to broadcast news of the resistance through large parts of the Soviet Union. In 1917 the people of Leningrad, then known as Petrograd, had been defiant in their support of the Bolsheviks, and now they were defiant in support of toppling the Bolsheviks' heirs.

Sobchak's ability to hold Leningrad was a critical blow to the coup. He showed the conspirators that even if they managed to take out Yeltsin, they still had an entire city standing against them. And not just any city, Leningrad was the Soviet Union's second largest and it was well-fortified.

In Moscow, the first edition of the underground Common Paper carried a Yeltsin statement raising the stakes in his stand-off, threatening the conspirators with the same fate he faced at their hands. He said the leaders of the coup d'état "are criminals guilty of high treason," an offense carrying the death penalty. He warned his people, "The order that the new-fangled saviors of the motherland are promising us will turn out to be an iron grip, with suppression of dissent, concentration camps, and arrests at night." The newspaper's front page called on citizens to disobey the Emergency Committee. The putsch is strong only thanks to the force of fear, it said.

Russian television, also barred from the airwaves, put its news programs on videotapes and entrusted them to pilots and passengers for distribution to twenty major cities around the country, according to Production Director Anatoly Lysenko. Television in the tiny central Asian republic of Kirgizia almost 2,000 miles away, however, was playing the news from the Russian White House regularly. And though the leading newspaper there carried all of the Emergency Committee announcements, it also ran a

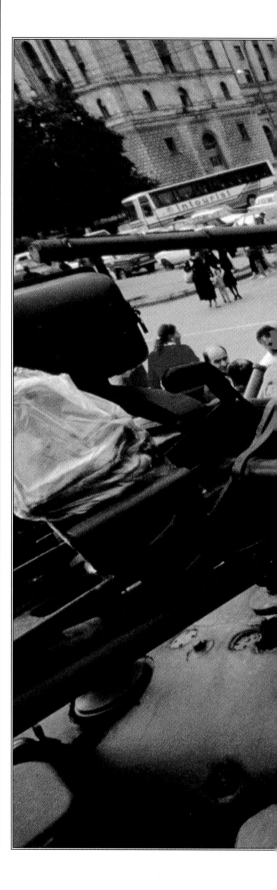

A young Russian peers inside a tank. Civilians left gifts of food for the soldiers, trying to convince the troops not to fight their own people. OVERLEAF: Thousands of coup demonstrators gather outside the Russian Federation Building.

BARRICADES
113

statement of protest from the paper's staff. Television in the Baltic states and Moldavia also reported developments from Moscow's White House. On the other hand, Ukrainian television did not use any of the tapes, Lysenko said. The president of the Ukraine was Leonid Kravchuk, a Communist who was also slow to criticize the Emergency Committee the day before.

Defying the state of emergency decrees, Russian television broadcast the news in two twenty- to thirty-minute bursts to the Far East and Siberia very early Tuesday morning.

Gas masks are kept at the ready inside the Russian White House as defenders watch the stand-off at the barricades from under the porticos.

Once discovered, the broadcasts were stopped. Gen. Nikolai Kalinin, the Moscow military commander, threatened to jail all Russian television news workers for thirty days for illegal transmissions, Lysenko said, but the arrests were never carried out.

By Tuesday, central television was only nominally under the control of the Emergency Committee. The plotters did not remove Lazutkin, despite his decision to show the resistance on the news the night before, and he grew increasingly bold. His staff allowed non-Soviet correspondents into the Ostankino television center to feed their reports to the outside world. With Lazutkin's permission, the workers from Soviet television secretly outfitted crews from the banned Russian television station. He even sent a remote broadcast van to the White House to set up to broadcast the Russian Federation Supreme Soviet the following day.

CNN requested central television help in setting up a microwave transmitter on the White House roof to carry live coverage of the demonstrations in front of the building. A technician showed up, but there was not enough gear available to make the transmission work properly.

As news of resistance spread, so did the strength of the opposition to the coup. By midmorning, tens of thousands of people were gathered at the centers of resistance: the Russian Parliament and the Moscow City Council. A rally called for Manezh Square next to the Kremlin was moved to the White House because Manezh was packed with tanks and troops.

At noon, 200,000 people filled the square on the side of the White House nearest the U.S. embassy. They perched in trees, on building ledges, and on the monument to demonstrators who had opposed the czar on this spot during an uprising in 1905. A cob-

blestone bridge that had been left in place to mark the earlier conflict was torn up, its paving stones once again put to use in building barricades. Unlike pro-democracy demonstrations before the coup, this one was liberally laced with protesters in their teens and twenties.

High above the nineteen-story building, a blimp defiantly flew the tricolored flag of pre-revolutionary Russia, now used as the symbol of the reform movement in the largest republic. A young man dressed in an antique military uniform with a gas mask on his belt waved a red Soviet flag with the hammer and sickle neatly cut out.

Former Foreign Minister Eduard Shevardnadze reminded the crowd of his warning in December that dictatorship was coming. "Unfortunately, I was right," he said. "But the junta won't succeed!" The crowd chanted his words back in response.

Other speakers told the crowd that their means of spreading the call to resist were still sharply restricted. "Every one of you can become a channel of information," said one. "Tell your friends, your relatives, your co-workers, that democracy makes its stand here!"

Leaflets fluttered down to the crowd from the balcony. They contained an appeal to the

Demonstrators practice donning gas masks in preparation for the attack on the White House that never came.

soldiers not to shoot, signed by Russian Vice-President Alexander Rutskoi, an Army colonel and respected Afghan war hero. "I call on your honor, common sense, and your hearts," the appeal said. "Today the fate of the country, its freedom, and democratic development are in your hands. Don't let there be bloodshed."

Yeltsin appeared with bodyguards holding bulletproof shields in front of his chest. His speech was serious and cautionary. "Yazov and Pugo have been repeatedly responsible for bloodshed in the Baltic republics," Yeltsin warned. "Their orders are illegal and no one should obey them!" But he urged this crowd to be careful, not to start any conflicts with the soldiers that could get out of control.

A block away along the riverbank, several more tanks faced the Russian White House, their allegiance uncertain. A crewman in one gestured toward the White House. "We have our own commander, and he's up there," he said. But his colonel said he was told to prevent disorder and that is what he intended to do, without favoring either side.

Top officials from Yeltsin's Russian government went to see Anatoly Lukianov, chairman of the USSR Supreme Soviet and widely suspected to be one of the plotters. Even more than the others eventually arrested in the conspiracy, he was known as a friend of Gorbachev. According to Rutskoi, Lukianov told the group Gorbachev was sick with a bad back and high blood pressure. "What kind of fools do you take us for? Are you trying to tell me that he issued a decree about the transfer of power because he had a bad back?" Rutskoi replied to Lukianov.

By Tuesday afternoon, the Emergency Committee had developed something of an emergency itself. There were several indications that the conspirators were losing heart. Prime Minister Pavlov was reported hospitalized with high blood pressure. Kazakhstan President Nursultan Nazarbayev, increasingly an important figure in the USSR, telephoned acting President Yanayev to seek guarantees that the White House would not be attacked. "Yanayev did not seem in touch at all," Nazarbayev told the Kazakh press. "He did not seem to know what was going on, why I was calling, or even who I was. He may have been asleep or something else."

Nazarbayev said that he also demanded Gorbachev be brought to Moscow to attend the Supreme Soviet session set for a week later. As a compromise, he suggested calling the Congress of People's Deputies into session and setting a date for a general election for president.

Vadim Bakatin, a member of Gorbachev's National Security Council, returned to his Kremlin office a floor above Yanayev and rescinded his resignation. He and Yevgeny Primakov, another Gorbachev aide, called on Yanayev to try to persuade the acting President to order the troops out of the city to avoid bloodshed. Bakatin and Primakov also wrote a statement condemning the coup and asked Foreign Minister Bessmertnykh to sign it as a third member of the National Security Council. Bessmertnykh refused, Bakatin said.

ABOVE: Anatoly Malikhin (left), leader of the coal miners union, and Alexander Korzhakov, chief of Yeltsin's bodyguards, consult in the Russian White House. OPPOSITE: Malikhin, weapon over his shoulder, consults by phone with striking miners.

Bessmertnykh said he refused because he was planning to hold his own news conference, which he did the following day.

Bessmertnykh, who suffered from bladder stones had had one such seizure in Helsinki several months before. Now, Bessmertnykh said, the pains returned. His doctor ordered him into a hospital. He refused to enter the hospital because this was a critical time in his country's history, and he signed a statement absolving his doctor of any responsibility. He was bedridden on Tuesday in his Moscow apartment when a statement from the Emergency Committee was delivered for his comment.

"It was a statement to all of the leaders of the world," Bessmertnykh said later, "but it was intended particularly for President Bush. It was a declaration of a new Cold War. It was Cold War language of the 1950s. If it had

relations with the United States would have gone down the drain. I wrote across the front 'Completely unacceptable. I do not agree. It would spoil our relations with the United States and aggravate the situation.' Then I gave orders to return it to those who sent it to us. It was sent through the KGB. I watched to see what would happen and they didn't publish it, even though it had a note on the bottom saying 'Send to TASS.'"

That afternoon he ordered a cable sent to all Soviet diplomatic missions reminding them that they were to accept no instructions from anyone but the Foreign Ministry without first checking. Gorbachev fired Bessmertnykh after the coup for failing to act decisively against the plotters. The diplomat, a veteran of thirty-four years in the foreign service, insisted that he had acted properly and said he had refused to support the Emergency Committee once he was sure it was illegal.

The only international support the plotters received came from North Korea, Cuba, Libya, and Iraq, hardly nations to give legitimacy to a coup. Yeltsin, on the other hand, worked the mainstream of international relations, dispatching a deputy foreign minister to consult with countries in Western Europe and to establish, if necessary, a Russian government in exile. Western leaders, in turn,

Moscovites eagerly seek information about the coup. Although newspapers were strictly controlled, leaflets provided news of the resistance.

ernment in exile. Western leaders, in turn, began dealing with Yeltsin rather than the Emergency Committee, which tried to block the contacts.

A log of the government communications system, operated by the KGB, tells a story of attempts by Western leaders to speak with Yeltsin:

1:42 P.M. WASHINGTON CALLS ON LINE OR-4. BUSH WANTS TO TALK TO YELTSIN. INFORMATION REPORTED TO VOLKOV [DEPUTY TO ANATOLY BEDA, CHIEF OF THE KGB'S 8TH DIRECTORATE, THE OFFICE OF GOVERNMENT COMMUNICATIONS]
2:07 P.M. ORDER FROM VOLKOV: DO NOT CONNECT.
2:17 P.M. WASHINGTON TOLD FOR A SECOND TIME THAT WE ARE TRYING TO LOCATE YELTSIN'S TELEPHONE SET AND YELTSIN.
4:55 P.M. ANOTHER REQUEST TO TALK TO YELTSIN. INFORMATION REPORTED TO VOLKOV.

It is hard to imagine officials in Washington believing that somehow the government had lost track of Boris Yeltsin's telephone, let alone the man himself. Actually the log shows that at 3:14 p.m. the previous day, Beda had ordered "all special telephone exchanges and telephone sets" switched off.

Two minutes after President Bush first tried to reach Yeltsin, President François Mitterand placed a call to Gorbachev, according to the log:

1:44 P.M. MPTS-1: MR. MITTERAND FROM PARIS CALLING TO SPEAK TO GORBACHEV. REPORTED TO VOLKOV.
2:07 P.M. SUGGEST PUTTING HIM THROUGH TO YANAYEV.
2:40 P.M. MITTERAND SPOKE TO MPTS OPERATOR, ASKING IF SHE HAD ANY INFORMATION ABOUT GORBACHEV; AFTER RECEIVING A NEGATIVE ANSWER, HUNG UP. REPORTED TO VOLKOV.

That evening, Mr. Bush also tried to speak to Gorbachev and had as much luck as Mr. Mitterand:

10:03 P.M. WASHINGTON CALLS ON LINE OR-4. BUSH WANTS TO TALK TO GORBACHEV. REPORTED TO VOLKOV.
10:17 P.M. VOLKOV: SUGGEST PUTTING HIM THROUGH TO ACTING PRESIDENT YANAYEV.
10:21 P.M. AMERICANS REFUSE TO SPEAK TO YANAYEV; WILL ONLY SPEAK TO GORBACHEV. REPORTED TO VOLKOV.

But Bush and Yeltsin finally got through to each other, and Bush told a news conference afterwards he had promised Yeltsin support in returning Gorbachev to power. Bush's televised news conference was specially designed to show the conspirators that the United States had another, legitimate leader to deal with. Yanayev could be ignored.

At 5 p.m., Yeltsin told British Prime Minister John Major by telephone that he wanted the West to demand that Gorbachev be freed and be examined by a doctor, and that Western leaders be allowed to speak with him. Then Yeltsin abruptly interrupted the

ABOVE: Tank crews accept food and anti-coup leaflets as protesters continue to attempt to sway them to the pro-Yeltsin side. BELOW: President Bush, flanked by Secretary of State James Baker (left) and U.S. Ambassador to the Soviet Union Robert Strauss, holds a press conference in the White House Rose Garden on August 20, after assuring Russian President Boris Yeltsin of "continued U.S. support."

A NATION IN CRISIS
MAP OF EVENTS

Although much of the news emanating from the Soviet Union centered around Gorbachev Yeltsin and the events in Moscow, there were other crucial events in the Republics that contributed significantly to the eventual failure of the coup. The events map at right highlights some of the most significant actions and reactions to the attempted takeover.

that tanks were moving toward the White House even as they spoke. "He said to me that he believed he had not very much time left," Major told a news conference after the call.

About one hundred tanks had been spotted, engines roaring, at an old airfield a few miles from the Russian Parliament. As fear of attack grew, women were evacuated from the White House and the doors sealed. Guards piled furniture in the stairwells and prepared fire hoses for use. Workers were ordered away from the windows as thirty-eight specific reports came in of snipers in nearby buildings. Gas masks were distributed. Everyone remembered that when troops attacked demonstrators in Georgia two years earlier, hundreds of people had suffered nerve damage from a gas that the Army later refused to identify.

Even as worry about an attack increased, Yeltsin's defiance continued to attract support domestically. The Ukrainian leadership finally voted to condemn the coup, and Moldavia's president told a rally of 50,000 in Kishinev that his government supported Yeltsin. Tens of thousands rallied in Minsk, the capital of Byelorussia, as well as in other cities across the country. On Tuesday evening, Central television and the Leningrad channel broadcast news of the resistance to large parts of the country.

News reports reaching the dacha in Crimea, encouraged Gorbachev and those with him, yet they still feared the actions of desperate men.

"The worst thing was that we had no [first-hand] information at all," one of Gorbachev's bodyguards, Boris Golentsov, told Soviet television. "Even if they had told us, 'We'll give you a car, a plane,' I don't know what decision we would have made... or where we would have gone without any

[direct] information or means of communication."

"We listened and analyzed, listened and analyzed — who was with whom, who was on strike, where there had been protests," presidential aide Chernyayev told the Los Angeles Times. "By late afternoon, the picture emerged that the plotters held Moscow and not much else of importance. Still, the President told me, 'We must defeat them. They must be beaten. We must not accept a compromise.'"

The strain was showing on Gorbachev's face. "You could barely see his eyes," Olga Lanina, his secretary, said.

But Raisa Gorbachev was having a tougher time. Lanina said that the President's wife suffered a nervous seizure Tuesday night which required medical attention. Nonetheless, Raisa Gorbachev asked another of the personal guards, Oleg Klimov, to help smuggle Gorbachev's four snippets of videotape to the outside world, she told a Soviet television interviewer.

"There's no way we can do it," he replied. "We are blocked by ships on the sea, and we are surrounded on land so thoroughly that you can't work your way past the guards and soldiers." Mrs. Gorbachev said they considered trying to break out with her husband surrounded by his loyal bodyguards, but feared the President could be killed in a gunbattle.

The opposing sides in the compound began sorting themselves out. Gorbachev's thirty-two personal bodyguards, all loyal to him, moved from the staff quarters to the guesthouse to reduce the chance of sparking a confrontation, Lanina said. They remained surrounded by a larger force of KGB security troops loyal to the conspirators. The opposing forces — both armed — continued to share meals in the same dining hall, coexisting uneasily. Gorbachev's bodyguard divided

LITHUANIA

AUG. 19: A naval blockade is put in place by the Soviet military. Communications and key buildings seized.

AUG. 20-21: Clashes with troops break out around parliament building. Coup collapses. As tanks withdraw from capital, gunfire is exchanged and one guard is killed.

AUG. 22: The Communist Party is outlawed and statues of Lenin are toppled.

LATVIA

AUG. 19: Naval blockade and key building seizures by military.

AUG. 20-21: Soviet "black beret" forces attempt to disarm guards at Council of Ministers building in Riga and order evacuations. Republic declares independence. Coup collapses. Troops withdraw.

AUG. 22-23: Communist Party is outlawed by parliament.

ESTONIA

AUG. 19: Military seizes communications and key buildings.

AUG. 20: Legislators barricade themselves in the parliament building and vote for immediate independence. Vacationing Foreign Minister Meri authorized to organize government in exile if parliament meeting is stopped.

AUG. 21: Independence declared. Coup collapses and military withdraws.

AUG. 22-23: Statues of Lenin are toppled.

RUSSIA

AUG. 19: ICBM missile launchers ordered to stand down by Soviet military to ease international tensions. Mines shut down as miners strike to protest unconstitutional state of emergency.

AUG. 20: Coup committee declared unconstitutional by President Yeltsin. In Leningrad, Mayor Sobchak and population called on to defend city council. 200,000 protest outside of Winter Palace. Troops are stopped from moving to the center of the city.

AUG. 21: 5,000 stand vigil through the night to protect the Leningrad city council building from possible attack.

AUG. 22: Miners return to work but refuse to ship coal until coup leaders are punished.

BYELORUSSIA

AUG. 20: A rally is held in Minsk forcing the legislature to meet. The Central Committee of the Communist Party supports the coup, but Supreme Soviet members oppose it.

KAZAKHSTAN

AUG. 20: President Nazarbayev denounces coup, resigns from the Politburo and Central Committee in protest. Demands that Gorbachev make a statement in public to prove the assertion of coup leaders that he is too ill to maintain his duties.

AUG. 23: Communist Party is outlawed by the republic.

HOUSE ARREST

AUG. 18: Gorbachev is placed under house arrest by the KGB police at his summer home in Foros.

AUG. 21: As the coup crumbles, four of the conspirators fly to see Gorbachev and are promptly arrested. Gorbachev leaves for Moscow.

UZBEKISTAN

AUG. 21: Orders by coup leaders are outlawed by President Islam Karimov.

AUG. 22: Karimov resigns in protest from Politburo and Central Committee.

AUG. 23: Communist Party activities are outlawed by the republic.

MOLDAVIA

AUG. 20: 50,000 protest the coup in Kishinev, the republic's capital. Thousands block entrance to the capital, as well as to government buildings and television stations. Prime Minister Muravski bans all pro-coup newspapers.

AUG. 23: Communist Party activities are outlawed.

KIRGHIZIA

AUG. 23: The Communist Party headquarters are nationalized by President Akayev.

UKRAINE

AUG. 19: Republican radio and television are shut down by order of coup leaders.

AUG. 20: Parliament declares all orders and directives of the new leaders null and void. 8,000 rally to protest the coup.

GEORGIA

AUG. 21: The republic appeals to the West to be recognized as a sovereign state.

AUG. 23: President Gamasakhurdia calls for a ban of the Communist Party and the nationalization of Party property.

Map labels

Arctic Ocean

NORWAY

SWEDEN

FINLAND

GERMANY

ESTONIA — Tallinn

LATVIA — Riga

LITHUANIA — Vilnius

Leningrad

POLAND

CZECHOSLOVAKIA

BYELORUSSIA — Minsk

Moscow

RUSSIA

HUNGARY

UKRAINE — Kiev

ROMANIA

MOLDAVIA — Kishinev

BULGARIA

Foros

Yalta

Black Sea

KAZAKHSTAN

Caspian Sea

Aral Sea

GEORGIA — Tbilisi

TURKEY

ARMENIA — Yerevan

AZERBAIJAN — Baku

UZBEKISTAN

KIRGHIZIA

Alma-Ata

Frunze

TURKMENISTAN — Ashkhabad

UZBEKISTAN — Tashkent

TADZHIKISTAN — Dushanbe

IRAN

AFGHANISTAN

CHINA

PAKISTAN

Outside the White House, defenders prepare food and continue the dialogue with soldiers and tank crews, many of whom ultimately turn their weapons to the defense of Yeltsin and the Parliament Building.

beach to swim, and General Generalov, in charge of enforcing the house arrest, sent one of his guards scurrying after them. Once on the beach, the guard took off some of his clothes, trying to pretend he was just out for a bit of sun himself, Lanina said. When Chernyayev left the beach, she recounted, the security phone rang and the embarrassed guard had to run over in his underwear to answer it and report on the movements of the President's aide.

Back in Moscow, the plotters spent Tuesday planning an attack on the White House. After the coup there were at least two investigations of what happened (one by the prosecutor general's office and one specifically into the activities of the KGB) and participants gave varying accounts. Some claimed the final attack order was rejected by lower-ranking officers, and others said the order was never actually given.

Defense Minister Yazov, KGB Chief Kryuchkov, and Interior Minister Pugo spent much of Tuesday trying to put together a new assault team to storm the White House. But as the Los Angeles Times later reported, field commanders repeatedly gave vague replies that they were unprepared.

At 2 p.m., General Grachev, commander of all paratroopers, attended a meeting in the office of Deputy Defense Minister Vladislav Achalov. Also present were General Varrenikov, commander of the ground forces and one of the conspirators who placed Gorbachev under house arrest at Foros; General Kalinin, the Moscow garrison commander; and General Karpukhin, head of the KGB Alpha Group; along with a number of civilians Grachev did not know. "We were told the government of Russia is standing up against the State of Emergency Committee, and there's no negotiating with them. We have to take action to force them to recognize

into two groups to stand guard day and night over the Gorbachev family.

Outside the compound, the entire scene was under the watchful eyes of more guards perched on the steep cliffsides and armed with machine guns, Lanina said. According to Gorbachev's son-in-law, "The outer guards were new men, specially brought in. They spoke to each other by radio using a new code, one that our guards didn't know."

That afternoon, Chernyayev, Lanina, the nurse, and the masseuse walked down to the have to take action to force them to recognize the committee," Grachev recalled. "They gave us this task: surround the parliament. They told me the paratroopers would be deployed around the American embassy, the Interior Ministry troops on Kutuzovsky Prospect, and the Alpha Group on the riverbank," Grachev said. That would effectively surround the White House.

The plan was to demand that Yeltsin's government give in to the orders of the new Kremlin leaders. If they refused, "The Interior Ministry troops would drive back the people surrounding the Parliament Building, and the Alpha Group would go through the gap and storm the building," Grachev said. At that point, he added, "I finally was convinced: If this happens, it will be a slaughterhouse." Returning to his own headquarters after the meeting, Grachev sent General Lebed, his deputy, to the White House. The conspirators' spies spotted Lebed there and reported to Yazov. Grachev's phone rang. It was Yazov.

"What's going on? Has Lebed turned traitor?" Yazov demanded.

"No," Grachev replied.

"So why did he go to the White House?" Yazov asked.

"To arrange security. We have to organize the deployment, food, explain where it is possible to sleep, to wash."

But Yazov was not satisfied.

Yazov also had trouble with his Air Force chief, General Shaposhnikov. Radio Echo reported that the Air Force had completely gone over to Yeltsin and that Shaposhnikov had been arrested.

Yazov summoned Shaposhnikov, who later described the scene: Yazov sat down, put his hand under his cheek, and screwed up his eyes. "What do you think I should do? Tell me honestly," the coup conspirator asked the general whose loyalty was suddenly doubtful.

"Honestly?" Shaposhnikov recalled saying. "All right. First, Dmitry Timofeyevich, we have to get out of this situation."

"How?" Yazov asked.

"With dignity," Shaposhnikov replied.

"And do you see a proper way?" Yazov continued, still giving nothing of his own opinion.

Shaposhnikov hesitated, wondering if he dared. He did.

"I do. Withdraw the troops and cancel the state of emergency."

"So, let's assume that. And the committee?" Yazov asked.

"The committee? Dissolve it — send them to the devil. Declare it illegal and, if necessary, arrest them," Shaposhnikov told Yazov, a member of that committee. "Give power to the Supreme Soviet and bring the President back."

At that moment, three other members of the high command entered the room. Yazov abruptly turned serious, walked to the other side of his desk, and asked Shaposhnikov, "Do you know why I asked you here?"

"My heart sank," Shaposhnikov said later. "I thought to myself, 'I have to be frank with him.'"

Yazov continued: "There are many democrats in the air force, and they are

LEFT: Air Force chief, General Shapnoshnikov, became one of the strongest pro-Yeltsin voices in the Soviet military. He successfully lobbied Defense Minister Yazov to avoid violence and withdraw troops and put the Soviet Air Force under his direct orders. BELOW: Yazov, one of the conspirators, finds himself under increasing pressure to take a "dignified way out" of the coup debacle. Later, Yazov insists that his was the primary voice against using force.

White House defenders represent a cross section of Soviet society including disabled veterans of the war in Afghanistan.

capable of doing anything. Can you guarantee that these people are under control?"

"Absolutely," Shaposhnikov replied.

"Then go and see to it," Yazov said.

Shaposhnikov, in trying to analyze this conversation, said he was inclined to think that Yazov was already wavering. Later, when it was safe, other generals claimed that they, too, had advised Yazov to withdraw the troops.

According to a prosecution tape obtained by ABC News, Yazov told investigators that he told Shaposhnikov, "Don't let the worst happen. Don't let any military aircraft — planes or helicopters — fly to Moscow." Yazov admitted to investigators later that

Shaposhnikov urged him to find a way out with dignity. But by that time, he said, "all my dignity boiled down to calling everybody and categorically prohibiting the use of force under any circumstances."

Shaposhnikov returned to his office, and ordered the entire Air Force to take orders from no one but him. He was worried. He continued to hear of plans for an attack on the White House. He and General Grachev talked during the late afternoon after Grachev attended the attack-planning session. According to Shaposhnikov, the paratroop commander was distraught.

"Just now, they have told me everything." Grachev said. "They are planning a real

we are going against our own people. Second, this is no local conflict. It will grow into a civil war. In this country, how many nuclear defense plants, chemical factories, atomic power stations are there? If a conflict arises, can you imagine what will happen? I have the impression that they want to use me. These bastards, they want me to give the order. I'll send them to hell. I won't give the order."

Shaposhnikov replied, "Pavel Sergeyevich, thank you. I have reached a decision, too. The planes aren't going anywhere. Let's work together. . . What are we going to do?"

"I'll resign," Grachev said.

"That's a bit difficult to do in the midst of a state of emergency," Shaposhnikov told him.

"I'll shoot myself, damn it," the paratroop commander said. "OK, so you kill yourself," Shaposhnikov responded. "What's the use in that?" The Air Force chief let the question sink in, and continued, "Grachev, hold off on the shooting. It would be better if we went to the White House."

But then Shaposhnikov called home to tell his wife what they were about to do. She advised against it. "If you go there," she reasoned, "Yazov — or if not him, someone else — will fire you. In that case, you'll lose control of your troops, and wind up with the exact opposite effect of what you want."

The two generals resumed their brain-

Major General Lebed, commander of the 106th Airborne Division, proved to be one of Yeltsin's strongest supporters among the Soviet military. The defection of him and his troops was a key factor in the coup's failure. BELOW: Muscovites remove cobblestones to erect a barricade between troops and the Russian Federation Building on the night of Tuesday, August 20.

Defenders construct a barricade blocking the movement of troops over the Kalinin Bridge near the Russian Parliament Building.

The two generals resumed their brainstorming. They discussed surrounding the Kremlin and taking the battle to the plotters.

"Let's take your paratroopers and surround the Kremlin and, what's more, arrest the junta," Shaposhnikov suggested. "We have enough force," Grachev agreed. "But we're missing something else."

"What?" Shaposhnikov asked.

"How many times have you been in the Kremlin?" Grachev asked. "Three times," said Shaposhnikov.

"And I've never been there," Grachev said. "If we send in the paratroopers, the KGB troops will shoot them right away, because they know the grounds," Grachev

pointed out.

Then Shaposhnikov suggested that if an order was given to storm the White House, he would go to the Kremlin and threaten an air strike on it if the plotters did not cancel the order in ten minutes. That melodramatic move was similarly discarded.

Finally, Grachev concluded it might be better simply to stay by the telephones "to interrupt any stupid orders," as Shaposhnikov recalled. Both men then called Yeltsin's headquarters to promise that the paratroopers and the Air Force would not attack and, in fact, would try to prevent any other troops from doing so. Grachev said he deliberately used a tapped telephone line to call a friend at the White House to say, "Tell everyone that the paratroopers won't touch them. They won't shoot." Afraid of arrest and court-martial, he then posted a guard at his headquarters.

By nightfall of this second day of confrontation in front of the White House, the crowd had grown even larger. It was raining ever harder. Some defenders huddled under makeshift plastic tents. Others cooked potatoes on campfires in the mud of what had been one of Moscow's few pristine, green lawns. Civilians distributed milk to the soldiers in the several dozen tanks and armored personnel carriers in front of the building. Others handed out canned seaweed — never a Moscow favorite, but one of the few foods normally available — and frozen fish sandwiches.

Yazov met with KGB and military officers again in the early evening. "We have to speed up," Yazov said, according to a Soviet newspaper account, that quoted a prosecutor's report. "We have helicopters and tanks — we will destroy them." They discussed a knock-out blow at the first and second floors of the White House with the help of helicopters. Shaposhnikov, by then in open defiance, sent word that he would send his airplanes against them, the newspaper said.

Vadim Bakatin, a Gorbachev loyalist who had been told by White House officials that an attack was anticipated, called Yazov at 8 p.m. to plead with him to prevent the attack. "I am not a person to take such a stupid decision," Yazov told Bakatin, according to his aide Vyacheslav Nikonov. Russian officials said later that the attack was called off because of Shaposhnikov's threat.

About 8 p.m., the conspirators were meeting in the Kremlin. Leonid Kravchenko, chairman of the State Radio and Television Company, went to the meeting to request authority to broadcast on more channels and

to plead that he not be held responsible for the Leningrad television station's independent reporting.

As he walked into the meeting room, Kravchenko recalled, acting President Yanayev said he wanted to go on *Vremya*, the 9 p.m. television news program, to tell the people that force would not be used against the White House. "A pall fell over the room," Kravchenko said. After a moment of silence, the debate resumed.

"We could soon be under attack ourselves," Kryuchkov said. "Why should we give assurances that we won't attack?"

"Is there a man in this room who intends to attack?" Yanayev asked. There was no reply. "I believe there is none," Yanayev said.

But Kryuchkov had not given up. The Defense Ministry might not have the stomach for an attack, but the KGB leader thought he could still make the decision and carry out an attack alone. At 8 p.m., he sent the following telegram:

TOP SECRET

URGENT

CODED TELEGRAM NO. 73218/325

TO: MOSCOW, CHIEF OF THE DEPARTMENT OF

SPECIAL FORCES OF KGB TROOPS. TBILISI,

KGB leader Kryuchkov proves to be one of the main proponents of an attack on the Russian White House and the use of force to maintain control. In preparation, he sent this telegram to border troops placing them under the authority of the department of special troops of the KGB.

COMMANDER, CAUCASUS BORDER TROOPS. VITEBSK, COMMANDER, 103D PARATROOP DIVISION NAKHICHYEVAN, COMMANDER OF THE 75TH MOTORIZED DIVISION CHUGUYEV, COMMANDER OF THE 48D MOTORIZED DIVISION MOSCOW, COMMANDER OF THE 27TH SPECIAL ARMORED TROOP COMPANY

FROM 8 P.M., AUGUST 20, 1991, THE 103RD PARATROOPER DIVISION, 75TH MOTORIZED DIVISION OF THE BORDER TROOPS OF KGB OF THE USSR, THE 48TH MOTORIZED DIVISION, AND 27TH SPECIAL ARMORED TROOP COMPANY OF THE KGB OF THE USSR ARE PLACED UNDER THE AUTHORITY OF THE DEPARTMENT OF SPECIAL TROOPS OF THE KGB OF THE USSR. THE ABOVE-MENTIONED DEPARTMENT SHOULD DO EVERYTHING NECESSARY TO PROVIDE HIGH COMBAT CAPABILITY OF THE UNIT LISTED ABOVE.

V. KRYUCHKOV

CHAIRMAN

COMMITTEE OF STATE SECURITY OF THE USSR

Obviously, the KGB chief was still considering a final effort to bring troops in from non-Russian areas many hundreds of miles away to carry out the attack on the White House without the approval of the rest of the Emergency Committee.

On the television news at 9 p.m., the Moscow military commandant announced a curfew starting at 11 p.m. It was widely assumed he wanted to thin out the crowd surrounding the White House before an attack. At 10 p.m., Interior Minister Pugo disbanded the Moscow police, who were deeply divided in their loyalties.

Officials at the news agency TASS were not informed of the curfew directly but heard about it on television. Anatoly Krasikov, who was in charge, left it up to individuals to decide whether or not to remain. The English Language Service decided to shut down, in what they considered a small protest strike. The Russian Language Service is not normally staffed with reporters at night, and it made no exception to its usual practice even though all knew that history was being made.

General Konstantin Kobets, the Russian defense chief, told the defenders of the White House that KGB troops were expected to surround the building at 1 a.m. Against what could turn out to be the massed might of the Red Army, the KGB, and the Interior Ministry, Kobets had only three hundred armed men inside the White House that night. There were another three or four hundred defenders inside who could make do with Molotov cocktails and the building's fire

hoses and, finally, with pieces of wood. Outside, he had tens of thousands of ordinary citizens, armed only with strength of will.

Men with loudspeakers told the crowd what to do when the attack came: Move aside to let the attackers through — and then surge around the troops, capturing them in the sea of bodies so they could be disarmed.

Inside the Kremlin and other Soviet government buildings, the Emergency Committee was in disarray, but that was not yet known in the White House, on the streets, or by the various military units. And so, as midnight approached, events moved

LEFT: Coup protesters camp out in the rain during the constant vigil outside the Russian White House. **ABOVE:** The Taman Division soldier who defected to Yeltsin's defense, mans his tank's machine gun in anticipation of an attack.

Day 4

STANDOFF

Moscow's Kutuzovsky Prospect has long been an avenue of conquest. Napoleon surveyed the city from a height on the roadway, relishing his conquest. Then he marched along the thoroughfare to the Kremlin at the head of his army. Every day, in more recent decades, the Communist Party leaders who conquered the country sped in their huge limousines down the unusually well-maintained avenue to their offices in the Party's Central Committee headquarters and the Kremlin.

At midnight Tuesday ten women

Violent confrontation erupts between the military and angry defenders in the early morning hours of Wednesday, August 21. Three civilians are killed. Vladimir Usov and Ilya Krichevsky die of bullet wounds to the head, after Dimitry Komar is killed trying to board an armored personnel carrier.

Day 4

8/21/91

1:00 am
Three civilians are killed when violence erupts between protesters and troops at the Kalinin Prospect underpass.

3:00 am
KGB Chief Vladimir Kryuchkov decides against storming the White House with KGB troops.

4:00 am
Leningrad Police Chief Arkady Kramerev receives call from a colonel who requests safe passage out of the city for himself and his 1,500 troops.

8:00 am
Defense Minister Dimitry Yazov meets with the Defense Board, which votes in favor of ordering all troops to withdraw from Moscow.

11:00 am
Tanks and APCs begin moving out of Moscow.

stood in the rain in the middle of Kutuzovsky Prospect's eight lanes in front of a barricade of buses, facing west. Tanks of the KGB's Vitebsk Division were expected. They held umbrellas and a huge sign that read, "Soldiers, don't shoot your mothers." Behind them, a few hundred yards from the White House, defenders packed trucks onto the Kutuzovsky-Kalinin Bridge over the Moscow River. When the tanks approached, the bridge full of vehicles would be set afire, a Russian legislator explained later.

On another likely attack route — a small street leading from the Garden Ring Road past the United States Embassy to the White House — demonstrators had picked up and moved dozens of American diplomats' cars to block the road. If Soviet tanks assaulted the democrats' stronghold by this way, they would have to crush a considerable amount of U.S. property.*

The armored column appeared on the Garden Ring Road in front of the American embassy at midnight. Inside Armored Personnel Carrier No. 536, a teen-aged private named Nikolai breathed the smell of greasy metal and sweaty bodies packed into a small space as he squinted through the four-inch-wide visor, trying to see where he was driving the massive fighting machine. The column was heading south through the Kalinin Prospect underpass. As it neared the other side, Nikolai saw a barricade of concrete, metal, and a dozen buses blocking the street.

Outside Nikolai's roaring APC, hundreds of White House defenders lined both sides of

---

* The American embassy's old building is situated on the Garden Ring. The controversial new embassy, said to be infested with electronic bugs and not yet used, is on a narrow street between the White House and the Garden Ring. Two rows of town houses for diplomats and other embassy employees flank the office building. Americans could view the events at the White House from windows overlooking it though they were evacuated to the embassy gym Tuesday night.

the walled ramp, yelling in anger and fear. Although the armored column was not heading directly toward the White House, the defenders assumed that this was the beginning of the long-awaited attack. Suddenly, the lead APC crunched into tens of thousands of roubles' worth of Moscow city buses, trying to batter its way through the barricades. The demonstrators no longer had any doubts. The battle was on.

As the first APCs rocked forward and back, ramming the barricades, demonstrators ignored the danger of tons of moving armor and climbed on board the vehicles. Frightened soldiers atop the APCs fired their machine guns in the air trying to scare off the crowd. Several demonstrators threw a tarpaulin over the visor of Nikolai's vehicle, blinding him. Then someone in the crowd threw a firebomb.

"I couldn't see anything," Nikolai told *Izvestia* later. "I opened the hatch, but someone hit me on the head. I ducked back into the vehicle and started to turn it around. Suddenly, smoke appeared inside. It was impossible to breathe. I tried to open the hatch again and couldn't. Someone was standing on it. There were already flames inside the vehicle, and my clothes caught fire.

"Finally, I managed to open the hatch, and I started to put out the fire," Nikolai said. "Most of all, I was afraid about the vehicle, because it was fully armed for combat and could explode at any moment."

Nikolai's sergeant, Yuri, remembered cobblestones flying through the air, and the "inconceivable noise" of a dozen armored vehicles and hundreds of people screaming.

Dmitry Komar, a medal-winning veteran of the Afghan war who had never been able to speak to anyone about his experiences there, tried to climb into the rear hatch of Nikolai's vehicle. A soldier leaned out another opening and fired shots. They missed. But

Komar fell, struck his head on the pavement, and died of the injury.

The crowd went wild, screaming, "Fascists! Shame! Shame!"

With weapons firing, Molotov cocktails in flight, people screaming, the armored vehicles backing and rearing, smashing again into the barricade of buses blocking their escape from the claustrophobic confines of the underpass — confusion prevailed. Vladimir Usov and others rushed to pull Komar's body away from the APC. A bullet struck Usov in the forehead and killed him. Nikolai's APC ran over Usov's dead body, crushing it.

Ilya Krichevsky, a 28-year-old former tank gunner who had gone out that night to talk tank crews out of killing civilians, instead died of a shot in the forehead as he stood in the roadway screaming at the APC crewmen.

Inside his APC, Nikolai had no idea what was going on. "I heard one of ours start to shoot overhead, to drive the people off the top. But at that moment, I didn't know any-

thing about anybody being killed."

The APC was in flames. Nikolai and the rest of the crew abandoned it. "With difficulty, we managed to fight our way through to another APC," the sergeant added. Nikolai and two other crewmen from APC No. 536 suffered burns. As the burning APC crashed into the nearest bus once more, the fire spread to the bus and flames leaped to the sky. Several of the other armored vehicles bashed the buses until they found themselves stuck in a mass of crushed metal.

By this time, the crowd was out for blood. They had just watched three protesters die. The civilians were not about to let the column of vehicles escape. Water trucks were driven into place at the other end of the

ABOVE: Defenders light candles and pray for peace. **BELOW:** Women stand in the rain across the eight lanes of Kutuzovsky Prospect where tanks are expected. Their banner reads, "Soldiers, don't shoot your mothers."

2:18 pm
Emergency Committee members Vladimir Kryuchkov, Dimitry Yazov, Oleg Baklanov, and Alexander Tizyakov leave Moscow by plane to visit Gorbachev in the Crimea.

4:45 pm
Russian Vice-President Alexander Rutskoi, Prime Minister Ivan Silayev, Vadim Bakatin, and Yevgeny Primakov leave for the Crimea in pursuit of the Emergency Committee members. They fear that Kryuchkov and the others might try to assassinate Gorbachev.

5:00 pm
Coup plotters are placed under guard by Gorbachev's bodyguards upon their arrival at his dacha.

6:38 pm
Communications at Gorbachev's dacha are restored, and the President makes his first call to Boris Yeltsin.

7:19 pm
Gorbachev phones U.S. President George Bush to say that he is back in power as President of the Soviet Union.

underpass, trapping the APCs.

Russian legislators Oleg Rumyantsev and Anatoly Alexeyev ran out to the confrontation armed with a megaphone. Rumyantsev, his lip dripping blood from an earlier encounter, talked with soldiers and then pleaded with the crowd, trying to stop the bloodshed. "We don't want any more deaths," he said. But he was not speaking just of deaths among the several hundred civilians and dozen armored vehicles in front of him. With a KGB division on the outskirts of town, he feared this confrontation would be the excuse to start storming the White House. "I am afraid the KGB will attack if this gets out of hand," Rumyantsev said.

Perhaps tens of thousands of lives hung on the legislators' ability to defuse this confrontation, to stop the soldiers from firing their guns, and to stop the crowd from throwing firebombs that could detonate the APCs' ammunition.

Finally, the military commander promised to order his men back into their vehicles, where they would quietly stay put until morning, when everyone would leave. There would be no attack by either side.

Rumyantsev told the crowd about the deal.

"No! No!" the demonstrators screamed, still charged with shock and anger over the deaths. Though the bodies had been removed, the blood of the victims still ran in the street, mixing with the rain. The soldiers could leave, the demonstrators yelled, but not with their armor and weapons.

The two legislators negotiated further. Finally, they turned again to the crowd. The soldiers would stay with their vehicles, and this unit would be turned over to the defense of the White House. A Russian legislator would ride on each vehicle to ensure that no more firebombs would be thrown.

"Do you agree not to attack them?"

Deputy Alexeyev shouted through the megaphone. There was a smattering of applause, though hardly enough to inspire confidence. "With each APC will be a Russian legislator," Alexeyev continued. "I ask you to preserve their health."

A few blocks north of this confrontation, six armored vehicles came roaring down the Garden Ring Road in the direction of their trapped comrades. Several hundred demonstrators ran out into the road and formed a line of people across the eight-lane avenue at Vosstaniya Square. Faced with the prospect of shooting or crushing dozens of people, the APCs stopped. Four turned and rumbled back from whence they came. The demonstrators surged around the two remaining.

"Don't shoot!" they begged the soldiers.

"That I can promise," replied one. "My personal decision is that I'm not going to touch anyone." He said they had been ordered only to occupy Vosstaniya Square for the duration of the curfew. And then he took a small tricolored Russian flag from inside his uniform and stuck it in the gun muzzle of his APC.

At 4:35 a.m., just before dawn, two officers drove up and spoke to the two crews. The soldiers told the civilians that they were being ordered back to their base and started their engines. Suddenly, all lights in the city went out, as least as far as the eye could see. Then a huge tank came roaring down the Garden Ring Road toward the demonstrators. People screamed and ran.

Endless seconds later, the tank reached its mates — and turned around. It was a false alarm. All three vehicles departed.

Back at the underpass, it took more than an hour to move the water-truck barricade and turn the nine APCs around. Finally, they came lumbering slowly out of the underpass,

each one carrying about two dozen people on top — demonstrators, Russian legislators, and soldiers. On the lead APC flew a white flag of surrender and the Soviet flag, its hammer-and-sickle insignia removed.

"They're our first captives," said legislator Alexeyev happily. As the column of armor approached the White House about 5 a.m., the crowd broke into cheers of triumph.

Lt. Col. Anatoly Chistyakov, political officer of the Taman Division, told *Izvestia* later that these APCs had never intended to attack the White House. They were only heading further south, to the positions they had been ordered to guard during the curfew. The commander on the scene decided he had to break through the bus barricade to get there, Colonel Chistyakov explained. He added that although obeying an order to enforce the

curfew, the division had refused to follow the verbally transmitted order of General Varrenikov "to prepare three tank companies for deployment in the region of the Kalinin Bridge," just in front of the White House.

"We had heard that very many people had gathered in the Kalinin Prospect region, and if we had allowed tanks to break it up, we could not have escaped disaster," Colonel Chistyakov said.

Those inside the White House heard the noise but could not see the confrontation on the Garden Ring Road. "I heard shots and saw tracer bullets outside my window," said Colonel Samoilov, of the Defense Committee in Yeltsin's government. "We thought it was an attack of the Spetznaz [KGB special forces]." The Russian chief, Gen. Konstantin Kobets, advised Yeltsin to

An armored personnel carrier tries repeatedly to smash through the barricade of buses and vehicles blocking the exit from the Kalinin Prospect underpass.

8:47 pm
Gorbachev phones state broadcasting chief Kravchenko and orders him to run a statement on the 9 o'clock news saying that "the President is in full control of the situation in the country now."

11:50 pm
Gorbachev and his family leave the airport at Belbek in the Crimea to return to Moscow.

escape to a safer place, but Yeltsin refused to leave the crowds of citizens who were ready to be crushed by tanks in his defense. "I'm not going anywhere," Yeltsin said, according to Kobets. "I'd rather die here,with you, in a fight to the death."

However, Yeltsin did take some precautions. He spent more than two hours hidden in the bomb shelter underneath the Russian Parliament Building. His personal bodyguards deployed around the vault as a last-ditch defense, said his aide, Viktor Ilyushin. Also, a helicopter remained on alert to swoop into the inner courtyard of the nineteen-story building to rescue Yeltsin, Samoilov said.

At the paratroopers' headquarters, midnight Tuesday came and went. General Grachev, the commander, said his troops were sup-

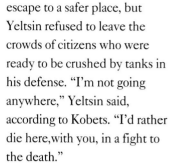

posed to start moving toward the White House at midnight to prepare to clear the way for an attack by the KGB Alpha Group. But General Grachev issued no command. Unconcerned by his decision to defy orders, Grachev waited, expecting to hear from an irate superior any second.

"What would have happened if I had agreed?" he said later to the Soviet Army newspaper. "We would not be sitting here.The 'victors' would be dying excruciating deaths from chemical and bacteriological warfare." That passage was the only suggestion that a Red Army military unit had the capability to use lethal chemical and germ weapons and could have been ordered to use them against its own people.★

About 1 a.m., Grachev said, he received a

call from General Karpukhin, of the Alpha Group, which was supposed to storm the White House after Grachev's paratroopers opened the way. As Grachev recalled it, Karpukhin complained that he could not reach his bosses. Grachev asked Karpukhin where he was.

"About two kilometers from the Russian Parliament," Karpukhin said. "I have evaluated the situation and made a decision." Then he fell silent. Grachev waited. "I won't take part in this storming. There will be no attack. I won't go against the people," Karpukhin said finally.

"At that dramatic moment, I tried to call Yazov," Grachev recounted for *Krasnaya Zvezda*. "Nobody answered. The Defense Minister was asleep." At 4 a.m., Grachev received a call from an officer relaying a message from Yazov: his paratroopers should withdraw — presumably from around the White House, since that is where they were supposed to be by that hour.

★ In the weeks after the coup several of the generals involved gave interviews to Soviet journalists that suggested horrifying scenarios — bombing the Kremlin, dogfights over the White House, the use of chemical and germ warfare. Military officers and civilians gave interviews to journalists who were not completely objective in their reports and that accounted for much unreliable information appearing in print. Rumors and self-serving accounts abounded.

"Tell the minister that the troops never moved in," Grachev said he replied.

Despite reports from numerous officers that they were ordered to attack the White House and refused, Vyacheslav Nikonov, an aide to Oleg Bakatin, who became post-coup KGB chief, said the post-coup investigation found no order to attack the White House was ever given. He said the only order to prepare for an attack was issued on Monday, not Tuesday. But Nikonov said that Tuesday night, after Marshal Yazov decided finally against an attack, KGB Chief Kryuchkov considered going ahead with only KGB forces. Kryuchkov decided against that course of action at 3 a.m. after meeting with his lieutenants in his KGB headquarters.

According to other accounts, Karpukhin's Alpha Group had already refused an order to prepare for an attack the night before.

In his own defense, Yazov told prosecutors later that he merely ordered troops to block intersections on Tuesday night, and that he barred the use of weapons. However, Kobets later obtained a copy of the minute-by-minute plan of attack.

Inside Yeltsin's headquarters, the fear of an attack grew despite various assurances coming in that there would be no violence. Army Chief of Staff Moiseyev called to say there would be no attack. At 1:40 a.m., according to some reports, Kazakhstan President Nazarbayev telephoned Yeltsin to say that Vice-President Yanayev had promised him there would be no attack. But such reports persisted.

Word spread of an attack at midnight. Then 2 a.m. Then 3 a.m. Throughout the night, Russian government radio, inside the

ABOVE LEFT: After long negotiation, the APCs turn from the barricades and move back through the Kalinin underpass carrying jubilant demonstrators, Russian legislators, and soldiers. **CENTER LEFT:** Among the heroes of the coup resistance was tank driver Nikolai Izreshia, one of the many soldiers who joined the ranks of the defenders. **BELOW:** Victorious demonstrators crowd atop one of the armored vehicles as it withdraws from the barricades.

White House, reported unconfirmed sightings of tanks and troops approaching the building. At one point, a column of buses rolled toward the White House along the riverbank. Everyone assumed they were full of troops and waited nervously. After about fifteen minutes, the buses left.

"The most terrible period was 1 to 5 a.m., Wednesday," said an ex-Army officer helping to defend the White House. "With just ten tanks and our defenseless people all around, we were just cannon fodder."

Gradually, the volunteer defenders of the White House outside the building and the Yeltsin government officials inside began to feel more optimistic. When they heard reports at 5 a.m. of two KGB divisions standing pat on the outskirts of the city and of other units that were withdrawing, a wave of relief surged through the crowd.

Anatoly Yakovlev, one of the many offspring of government officials who had gone to the barricades, broke away long enough to telephone his father, presidential aide Alexander Yakovlev.

"They've shriveled!" he shouted happily.

The children of many prominent and important people were at the barricades, including the son of Valentin Lazutkin, the first deputy chairman of Soviet television. His presence compelled his father to resign his position after the coup failed but the letter was not accepted. One young man in the crowd was Semyon Budyenny, grandson and namesake of the legendary old Bolshevik field marshal who organized the Red Army cavalry after the 1917 Revolution.

Supposedly no troops had entered Leningrad after an agreement was reached between Mayor Anatoly Sobchak and the military high command on Monday. But at 4 a.m., Wednesday, Arkady Kramerev, the city's police chief, received a phone call. A colonel

The tank attack expected and feared throughout the night fails to materialize, as orders to deploy the division to just in front of the White House are ignored by the officers in direct command.

Bystanders try to free the body of Dmitry Komar from an APC after the young Afgan War veteran fell and suffered a fatal head injury.

told him he had 1,500 paratroopers concealed in a military institute in the center of the city. They wished to leave, the colonel said, and asked the chief for safe passage. Kramerev told The New York Times that he was so happy for them to go that he sent extra vehicles so they could get out of town faster.

In Moscow the long, dangerous night finally gave way to daylight. General Shaposhnikov, the Air Force chief, called a meeting of his deputies at 6 a.m. and asked each for an opinion. They were unanimous, according to Executive Officer Pyotr Deinekin. "Withdraw the troops immediately. Have Yazov quit the Emergency Committee. Ask the Russian leaders to take down the barricades and sit down at the negotiating table."

The full Defense Board met two hours later. Defense Minister Yazov spoke for a long time and not very coherently, according to Shaposhnikov. The defense minister called his fellow Emergency Committee members Pavlov and Yanayev "bad people,

drunks, who dragged me without knowing where they were going. And behind me stands you, and behind you, the soldiers who are in their tanks. And this is shameful for the Army."

Several generals spoke in favor of troop withdrawals from Moscow. Finally, the Defense Board voted to remove the troops. Yazov promised to convey the Defense Board's opinion to the Emergency Committee. "Probably, I will give the order to withdraw the troops," Yazov added. "But I must tell you, I won't leave the committee. I cannot be a traitor twice. This is my cross, and I will carry it to the end," Yazov said, according to Shaposhnikov.

The generals asked Yazov to issue the order by 11 a.m., when the Russian Parliament was due to open a special session on overturning the coup. Yazov did nothing — although he told prosecutors later that he ordered the troops to withdraw "to end the disgrace." Finally, Shaposhnikov himself called the Russian Parliament, and had a secretary take a note into the session announcing that the troops were leaving. Vadim Bakatin, a key Gorbachev aide as well as a Russian Parliament member, read the note aloud.

The coup was indeed shriveling, and with the same uncertainty with which it started. Yazov's executive officer said no one ever issued a written withdrawal order. A verbal order from the Defense Board simply went to the teletype operators. The armed forces command tried to contact the Emergency Committee, but the members' adjutants refused all calls. Finally, the military leaders heard that key committee members were flying to see the President.

At 11 a.m., tanks began moving out of Manezh Square next to the Kremlin. The crewmen were delighted to be going. "It's all over. The Army was disgraced again," an armored unit commander by the name of Oleg Skobelev told *Izvestia*.

But confrontation was not over everywhere. Tanks still roared into a central square in Riga on Wednesday as the Latvian Parliament voted for full independence from the Soviet Union. That night, there was one final outburst of violence in Lithuania. A handful of Soviet troops inexplicably attacked the Lithuanian Parliament Building. One Lithuanian guard was killed.

In the annals of government takeovers, this coup d'état must hold some record for strangeness. Throughout the four days so far, Gorbachev loyalists telephoned the anti-Gorbachev forces repeatedly. Opponents met with each other and worked in adjacent offices in the Kremlin. Bodyguards and jailers took meals with each other at Gorbachev's Crimean dacha.

As the fortunes of the conspirators shifted, Gorbachev's supporters in the Kremlin switched from the defensive to the offensive. They began preparations for the return of the President to Moscow. By noon on Wednesday, they were drafting speeches for him. Yanayev's anti-Gorbachev guards patrolled the Kremlin corridor where they worked. One of those speech writers was Vyacheslav Nikonov, whose boss was Valery Boldin — Gorbachev's chief of staff, but also one of the key conspirators against the President. Nikonov wrote as Boldin worked in the office next door.

On Wednesday morning, Yeltsin talked to KGB chief Kryuchkov by telephone and suggested that they go together to visit Gorbachev in the Crimea, Yeltsin aide Ilyushin said. Yeltsin later claimed he duped Kryuchkov into making the trip but did not elaborate. After the call Yeltsin met with his security council. He was worried that the plotters might still prevail. According to Russian Vice-President Alexander Rutskoi, Yeltsin said: "I've got to fly to Foros now to pick up Gorbachev, because these bastards won't give up their attempts to attack. These bastards will bring back fascism."

ABOVE: A moscow firefighter prepares to use a water hose at one of the many blazes resulting from the clashes at the barricades between demonstrators and the military. BELOW: A wounded protester is carried from the confrontation near Garden Ring Road.

Yeltsin's deputies and advisers argued against his making the trip, citing the risk of capture by the conspirators. Instead, it was decided to send Vice-President Rutskoi, who was an Air Force colonel, and Prime Minister Ivan Silayev, along with a detachment of thirty-six armed Russian Federation policemen. And so began the chase scene that led to the coup's conclusion.

According to Rutskoi, Silayev telephoned Kryuchkov and invited him to fly with the Russian leaders to the Crimea. The KGB chief replied that he was in his car on the way to his dacha and that he would return to Moscow for discussions. Kryuchkov then suggested they all fly together to visit Gorbachev the next day. He agreed to speak to the Russian Parliament at 1 p.m., Yeltsin said.

"In fact, he went to the airport and flew to the Crimea," Rutskoi said, "and we had to chase after him."

KGB logs show that Kryuchkov had been busy all morning phoning the men who would be arrested as his fellow conspirators: Yanayev, Pugo, Lukianov, and Kryuchkov's own deputy KGB chief, General Ageyev.

Flowers are strewn over the bloodstained road where demonstrators and soldiers clashed and three were killed.

Valentin Karasev, Gorbachev's public relations adviser, was working in his Kremlin office and heard that Kryuchkov and several other conspirators were en route to the airport. He tipped off Yeltsin. Russian police tore after them, hoping for an arrest, but a four-mile-long column of armor heading out of Moscow slowed them.

The presidential jumbo jet took off at 2:18 p.m., minutes before the police arrived at the airport. On board were Kryuchkov and three other members of the Emergency Committee: Yazov; Oleg Baklanov, Gorbachev's deputy chairman of the National Security Council; and Alexander Tizyakov. Heading to Foros with them were Anatoly Lukianov, the parliamentary chairman who was widely suspected of complicity in the coup, and Vladimir Ivashko, Gorbachev's deputy general secretary of the Communist Party.

Rutskoi and Silayev, now joined by Bakatin and Yevgeny Primakov from Gorbachev's staff, headed for the airport about 4:45 p.m. to give chase. Word of their mission spread through Moscow, and by the time they took off they had a handful of Western and Soviet journalists on board the plane as well. The officials were worried that Kryuchkov and company were bent on doing violence in the Crimea, perhaps even assassinating Gorbachev. The pursuers were two-and-a-half critical hours behind the traitorous KGB chief.

The coup was collapsing. One after another, key groups condemned the Emergency Committee. The Supreme Soviet leadership, the Communist Party, and the Soviet Peace Committee were at the head of the list. The leaderships of the national legislature and the Party had done nothing to help Gorbachev until this point.

Karasev called TASS and Soviet television

and ordered them to stop obeying the conspirators and start obeying him. They agreed with alacrity. Nikonov walked into the Kremlin office where the KGB communications staff had been issuing the plotters' announcements for three days and handed them a notice saying the prosecutor had begun a criminal investigation into the coup.

"Did you approve this with Boldin?" asked one of the shocked staffers, according to Nikonov.

"No," he replied. "I did not, and I will not. But you should send this." They did.

At 5 p.m., TASS sent that announcement. A few minutes later, Yanayev's staff sent TASS a statement signed by the Emergency Committee denying that its members had been arrested. For the first time, TASS did not transmit a committee statement.

The scene in the Kremlin had its comic aspects: Karasev called the commandant of the Kremlin and ordered him to disarm the guards of Boldin, Yanayev, and Vasily Starodubtsev, the Peasants Union leader who was a last-minute addition to the Emergency Committee. Karasev said the three should not be allowed to leave the Kremlin. The commandant accepted the order, Nikonov said. But when Gorbachev's communications were restored, the President called the com-

As day breaks, the battered vehicles and charred remains of the barricades provide grim evidence of the violence of the night before.

mandant and ordered him not to allow the three men into the Kremlin. So the commandant freed them to go. Boldin left. Yanayev and Starodubtsev remained in their offices to await their fate.

Prime Minister Ivan Silayev is one of a contingent of Yeltsin supporters sent to Foros to free Gorbachev. OPPOSITE: Flowers are laid at a memorial in Garden Ring Road as a tribute to those killed during the tragic events of the night before.

In the plane headed for the Crimea, the pursuing rescuers knew that Gorbachev was still alive but little else, wrote Igor Sichka, a *Komsomolskaya Pravda* correspondent on the plane. Speculation was that the Moscow troop withdrawals might be merely a change in tactics. It was now clear that generals had issued the withdrawal order, not the Emergency Committee conspirators. That meant the KGB troops could still be in the city, ready to attack when everyone's guard was down.

They worried that Kryuchkov might kidnap Gorbachev and move him. They feared their own arrival could set off a gun battle. "Who knew whether the conspirators were trying to use the slightest excuse to provoke firing and in this way physically eliminate the President, throwing the blame on us? These guys have nothing left to lose," Sichka wrote, based on an airborne interview with Bakatin, a loyal Gorbachev aide.

For a time it appeared that their plane might not be able to land at Belbek, the military airport nearest to Gorbachev's dacha. The local military authorities claimed the conspirators' plane was damaged and blocking the runway, Air Force staff aide Pyotr Deinekin said later. From the plane, Rutskoi radioed for a detachment of marines to be sent to the airport to guarantee the Russians' safe landing. Rutskoi later said that Soviet

marines stationed at the airport had orders from the conspirators — or their supporters — to shoot down any plane making an unauthorized landing at Belbek. Those troops were withdrawn only twenty minutes before the rescuers' arrival. "If we had landed a bit sooner, we would have been wiped out by grenade launchers," he said.

Finally, a decision from the military high command in Moscow forced the local authorities to allow the second plane to land at Belbek. The presidential jumbo jet was on the ground, but the conspirators were long gone.

Rutskoi at first considered three military plans for freeing Gorbachev. The first was to stop ten kilometers from the dacha and send an ultimatum demanding a meeting with the plotters. The second was to surround the dacha and then send the ultimatum. The third was to storm the dacha. As the men on the airplane thought about it, however, the military options did not offer much hope.

"The blockade of the President's dacha was a serious undertaking. There were warships cruising off the coast. The road was blocked," Rutskoi said. "We didn't know what condition the President was in. They could have given him all sorts of injections, as is often done in the Soviet Union. And with his wife, daughter, and grandchildren there, the plotters could have threatened his family."

The rescuers eventually decided to leave the armed men behind for fear of sparking a battle that could leave Gorbachev dead. They were to take action if Rutskoi did not call with news within three hours.

There were small hopeful signs at the Gorbachev dacha Wednesday that the situation might be changing for the better. At sea, several naval ships that had been in the area for two days suddenly sailed off at mid-after-

President's bodyguards reported, "Some people in camouflage uniforms are crawling toward the dacha." The frightening figures in the dusk were unidentified and assumed to be loyal to the conspirators. One of Gorbachev's guards picked up a telephone and called the troops on the perimeter: "Who is crawling out there?" he barked. "If they move another inch, we'll shoot them! Send them back! In the opposite direction!"

After a few moments, the word came to Gorbachev with relief: "They're crawling back the way they came."

At 6:38 p.m., the same KGB officer who had cut presidential communications on Sunday ordered them restored. Gorbachev got his first call out to Yeltsin.

"It turned out that someone had ordered the telephone operator to make only one phone connection," Gorbachev said later. But the operator had ignored the two officers standing behind her. "She did what I asked, and connected me with everyone," Gorbachev recounted. "The officers undoubtedly understood, but did not interfere." After Yeltsin he called the presidents of Kazakhstan, the Ukraine, Byelorussia, and Uzbekistan — the largest Soviet republics after Russia.

At 7:19 p.m., Gorbachev telephoned Kennebunkport, Maine. George Bush was out in his boat and had to hurry back to shore to take the call. Gorbachev told the American President that he was again in charge. But things were far from secure. The Russian Parliament group had not yet arrived, and Gorbachev did not know the loyalties of the people he had to rely on, even of the guards around the dacha. The President still had to fly back to Moscow, wondering if he might be shot out of the sky.

Though the chilly rain continues into Wednesday morning, daylight brings an easing of tension among the crowd around the White House as the threat of a major attack seems to lessen.

KGB director and coup leader, Kryuchkov, contemplates his fate as he returns to Moscow on Gorbachev's plane. Ten minutes later he was under arrest.

"Everything was still dangerous, and they could have destroyed me en route," Gorbachev said.

Not knowing whom to trust, Gorbachev soon made an error. One of his first calls that evening was to General Mikhail Moiseyev, armed forces chief of staff, appointing him Defense Minister in place of Yazov and ordering him to secure Gorbachev's safe return to Moscow. Moiseyev was fired two days later, accused of being a coup sympathizer. He had signed an order during the coup directing commanders to take decisive action against coup resistors trying to "penetrate" military units.

While Gorbachev began to reassert control

at the compound, his Russian rescuers sped through the dark along the Sevastopol-Yalta seaside highway. Some of them were armed, but only with handguns. Others were unarmed. They did not know if they would encounter enemy gun fire.

"We didn't know anything," correspondent Sichka said.

When they arrived they left their cars at the gate and walked into the compound. Silent men with automatic weapons watched them enter. Rutskoi and the others did not know their allegiance. The officials went straight toward the family residence. The journalists were diverted to the service entrance and led to the staff quarters where they waited.

As Rutskoi approached the dacha, he thought about the possibility that Gorbachev himself was behind this coup. "You understand that speculation was rife in Russia… that all this was a game on the part of Mikhail Sergeyevich. You can't hide it; they were saying such things. But when Mikhail Sergeyevich came out to meet us with his aides, it was clear from his face that he was happy to see us," Rutskoi said.

Gorbachev "hugged us and kissed us," Silayev said. Russian legislator Vladimir Lysenko described the President as looking exhausted from his ordeal, white, with sunken cheeks.

"I was walking away from my own funeral," Gorbachev described the scene to Soviet television. "I was so happy about what happened, that we were able to overturn the coup."

Raisa Gorbachev "seemed like someone who was about to have a heart attack, almost dying — as if she had seen what fate had in store for her," Rutskoi said. Lysenko said she was unsteady as she walked toward them.

Finally the journalists were allowed in to see Gorbachev, in a sitting room in the dacha. "He was very excited, incoherent, using broken phrases," Sichka said.

"I made no deals," Gorbachev told the reporters. He told them that if the conspirators forced him to turn over power, "I would have to finish myself off. There could be no other way out."

Gorbachev refused to meet with the men he called "traitors" — the Emergency Committee members — but he did agree to receive Lukianov, the Parliament chairman who had been a law school classmate, and Ivashko, Gorbachev's deputy in the Communist Party. Chernyayev witnessed the meetings.

Ivashko tried to explain that he had head-ed off a meeting of the Communist Party leadership scheduled for Tuesday that would have formally ousted the President from his post as chairman. Ivashko, however, had an excuse for his basic inaction: He had crawled out of a hospital bed to fly to Foros and still had his throat bandaged. Gorbachev gave him short shrift.

When Lukianov tried to tell Gorbachev he had worked against the conspiracy, the President ripped into him. "Listen, we've known each other for forty years. Don't try to make a fool out of me! You should have thrown yourself in front of the guns! You delayed the Supreme Soviet for six days, a week! What are you telling me, you did this, you did that! The very next day you should have summoned the Supreme Soviet if you're on the side of legality and the President," Chernyayev quoted Gorbachev as saying.

At 8:47 p.m., Gorbachev called state broadcasting chief Kravchenko and dictated a statement for the 9 o'clock television news.

"President Mikhail Gorbachev said today he is in full control of the situation in the country now and that his communications links to the nation, cut off by adventurist actions of a group of state officials, have been restored," the news announcer said.

A little later, Rutskoi went to the airport at Belbek to arrange for the President's safe return to Moscow. They were still exercising care. "We prepared both planes for take-off… to confuse them. We were afraid it would not be possible to fly on the presidential plane, because one could expect anything from

A tired, but smiling Gorbachev responds to reporters' questions after his rescue. He is accompanied by Prime Minister Silayev (right) and Vice-President Rutskoi (center, hand raised).

ABOVE: Exhausted, Raisa and her granddaughter depart from the plane, back in Moscow after their ordeal in Foros. BELOW: A loyal bodyguard surveys the crowd at the VIP terminal awaiting Gorbachev's arrival.

these traitors," Rutskoi said.

It was approaching midnight when the convoy of ZIL limousines and Volgas raced up to the presidential jumbo jet parked on the apron at the military airfield. Although Gorbachev's car stopped, he stayed inside, and rode on to board the smaller Russian plane a half-mile away. The trick was meant to confuse watchers into thinking he was on his own presidential jet.

Kryuchkov was put onto the Russian plane with Gorbachev. Yazov and the others flew on the jumbo jet along with a contingent of the armed Russians. Kryuchkov's bodyguard did not interfere when their boss entered the Russian plane. He was quiet and appeared to be depressed, witnesses said.

Gen. Andrei Dunayev of the Russian Interior Ministry asked him, "Do you know what kind of punishment awaits you?" Kryuchkov looked surprised, Dunayev said later. The KGB chief replied that a trial for the committee members would bring no glory or authority either to the Soviet Union or Russia.

Later, in custody, Kryuchkov told Dunayev, "It's unfortunate that Mikhail Sergeyevich would not see me. I would have explained everything. I didn't do anything against him."

Gorbachev and his exhausted family rode in the forward compartment, ignoring Kryuchkov.

On arrival in Moscow, Rutskoi was still worried. He told the pilots, "If everything has gone wrong… if it's not our side waiting for us… then we'll turn around and fly away again."

The plane rolled to a halt in front of the VIP terminal at Vnukovo Airport. Rutskoi's own chief bodyguard was the first to step out of the jet. Rutskoi told him, "If they open fire, you use your machine gun to cover us, and we'll have a chance to escape."

When Rutskoi stepped through the hatch he saw the crowd of reporters and Russian officials, but he also saw armored personnel carriers of unknown loyalty, and armed forces Chief of Staff Moiseyev and Foreign Minister Bessmertnykh.

"It was disgusting to look at them," he said. "They were standing there to greet the President, and they had not said anything in his defense."

Once they were off the plane, Rutskoi ripped into General Moiseyev for complying with the orders to bring tanks into the capital. "With modern tanks, you can destroy houses, destroy everything… How much do have to hate your own people to give this command?"

Gorbachev emerged, followed by his wife, clutching granddaughter Oksana, and Irina, carrying Anastasia. The President looked exhausted. He was pale.

"The most important thing is that everything we have done since 1985 has already brought tangible results," he told reporters. "Society, our people, are now different."

He thanked those Soviet people who had saved his life. He specifically included his former enemy, Boris Yeltsin.

Gorbachev's aide, Yevgeny Primakov, tried to pull him through the crowd. "Don't hurry," Gorbachev said. "I want to breathe the free air of Moscow."

Yazov got off the second plane, followed by numerous Russian police running to catch up with him as he strode toward the VIP terminal. Barannikov slapped him on the shoulder and said, "You're finished." Yazov acted as if he didn't hear the words. Then he saw an armed guard in the doorway, and the light finally dawned.

"I see… it seems that you are going to arrest me," the defense minister said, his voice cracking.

At the Kremlin, Gorbachev aide Veniamin Yarin ordered guards on the office door of Vice-President Yanayev. Yarin said later that

Yanayev was drunk. "There was fear in his eyes… He said he had been threatened with Lefortovo Prison if he did not cooperate."

At the White House, tens of thousands of protesters were still on alert, and word ripped through the crowd that Gorbachev was coming straight from the airport to thank them. The expectation was so great that when Rutskoi returned, people who could see only a black limousine cried, "Gorbachev is here!"

Unfortunately Gorbachev and his family were so strained by their ordeal that it never occurred to them to go anywhere but home. That was a major political mistake. The President would make other miscalculations before he realized just how drastically his country and its power structure had changed in only three days.

Gorbachev and family return to Moscow at 2:15 a.m. Thursday, August 22.

Aftermath

Moscow erupted in joy Thursday morning. In the streets, pedestrians smiled and laughed with strangers in a manner utterly alien to the gloomy, reserved Soviet capital. Fear disappeared. The troops and tanks were gone. Gorbachev was back in the Kremlin.

On that day after the coup collapsed, Gorbachev said he had returned from his brief Crimean captivity a different man in a different country. Yet he had no idea how very different his country and his position in it actually were. When he awoke that morning, he was well on his way to becoming a relatively powerless figurehead in a fragmented nation

In front of St. Basil's on Red Square, Muscovites parade a giant "new" Russian flag produced by one of the city's post-coup entreprenuerial enterprises.

where suddenly empowered subordinate republics were taking control away from the central government and the Communist Party.

On that aftermath Thursday, Yeltsin spoke to his people from the balcony of the White House once again, but this time in triumph. He thanked them for "inflicting a crushing blow" against those who would steal the government. "Your weapon was the enormous will to defend the ideals of freedom, democracy, and human worth," he said. Then came the politics. The coup, he said, proved that the entire central government was stuck in the discredited old ways and must be changed. "At any moment, they [Gorbachev's government] will seek to restore their dictatorship over the republics." He called for the immediate formation of "a government of national accord."

The crowd, heady with victory and relief, streamed out of the barricaded square and marched to the Kremlin, Red Square, and the KGB, waving new Russian flags. Other Muscovites abandoned their offices, apartments, and jobs to join the celebration.

"What would have been my son's fate if this had not happened?" said fifty-year-old historian Larisa Yakovleva, panting as she hurried from the Museum of the History of Moscow toward the chanting crowds on Dzerzhinsky Square, site of the notorious Lubyanka, the KGB headquarters. "We are all so happy!"

On that square, hundreds of people whistled and chanted, "Down with the Communist Party." A young man in a tank driver's uniform climbed the statue of Felix Dzerzhinsky to install a Ukrainian independence flag, desecrating the monument to the founder of the Soviet secret police and defying the KGB with a symbol of freedom.

Around KGB headquarters, thousands of citizens stabbed their fists in the air in anger, shouting, "Executioners!" at the shadowy figures behind curtained windows and exorcising the dark spirit of decades of terror that had come from the building. With the KGB chairman himself under arrest, the agency had suddenly lost its immunity from public complaints and criminal prosecution.

Some demonstrators even painted the slogan, "Down with the KGB," on the facade of the once-feared agency's headquarters. Inside, KGB agents worried that the crowd might try to storm the building. "We knew we could not use weapons. There had been enough bloodshed already," said Maj. Gen. Alexander Karbainov, a KGB spokesman.

Several Russian legislators arrived and calmed the crowd. To appease the protesters, Moscow Mayor Gavril Popov promised to have the huge statue of the hated Dzerzhinsky removed safely that same day.

The people of the capital were still nervous. Just before dusk thundering noises like artillery fire shook the city. Was it one last stand by the coup supporters? Was the euphoria of freedom a short-lived illusion? It turned out to be only fireworks set off by celebrators.

By midnight, construction cranes were lifting the fourteen-ton statue of "Iron Felix" off his pedestal in Dzerzhinsky Square. They had him by the neck. A crowd of 3,000 cheered and set off flares in joy. When he was down, demonstrators kicked at his face.

"I spit on that son of a bitch!" said Paul Shebalin, an American from San Francisco whose father fought Dzerzhinsky and the other Bolsheviks as they were consolidating power after the 1917 Revolution.

"We are all sick of the Communists. They have been strangling us for seventy years," Alexander Filippova, a pensioner, told The New York Times.

Mayor Popov was the first to sense the mood of the people and realize the time had come to kill off communism. He moved quickly to suspend the Party's activities in the capital — and set off a firestorm of similar moves over the next two days.

Gorbachev was not as sensitive to the Party's vulnerability. At a press conference Thursday evening, Gorbachev continued to defend the Party. "Everything was done to break me," he said, detailing how his communications were cut, his dacha surrounded, his family implicitly threatened. "These people might have done almost anything," he said. Yet he still insisted that the Communist Party was salvageable, an opinion he would hold for two more days. For months there had been rumors that Gorbachev would quit his position as Party general secretary in a move to diminish the organization's influence.

Now, when it was clear that the coup was the Party's last grab for its old power, he was still talking about restructuring it.

"He'd been through an earthquake," said his long-time friend Yakovlev. "He came out in a state of shock. Anybody who wasn't in Moscow did not understand how the psychology of the city had changed."

Yeltsin became the President's teacher. From the very first hours of the coup on Monday morning, Boris Yeltsin had seen his opportunity and seized it. Neither he nor his lieutenants stood on ceremony. To the extent that they could, they ran not only the Russian Federation but the entire USSR. They gave orders to military commanders who were supposed to be under the authority of Dmitry Yazov, the defense minister who was one of

A city celebrates: "Moscow Day," August 30, 1991, included fireworks over the Kremlin and, a first, a rock concert next to the Kremlin Wall.

8/24/91

The Ukraine declares independence.

Gorbachev resigns as Party general secretary and turns all property of the Communist Party over to the government.

8/26/91

At a meeting of the Supreme Soviet Gorbachev attempts to preserve a political and economic union of former Soviet republics but is rejected by independence-minded republics.

9/2/91

Congress of Peoples' Deputies votes to dissolve the Soviet Union.

the plotters. They were in touch not only with Emergency Committee members and their cohorts but also with Gorbachev loyalists. And it was Yeltsin who began dealing with other governments and their leaders, such as President Bush and British Prime Minister John Major. It was clear for all the world to see that Boris Yeltsin was the man with pivotal power in the fractured USSR.

Gorbachev went to the Russian Parliament to thank his rescuers for restoring him to power. The legislators had other ideas. They emphasized in a raucous session broadcast on national television that the republics would be exercising the power in the future. They interrupted Gorbachev repeatedly, asking brazen questions and demanding the prohibition of the Communist Party. They called it a "criminal enterprise."

Yeltsin forced Gorbachev to read aloud a record of Monday's cabinet meeting, where all but two of his own ministers betrayed him or at least turned a blind eye to the schemes of the coup plotters. When Gorbachev protested the humiliation, saying he had not read the document. Yeltsin was merciless, insisting: "Well, read it now."

Gorbachev did so, acknowledging the defection of one after another of his top officials: "Sichev actively supports…. Panyukov hemmed and hawed and finally supported…. Stroganov actively supported the committee and reported that his staff is calling the machine factories and urging them to support it…." The list was from notes taken at the meeting by one of the cabinet members who remained loyal to Gorbachev.

Yeltsin forced Gorbachev to promise publicly he would accept all the emergency decrees Yeltsin had approved during the coup. Then Yeltsin informed the Soviet President that one of those decrees transferred ownership of all property in Russia from the central government to the republic.

The blindsided Gorbachev had suddenly become a kind of tenant-leader in his own country. Technically, his government no longer even owned the Kremlin. But that was just the beginning. Yeltsin whipped out a document. "On a lighter note," he said, "shall we now sign a decree suspending the activities of the Russian Communist Party?" He signed with a flourish, and the Parliament broke into an ovation.

Gorbachev was stunned. "I think you'll be… I don't know what you're signing there," he stammered. Finally, he argued that it would be undemocratic to prohibit the entire Party. He was beginning to come round, however. He announced cryptically that he had just agreed to an order sealing Communist Party headquarters because "something is going on [there] that must be stopped."

In fact, 2,000 protesters had surrounded the Party headquarters complex near the Kremlin and were insisting that no one be allowed to leave with documents that might prove the Party's criminal involvement in the coup. With Gorbachev's acquiescence, the vast Party bureaucracy was locked out of its main office complex, and the Party was effectively shut down.

Simultaneously, officials across the huge Soviet Union launched separate attacks on the Party. Within minutes, TASS was churning out report after report: Kirgizia confiscated the Communists' republic head-

quarters; Moldavia and Tadzhikistan banned Party groups from government agencies; the acting head of the KGB barred the Party from its position of pervasive influence in the secret police. People pulled down statues of Lenin and other Bolsheviks who were heroes only to the Communists; Yeltsin suspended six Party newspapers, including *Pravda*. Party bosses, sensing a rout, began to resign.

It took Gorbachev another day to go all the way. When he did, it was with a vengeance. Saturday, he quit as Party general secretary, the position from which Stalin, Khrushchev, Brezhnev, Andropov, and Chernenko had ruled before him. He did not merely quit. He turned on the Party that had first nurtured him for years and then betrayed him in a few days. He accused Party leaders

In the aftermath of the coup, Yeltsin emerges as a hero, triumphantly addressing the people of Moscow at the rally of victors in front of the White House.

ABOVE: With the balance of power clearly shifted to Yeltsin, the two leaders confer prior to the meeting of the Congress of Peoples' Deputies. BELOW: With demonstrators in the the street shouting, "Executioners!" and "Down with the KGB!" two officials watch the scene from inside KGB headquarters.

and their mass media propaganda bureaucracy of supporting the conspirators. He gave the Party's vast property holdings to the government and banned it from activity inside the government, the military, the judicial system, and the KGB: the very sources of its stranglehold on Soviet society. And he urged the Party leadership to disband.

The orders shut down everything from 5,000 Party office buildings and 30,000 Party organizations to hundreds of special resorts, schools, clinics, stores, and even a private liquor factory run by the Tatarstan Party elite for its own use. Gorbachev's turnabout in just twenty-four hours was complete, and it would be fatal for the institution that had ruled and terrorized the Soviet Union for seven decades.

Not only were all the coup leaders top figures in the Communist Party, but the Party organization tried to implement the takeover. Moscow city officials reported

that Party officials had pressured them to follow the plotters' orders. Other Party organizations across the land moved to retake their pre-perestroika positions of power from the legally elected authorities. After the coup failed, Party officials burned and shredded whole truckloads of documents, according to media reports. Republic-level Party chiefs in Latvia, the Ukraine, and Lithuania were accused of criminal actions in the coup along with the national leaders.

In the next few weeks, there was a wave of national revulsion with communism. For example:

• The Lenin Museum in Moscow was closed.

• The Young Pioneers, the organization intended to start indoctrination of children at kindergarten age, voted to remove itself from Party domination.

• Communist parties in Kazakhstan and Armenia were disbanded.

• The Museum of the Revolution in Moscow, dedicated to the Communists' ascension to power, added a new exhibit to depict their demise in the August coup.

• Russian governmental offices moved into the Communist Party headquarters to take advantage of its superb communications and computer facilities.

• Statues of Party leaders were removed from their sites in Moscow and unceremoniously dumped on a back lot behind the Tretyakov Gallery where the citizenry could view them fallen in disgrace.

• Leningrad's mayor proposed

removing Lenin's body from its famous Red Square mausoleum and finally burying the remains near his mother in a Leningrad cemetary.

• Even Gorbachev's dacha at Foros, the subject of some criticism for its extravagance, was given to the state.

Yeltsin struck hard at the Party-controlled media. He not only shut down six Party newspapers, but he confiscated more than one hundred Party printing plants. Within a few days, most were allowed back in business as independent or private publications. *Sovietskaya Kultura* became simply *Kultura*. *Pravda* came back on the newsstands without the Order of Lenin Medals on its masthead and also without the famous Karl Marx quotation, "Workers of the World, Unite."

Faced with competition from a raucous free press, the propaganda behemoth *Pravda* now saw its circulation drop drastically. The era of free-for-all press competition had begun. More than seven thousand new publications were registered. Though many of those had difficulty starting up and making arrangements to be printed, hundreds did begin publication.

Within days, the search began for the enormous sums of money thought to have been accumulated illegally by the Party. Suspicions of misappropriation were intensified when a Communist Party business manager leaped to his death from his office window after the coup failed. It was likely to be a long search. For years, the Party and its youth group, the Komsomol,

had been quietly investing in the new private businesses of the Soviet Union. The Komsomol used its connections and funds to start thousands of businesses not owned by the youth group itself, but by individual members.

After the coup, a Soviet business group charged in the newspaper *Commersant* that the Party had secreted $100 billion in banks outside the country, much of it stolen from the state by buying Soviet raw materials at heavily subsidized domestic prices and selling them abroad for world prices. Since Party members ran all government agencies controlling such transactions, it would have been easy, the accusers charged.

Komsomolskaya Pravda, the newspaper of

The Moscow city Party Committee Building is sealed by government decree, beginning a backlash against the Communist Party that would sweep the Republics.

the Party's youth group, quickly became a leader in investigative reporting. It charged that the Party transferred funds into private businesses that it secretly owned.

The Party was over.

It took four days for the coup to run its course and collapse. It took only three more days for

A Moscow city official announces to the crowd that Communist Party Central Committee headquarters is being sealed to protect evidence related to coup involvement.

remnants of Soviet political unity to disintegrate as well.

The Baltic republics, for example, moved swiftly to seize real independence while the central government in Moscow was in disarray. Lithuanian authorities banned the Communist Party there on Friday. Most Lithuanian Communists had chosen months before to change their party's name and ideology and support independence. The surviving Communist Party was now a rump organization still trying to recapture the past. Lithuania and Latvia froze or confiscated Communist Party property and ordered criminal investigations into what was widely assumed to be the Party's involvement in months of anti-independence violence.

Estonian radio and television resumed operations, and a three-mile-long line of military vehicles streamed out of the capital city of Tallinn. By Friday, this convoy sent in at the beginning of the week had left the republic. Crowds jeered as soldiers abandoned the television headquarters and tower in Vilnius, Lithuania's capital, which had been occupied since January.

Gorbachev discovered at a Kremlin meeting on Friday morning that republic leaders would no longer take orders from him. Instead, they started to create a government that met their needs, which turned out to be not much of a central government at all. Soon, the cabinet of fifty-six ministers would be ousted. The republic leaders bothered to replace only a handful.

They decided together to oust the men

Gorbachev had just named to head the Defense Ministry, the Interior Ministry, and the KGB. They replaced men whose allegiance was doubted with three who actively fought against the coup: General Shaposhnikov, the Air Force chief, became defense minister; Lt. Gen. Viktor Barannikov, Yeltsin's interior minister, became head of the USSR Interior Ministry; and Vadim Bakatin, a Gorbachev aide, became KGB chief, even though he reminded the leaders he had repeatedly called for liquidation of the secret police agency.

On Saturday night, the leadership of the Ukraine delivered the coup de grace to the USSR. That republic, the second largest in the union after Russia, declared independence. When the six tiny republics of Lithuania, Latvia, Estonia, Georgia, Moldavia, and Armenia declared independence, that was manageable. Together, they amounted to only 10 percent of the Soviet Union's population, area, and economic might. But the Ukraine, with its rich farmlands and population of fifty-two million, was a critical industrial and agricultural area.

The Ukraine's decision set off a chain reaction of six similar independence declarations: Byelorussia on Sunday, Moldavia on Tuesday, Azerbaijan on Friday, Kirgizia and Uzbekistan on Saturday, and Tadzhikistan on September 9.

Declaring independence, of course, is only part of the process of gaining it. A further key step is winning international diplomatic recognition. Nearly eighteen months had passed since Lithuania had issued its declaration, and its people were free only in their own minds. Soviet troops and Soviet bureaucrats still controlled most of the territory and the economy.

Yeltsin changed all that. On Saturday, August 24, as the world was trying to comprehend the shattering of the Communist Party

and the declaration of the Ukraine, Yeltsin's government granted diplomatic recognition to Estonia and Latvia. He had already done the same for Lithuania just before the coup, but without significant international effect.

With Russia recognizing Baltic independence and the Soviet Union splintering further, foreign governments stopped worrying about offending the Soviet government or damaging Gorbachev. First came the republics' Scandinavian neighbors; then the twelve nations of the European Community gave diplomatic recognition to the Baltics. Only the United States among major Western nations had not yet taken action to recognize freedom for the three republics, even though it was national policy during the Cold War years to call for the liberation of these captive nations.

Gorbachev, still far behind the rush of history on Monday, August 26, opened the special session of the Supreme Soviet legislature with a program that would have been radical before the coup. He asked for quick national elections for President and Parliament,

The statue of KGB-founder, Felix Dzerzhinsky, is pulled down to the cheers of thousands of demonstrators celebrating the victory of democratic forces in front of the KGB headquarters in the center of Moscow.

immediate signing of the Union Treaty, legal secession for republics that declined to join the new union, and stronger control over the KGB and military.

Gorbachev apparently remained hopeful he could salvage the document that had stimulated the Old Guard to mount its coup. The latest draft of the Union Treaty surrendered much power and authority to the autonomous republics and limited the role of the central government. But even this was no longer acceptable to the republics. They wanted complete independence.

One republic leader after another stood up to say it was already too late to salvage the Soviet Union as a single country. "The whole of the central government has completely outlived itself. It is dead. It has committed suicide," said Armenian President Levon Ter-Petrosian. "To re-animate the cadaver would mean a return to the danger of catastrophe," he said, referring to the fact that both the national Parliament and the Cabinet of Ministers had failed to oppose the coup.

Anatoly Lukianov is surrounded by journalists after he resigns under pressure from his position as Speaker of the Supreme Soviet. He steadfastly denies betraying his long-time friend Gorbachev in spite of mounting evidence that he supported the coup. OPPOSITE: Gorbachev thanked the world community for its support at the opening session of the International Conference of Human Rights in Moscow on September 11, 1991.

"The situation has radically changed," said Kazakhstan President Nursultan Nazarbayev, who until that moment had been Gorbachev's primary ally in efforts to preserve the union. Nazarbayev said the Union Treaty — which the conspirators had been trying to block as too radical — now did not go far enough. He said there was no longer a need for a national parliament or cabinet. He said that republics should have their own armies and foreign policy.

"The coup was like a political Chernobyl," said Ukrainian legislator Yuri Shcherbak. "The old Stalinist union collapsed, the single and indivisible Communist empire collapsed." Kirghiz and Uzbek leaders stood up to agree.

Gorbachev did realize that the Baltic republics were gone and he could no longer do anything to stop their secession. He gave his personal recognition by promising negotiations with republics choosing not to sign the Union Treaty.

Struggling to contain the damage, Gorbachev met on Tuesday, August 27, with the presidents of Russia, Kazakhstan, and Kirgizia. He took their advice to begin immediate negotiations on two kinds of union: one political and one economic. Republics could join either or both.

Publicly Gorbachev pleaded for unity in the Supreme Soviet. But privately he was negotiating terms of a new union that would not have the cohesion he once sought. He was now over his post-coup dispirited weariness. In an impassioned speech, he said the Soviet Union was "on the point of collapsing" and said he would resign if that happened. Legislators took the warning with a yawn. If the union was falling apart, then Gorbachev's resignation no longer seemed much of a threat.

Nor did the coup enhance Gorbachev's personal popularity. One week after the coup, Gorbachev had an approval rating of just 4 percent as opposed to Yeltsin's 74 percent in one poll. In a Moscow and Leningrad survey, 77 percent blamed Gorbachev for appointing the conspirators to office. Reporters during the coup came across person after person in the besieged White House who said they were risking their lives for democracy, not for Gorbachev.

From the time he came to power in 1985, Gorbachev had developed the Western

ABOVE: A mourner displays the photograph of one of the coup victims at the mass funeral held for the three young men. BELOW: Gorbachev places a flower on the coffin of one of the victims after bestowing on the three men the country's highest honor, Hero of the Soviet Union.

politician's penchant for "pressing the flesh," for winning approval through personal grass-roots contact with the people. The instinct seemed to abandon him during the coup, and when he returned from the Crimea on Wednesday he failed to see the need to go immediately to the barricades to join in solidarity with the crowd there. But he did speak at the public funeral of the three Moscow coup victims, despite the real danger of an assassination attempt. He gave the three victims the country's highest honor by naming them Heroes of the Soviet Union.

Eduard Shevardnadze, Gorbachev's former foreign minister and now a leading democrat, suggested that the three young men should be buried as heroes in the Kremlin wall and that the ashes of the Stalinist "heroes" who had been interred there could be booted out to make room for them. Gorbachev would not go that far.

Gorbachev's stiff, formal speech at the funeral also contrasted with Yeltsin's humble plea to the parents of the victims. "Forgive me, your president, that I could not defend and save your sons," Yeltsin said. The Russian president also walked several hundred yards with the funeral procession, as the nation watched on television.

While the USSR Supreme Soviet debated its own inaction during the coup, the aftershocks continued. The members of the Emergency Committee and several other alleged plotters were formally charged with treason, which could carry the death penalty.

Interior Minister Boris Pugo, one of the key figures in the conspiracy, shot himself in the head while officials were on their way to arrest him. Another close Gorbachev aide Marshal Sergeye Alchromeyev hanged himself in his Kremlin office downstairs from Gorbachev's suite — leaving his colleagues puzzled. None believed the elderly general could have been involved in the coup. TASS knew about, but did not report, a dozen other suicides.

At Gorbachev's request, the legislature fired the entire cabinet. That included Foreign Minister Bessmertnykh, who argued publicly that he had tried to protect Gorbachev's international policy and the Soviet Union's standing in the world during the crisis.

General Shaposhnikov, the new defense minister, said he would retire 80 percent of the top officer corps and replace them with men of the post-Stalin generation.

With the country disintegrating, the republics began planning creation of their own armies, raising the specter of civil war. Disintegration also meant control of Soviet nuclear weapons could fall under several governments. The Ukraine's insistence that it preferred to be nuclear-free meant nothing in the short term because there were too many nuclear weapons spread across the republic. Missile silos could not be rebuilt overnight, and it would take time to move such dangerous weapons.

At the KGB, Bakatin fired the entire top management and brought in outsiders to keep the secret police under control. He

quickly fragmented its centralized power, transferring most of its 250,000 troops to the military. The border guard was turned into an independent agency. The presidential protection force, the anti-terrorist Alpha Group, and the government communications staff were transferred to the President's control, so that the KGB chief would not again have sufficient power to capture the President, cut off communications, and overrun the capital with weapons of war. Bakatin also promised to pull the agency out of the business of spying on Soviet citizens.

In the Interior Ministry, Barannikov began transferring most of his ministry's power to the republics and ordered the police to stay out of politics.

Parliamentary Chairman Lukianov told the Supreme Soviet he was not a part of the coup conspiracy, but the legislators gave him no more mercy than Gorbachev had. Many said that in conversations during the coup, Lukianov had confirmed Gorbachev's "illness" and refused to arrange for Gorbachev to speak on television. Investigators found a draft agenda for the legislature in Lukianov's office, calling for confirmation of the state of emergency. Within days, Lukianov, one of Gorbachev's oldest personal friends, was in jail.

Gorbachev and Yeltsin turned the official media upside down as well, dumping Kravchenko from state broadcasting and replacing him with the radical editor of the Moscow

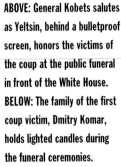

ABOVE: General Kobets salutes as Yeltsin, behind a bulletproof screen, honors the victims of the coup at the public funeral in front of the White House. BELOW: The family of the first coup victim, Dmitry Komar, holds lighted candles during the funeral ceremonies.

A huge crowd of mourners form a funeral procession from the Kremlin to the cemetary. Of the hundreds of flags displayed, most were independence flags of the republics.

News, Yegor Yakovlev. The new man promptly left viewers gasping by beginning the evening news show with a film clip of a meeting where he announced the firing of KGB agents in the radio and television system and the rehiring of the journalists who had been fired by Kravchenko for refusing to submit to censorship.

Gorbachev sent his own press secretary, Vitaly Ignatenko, to take over TASS, after Yeltsin had fired the previous director-general and announced that all of its property belonged to Russia. In a compromise, Yeltsin was given control of Novosti, the second Soviet news agency, one known for KGB personnel.

Yeltsin's big blunder of the week came when he raised the possibility of redrawing Russia's borders with seceding republics. Kazakhstan's Nazarbayev retorted, "Well, then, that's war. That's civil war." For Kazakhstan, boundaries were a life-or-death issue. Huge tracts of its territory, including the resource-rich northwest, were occupied primarily by Russians and might be claimed by a resurgent Russia. The Ukraine, too, quickly objected. Of Russia's twenty-three boundaries with other republics, only two are uncontested. And so Yeltsin's remarks sent shudders through leaders of the neighboring republics.

Gorbachev sought political advantage from the statement, saying he rejected any review of existing borders. The leaders of the other republics quickly saw a place for him as mediator and countervailing force to a powerful Russia and Yeltsin, its charismatic leader.

Yeltsin was forced to send a high-powered delegation to the Ukraine to calm the fears. The delegation, led by Russian Vice-President Rutskoi and Leningrad Mayor Sobchak, did more than that. Within a day, the Russians and Ukrainians not only had agreed on their existing borders, but also had worked out an economic and military alliance that covered two-thirds of the Soviet population and left no role for the central government led by Gorbachev. Just to make the demise of the Kremlin leadership absolutely clear, the two largest republics invited "other former subjects of the USSR" to join their alliance.

In the week after the coup, the USSR's Supreme Soviet voted itself out of business and ratified Gorbachev's decision to shut down the Communist Party by suspending its activities. Even though 80 percent of the Soviet parliamentarians had been elected as Communists, they accepted overwhelming public opinion and barred the Party from operation until the prosecutor finished investigating its role in the coup.

The legislature also recommended that its parent body, the 2,250-member Congress of People's Deputies, elect an entirely new 542-member Supreme Soviet during its meeting the following week.

Over the weekend, the Soviet Union unraveled further, as Azerbaijan, Uzbekistan, and Kirgizia brought the number of republics declaring independence to ten of fifteen. The Russian delegation in the Ukraine had flown on to Kazakhstan and agreed there to an economic alliance. Meanwhile, the republics were quietly working out their own plan for formal dissolution of the union to prevent uncontrolled disintegration. With Gorbachev's help, they would spring it on the unsuspecting Congress.

On Monday morning, September 2, Gorbachev and the leaders of ten republics opened the Congress with a preemptory strike. Nazarbayev read out a plan to end the Soviet Union. The coup had wrecked the process of renewing the Soviet Union, and "brought the country to the brink of catastrophe," Nazarbayev said. The ten-republic

plan was necessary "to prevent further collapse of the structures of power, pending creation of a new political system."

He called for a transition period, during which each republic would define the form of its relations to the new union, and each would be recognized as a sovereign state. As one deputy put it, the new entity would be "not a country, not an association, but something the world has never seen." The proposal also called for replacing the Communist-dominated Congress during the transition period with a new legislature chosen by the more radical republic legislatures. To stave off conflicts over borders, the proposal recognized existing frontiers.

The statement was signed by Gorbachev and the leaders of Russia, the Ukraine, Byelorussia, Kazakhstan, Uzbekistan, Azerbaijan, Kirgizia, Tadzhikistan, Armenia, and Turkmenistan. Missing were only the five small states farthest along on the road to independence: the three Baltic republics — Estonia, Latvia, Lithuania — and Georgia and Moldavia.

Left gasping, the legislators were sent off to caucus by republic, where the republic leaders could pressure them into agreement. As they obediently shuffled out of their seats, several supporters of a strong central government yelled at them to stop leaving.

"This is an attempt at an unconstitutional coup!" said Col. Viktor Alksnis, a legislator known as "the black colonel" for his hard-line views. "Why should ten people decide for thousands?" he shouted, but few heard him.

The proposal made no mention of the

Photographs of the three men killed were carried at the head of the funeral procession and left at the cemetary to mark the graves of the three victims. Left to right: Vladimir Usov, Ilya Krichevsky, and Dmitry Komar.

Baltic republics. Instead, it proposed Soviet support for any republic seeking to be recognized as a subject of international law — obscure language implying diplomatic recognition. That was enough to satisfy the Bush administration. Now President Bush finally added the United States to the parade of nations granting full recognition to the Baltic republics. He said he had delayed the announcement three days at the personal request of Gorbachev.

Over the next several days of the Congress, Gorbachev and the republic leaders let the legislators carry out a stormy debate. Even some of the progressive legislators complained that it was undemocratic essentially to dissolve the legally elected Parliament and suspend key parts of the Constitution. "We've gotten used to this big country, and now we're supposed to vote so that there will be a lot of separate countries," complained lawmaker Alexander Belogolov.

Outside the Kremlin on Red Square, however, legislators had to walk a gantlet of protesters demanding, "Congress of Servants of the Communist Party — Dissolve!" The protesters were speaking their minds clearly. Viktor Durnov was an example: "We've heard nothing but slogans and words…We need new elections." One of the legislators, Vasily Tso, walked through the crowd and said he sympathized with them, "There is a huge legislative vacuum, and we need to stop the complete collapse."

Whenever debate inside the Kremlin got out of hand, the leaders called a recess to rewrite a disputed proposal behind closed doors. Then they would hold more caucuses in which the republic leaders could pressure their delegations. The coup, Gorbachev argued, had left the country "on the edge of an unmanageable breakup," and the Union Treaty draft of the ten republic leaders was

now the only way to make the inevitable split peaceful.

Isolated cases of inter-ethnic violence were already rising across the country, and numerous legislators warned that the Soviet Union could dissolve into civil war. The Soviet lawmakers could watch on television every night and see the Yugoslavian civil war developing. That was a frightening prospect. The Soviet Union had a huge arsenal of nuclear weapons, some of which could fall into the hands of warring ethnic groups. In fact, one version of the Nazarbayev proposal called for quick negotiations on liquidation of tactical, or small, nuclear weapons. Another version called for seceding republics to sign the International Nuclear Nonproliferation Treaty.

Across the country, there were dozens of disputes over one ethnic group's occupation of the traditional homeland of another. The violence surrounding the Armenian population in Azerbaijan's Nagorno- Karabakh area was only one example. Georgians were pitted against Ossetians in Georgia. Tensions also exist between Russians and Ukrainians, Estonians, Latvians, and Lithuanians in each of those republics. As the Soviet Union broke up, the myth of unity was disproved.

Some republics appeared likely to use the escape from Kremlin control to roll back Gorbachev's reforms and revert to a strong dictatorship. Reformist legislators cited Uzbekistan as a likely example, since its Communist Party still controlled the press, the government, and the economy. Leonid Kravchuk, the Ukrainian president, a lifelong Communist, quit the Party and threw his support to independence only when it became politically expedient. In Georgia,

OPPOSITE: A rally in the Ukraine around a defaced monument to Lenin. ABOVE: A fatigued Gorbachev presides over a marathon last-day session of the Congress of Peoples' Deputies on September 5, 1991, where a transitional government is created, giving more power to the republics.

violence broke out between protesters demanding the resignation of President Zviad Gamsakhurdia — who had been democratically elected but was accused of turning into a dictator — and his supporters.

Gorbachev warned the Parliament that if it

did not accept the republic leaders' proposal to stave off this nightmare vision of civil war, "the people will reject this Congress." Legislators were aware, however, that the plan would remove them from their cushy positions. "You will stop being

ABOVE: Gorbachev poses with his new allies, pro-democracy, reformist legislators who opposed the coup and helped shaped the agreement to dismantle the Soviet Union. BELOW: Khazakhastan President Nursultan Nazarbayev is regarded as one of the new Soviet Union's most powerful political figures and a counterbalance to dominance by Russia.

deputies several days after the Union Treaty is signed, as you cannot be a deputy in a nonexistent country," Alexander Zhuravlev, a Byelorussian legislator, warned his colleagues. In the end, the legislators were given a sop: they would retain their privileges of priority train and plane tickets, as well as their 300-ruble monthly salaries. The new legislature would retain the Supreme Soviet name, even though it would hardly resemble the body it replaced.

By Wednesday night, the Congress was still resisting. Gorbachev won preliminary votes, but not by the two-thirds margin he would need on the constitutional amendments necessary to put the plan into practice. He passed the word that he would put the plan into action by decree if necessary. But that would leave the country with two governments, one semi-dissolved and the other of doubtful legality.

By Thursday, September 5, Gorbachev was again manipulating the legislators like a puppeteer. He rammed through each segment of the proposal, barring further debate

or amendments. When he did not have enough votes on a key point, he suggested changing the constitution immediately to eliminate the requirement for a two-thirds majority.

The men and women who had been elected Soviet legislators from Latvia came to his aid, casting votes in favor even though they rarely even showed up for what they now considered the parliamentary sessions of a separate country. "They didn't have four votes," said Latvian legislator Yuri Boyars afterwards. "We decided to help him because it was in our political interest to reform the Soviet Union." On the next vote, the amendment passed.

Overnight, there had been a key change in the proposal to satisfy separatist republics: It now spoke of a new, voluntary union based on "independence," not just sovereignty. The final draft called for immediate negotiations with republics choosing not to join the union — expected to be the Baltics and Georgia.

With the critical points decided, the rest was formality. Gorbachev suggested leaving a proposed declaration of human rights for the new Supreme Soviet to consider. The Congress shouted him down and passed it on a voice vote with no debate.

As the session was about to end, Leningrad Mayor Sobchak strode to the microphone and suggested it was time to move Lenin's embalmed body out of the Red Square mausoleum and bury him next to his mother in a Leningrad cemetery. Thus the adoration of the Communist state's founder would be ended. Conservatives rose to object, and Gorbachev quickly put the question off until the first session of the new Supreme Soviet. The Congress was over.

"The Soviet Union is finished," said reformist legislator Arkady Murashev with a happy grin.

As the meeting broke up, Russian President Yeltsin walked past Gorbachev to shake hands with Kazakhstan President Nazarbayev, for the real victors were the republics, which gained all the power lost by the Kremlin. Finally freed of the stultifying central government, the republics expected to be able to pursue greater democracy and quicker economic reform.

Gorbachev would retain power over foreign policy and the military, the police, and the KGB, at least for a transition period, which leaders said could last from two months to two years. While Gorbachev posed for photos with a group of democrats —once again his allies— he told them, "You have entered the transition period!"

The next morning, the Russian legislature met and formally approved the results of a June referendum in Leningrad, returning to the country's second-largest city its old name of St. Petersburg. Simultaneously, Gorbachev and the republic leaders met for the first time as the State Council. Their first big decision was to ratify recognition of the Baltic republics' independence.

As a result of these early September gatherings, the old USSR was no longer. The coup plotters wanted to dismantle the reform. Instead, they detonated the charge that blew up the authoritarian structure they wanted to rebuild. Now the reformers had the opportunity and responsibility to pick up the pieces in a country that had fallen so far that it had no name, no national day to celebrate, no national anthem, no single political leader.

"This is a real people's revolution," said Alexander Yakovlev, the Gorbachev aide who foresaw an attempted coup and resigned from the Party to underline its resistance to democracy. "Freedom has triumphed at last." Now the hard work would begin.

A demonstration by Azerbaijanis following the election of Ayez Mutalibov, September 8, 1991. Although heralded as a democratic election, long-time Communist Mutalibov was the only candidate on the ballot and is unlikely to be a champion of democratic reform.

History

The rise of Mikhail Gorbachev and his attempt to reform Soviet society did not spring full-blown on an unsuspecting country. In fact, the seeds of reform were sown by Nikita Khrushchev starting in the 1950s, and the need for reform was as old as the Communist system itself. The system brutalized the Soviet people, and never lived up to the promises it made. The coup attempt of August 1991 became the Second Russian Revolution.

When Russian President Boris Yeltsin and other leaders barricaded themselves inside the Russian Parliament Building, determined to

Czar Nicholas II ignored the growing unrest that would ultimately sweep him and his family from the throne of Russia and open the door for the Bolshevik takeover in 1917.

ABOVE: The attack on the Winter Palace in Petrograd on November 7, 1917, ends czarist rule. OPPOSITE: Revolutionaries ransack and burn a czarist government building in St. Petersburg.

reverse the August 18, 1991, coup, they were fighting Soviet history. In more than seven decades of vicious dictatorship, tens of millions were killed by firing squad, torture, starvation, or other acts of inhumanity, and tens of millions more were imprisoned or internally exiled — done at the order, or whim, of their leaders.

Yet until 1991 Soviet citizens had not stood up against the system in sufficient numbers to threaten it seriously or to try to reform it.

Historians say that perhaps as many as 47 million people were killed by the actions of their own government during the thirty-five

years that Vladimir Lenin and Josef Stalin ruled. And that does not even include the 16 to 26 million people estimated to have died in World War II.

Millions claim they had no knowledge of the terror. Some are convinced it never really happened. Unceasing propaganda campaigns created and perpetrated a massive cover-up.

The Bolsheviks seized power on November 7, 1917, when a provisional government was floundering, trying to deal with war and food shortages after a spontaneous street revolution ousted Czar Nicholas II six months earlier. Lenin marshaled public anger over aristocratic control, lack of food, and the two million killed in the three years of World War I.

"Peace! Land! Bread!" was the electrifying slogan of the Bolsheviks. They fulfilled none of those promises.

Lenin ended the war with Germany by giving up huge amounts of territory. But the country was quickly engulfed in civil war, with the Bolsheviks fighting off various challengers. To provide bread for factory workers in the cities, Lenin's men confiscated grain from the peasants, leaving them nothing to eat or plant. The death toll mounted to more than 5 million between 1918 and 1922.

The promise of land was the greatest hypocrisy. Within a few years, Stalin would nationalize all land and force peasants to work on collective farms. Private farmers with a few acres of their own were exterminated, as officials confiscated their land and exiled or imprisoned them.

The first to feel the benefits of the 1917 Revolution were the intellectuals. For a short time freedom of expression flourished. But within two months of their seizure of power, Lenin and his men began to create the system of total dictatorial control that rendered opposition meaningless.

They quickly confiscated all printing presses and paper. Under Bolshevik power, the Communist Party owned the presses. The Bolsheviks introduced arbitrary courts, eliminating any possibility of challenge through the legal system. They created the Cheka secret police — eventually renamed the KGB — and ordered it to fight the press, saboteurs, strikers, and the Communists' political enemies.

Lenin's crimes, however, were quickly overshadowed by those of his successor, Stalin. Once he had power, Stalin moved

quickly to industrialize the Soviet Union and
nationalize everything in it, fulfilling the
Communist vision of the future. Land, housing, farm animals, and fine art all became the
property of the state.

Stalin succeeded, but at terrible cost. To
collectivize farms, he forced farmers to cooperate by setting impossible quotas for grain;
and when told this was causing starvation on
the farms, he refused to back down. The
result was a famine that killed from seven to
fourteen million citizens. Despite the famine,
Stalin exported grain to pay for imported factory machinery for his crash industrialization
program.

When the 1937 census showed a population decrease, he had the census chief
arrested and the results sealed away in the
archives. To cover up the famine, peasants
were barred from travel to cities, and city
dwellers were kept from the countryside.

Then Stalin began a massive and deadly
purge, ordering executions and imprisonment
of millions of the best and brightest in Soviet
society — soldiers, engineers, builders, diplomats, intelligence agents, and Party, government, and business leaders. Estimates of
those imprisoned run to more than ten
million, most of whom died in confinement,
either from the harsh conditions or from execution. In the Army, the purges in the officer
corps left the nation unprepared to fight
World War II.

Soviet citizens were terrified, and silent. In
the Ukrainian village of Bykovnia, near Kiev,
villagers witnessed as night after night from
1936 to 1941, trucks hauled a mysterious
cargo dripping blood into the nearby forest.
*By 1989, when Gorbachev's reforms had finally
begun to reassure people that they could speak out
with impunity, dozens of elderly peasants blamed
their own government for the skeletons in the forest,
each with a single bullet hole in the skull. The mass
grave of Bykovnia was at first attributed to the*

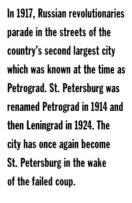

In 1917, Russian revolutionaries
parade in the streets of the
country's second largest city
which was known at the time as
Petrograd. St. Petersburg was
renamed Petrograd in 1914 and
then Leningrad in 1924. The
city has once again become
St. Petersburg in the wake
of the failed coup.

Nazis. Finally the Soviets confronted the fact that up to fifty thousand people had been killed by Stalinist agents and buried there.

Stalin thought he had saved the Soviet Union from attack in 1939 by signing the Molotov-Ribbentrop pact, in which the Soviet Union and Germany promised not to fight each other, allowing Hitler to invade Poland, starting World War II. In June 1941 Hitler invaded the Soviet Union anyway. Stalin had left his nation unprepared, trusting Hitler when he trusted no one else.

Hitler's armies swept through the Soviet Union, their Panzer tanks slicing easily through an army that still used masses of horse cavalry. The Nazis made it all the way to the defenses of Moscow and Leningrad in 1941, and came to within tens of feet of the Volga River at Stalingrad in 1943. Only the winter weather and last-ditch stands by the Red Army and the Soviet people stopped them, and then turned them back.

While the Soviet people made this super-human effort, Stalin continued his terror. He pulled troops and trains from the front to capture and transport hundreds of thousands of people to Siberia and Kazakhstan. They represented ten nationalities that Stalin said could not be trusted. While local men were at the front, troops moved into villages in the Caucasus Mountain region of Checheno-Ingush (still an ethnic flash point today) on a February night in 1944. They rounded up everyone left — women, children, and the elderly — and stuffed them into open trucks. They raced down the mountains on icy dirt roads carved into the cliffs. Survivors from the village of Itum-kale remember that some victims bounced out of the trucks into the river gorge below.

Stalin drew boundaries between ethnic homelands with deliberate disregard for settlement patterns in order to divide and rule. Mass deportations continued from places like the Baltic republics, to crush a strong partisan resistance to the Soviet takeover of their once-independent countries. He set the stage for the violent ethnic conflicts that emerged when Gorbachev's reforms drew back the curtain concealing decades of suppressed rage.

At the 1944 Yalta Conference, British Prime Minister Winston Churchill and United States President Franklin Roosevelt gave Stalin tacit hegemony over Eastern Europe. Just a few months after the war ended, the Iron Curtain descended and the Cold War began. Though the worst horrors in the Soviet Union eased with Stalin's death in 1953, totalitarianism and the "need" for sacrifice remained features of the system until Gorbachev became leader.

After a brief but sinister power struggle, Nikita Khrushchev succeeded Stalin and made the first moves toward both political and economic reform. In a secret speech to a Communist Party Congress in 1956, he exposed Stalin's excesses. Word of Khrushchev's criticism spread. For a time he allowed a cultural thaw in which writers like Alexander Solzhenitsyn wrote revealing novels about life under the terror. Others began

OPPOSITE: Lenin addresses the crowd gathered in Red Square on November 7, 1918, the first anniversary of the Socialist Revolution. **BELOW:** Lenin parades through Red Square in the center of a coterie of military commanders.

ABOVE: Leon Trotsky, one of the major figures of the Bolshevik Revolution, wrote pamphlets, tracts, and speeches that brought the philosophy of the revolution to the people. He was deported by Stalin in 1929 for "anti-Soviet actions" after a struggle for leadership. BELOW: Felix Dzerzhinsky (center) held a variety of positions in Lenin's government and founded the secret police. Strongly to the left, he vehemently opposed self-determination for the nationalities.

exposing some of the Communist society's faults. Economists were allowed to explore the concept of prices as a market regulator rather than central planning.

But Khrushchev did nothing to lift the huge burden of Cold War expenditures. In fact, by provoking the Cuban missile crisis in 1962, he spurred the arms race that would later help bankrupt the country. Khrushchev was ousted in a coup in October 1964 that was, outwardly, remarkably similar to the August 1991 move against Gorbachev. He was betrayed by his closest associates and when he appealed the decision to the Communist Party Central Committee — a tactic that had saved him years before — he had no support. That he was allowed to leave office and live out his years was a strong indication of a shift in the ruling class's attitude.

Nonetheless, when Khrushchev was removed, the Soviet people were silent. The oppressive Communist Party hierarchy kept leadership matters to itself. The people expected no voice in such decision making and asked for none. *But when the 1991 conspirators struck at Gorbachev, hundreds of thousands of Soviets spoke out. They were backed by elected leaders, by journalists determined to publish or*

broadcast, and by two years' experience of mass demonstrations of grievances. Gorbachev's own reforms had transformed the country.

Khrushchev's successors, Leonid Breznev and Alexei Kosygin, also flirted with economic reform, but after a few years, they gave up the idea and Kosygin was eased out of power. The so-called period of stagnation had begun, and Brezhnev presided over the collapse of the Soviet economy. By the 1970s, factories built in the 1930s and others moved from Germany after the war were wearing out. The Soviet economy, snarled in bureaucracy and Communist prohibitions, could not replace them. There were few incentives for workers to make anything better, faster, or easier.

Oil and other natural resources staved off disaster. Huge reserves were discovered in western Siberia, and exports of oil at the inflated prices imposed by the Organization of Petroleum Exporting Countries propped up the Soviet economy with more than $40 million a day.

While the military sector continued to grow in a vain attempt to keep pace with the Western nations, the rest of the economy deteriorated. Factories choked on impure raw

materials. Government mismanagement crippled the production, harvesting, and distribution of grains, compelling expensive imports to keep bread on the table.

When Brezhnev died in 1982 and former KGB Chief Yuri Andropov assumed the leadership, he sought to clean up much of the corruption, to reverse the slothfulness and instill a work ethic in Soviet society. But he was a sick man and he lasted only a little more than a year in office. His hand-picked successor Mikhail Gorbachev was denied the top job when Andropov died, but in March 1985, Gorbachev succeeded Konstantin Chernenko, the last gasp of the Old Guard.

By the time Gorbachev took office, the economy had been shrinking for four years. Corruption was rampant. Soviet citizens needed to trade favors or bribes to achieve everything from good medical treatment or a

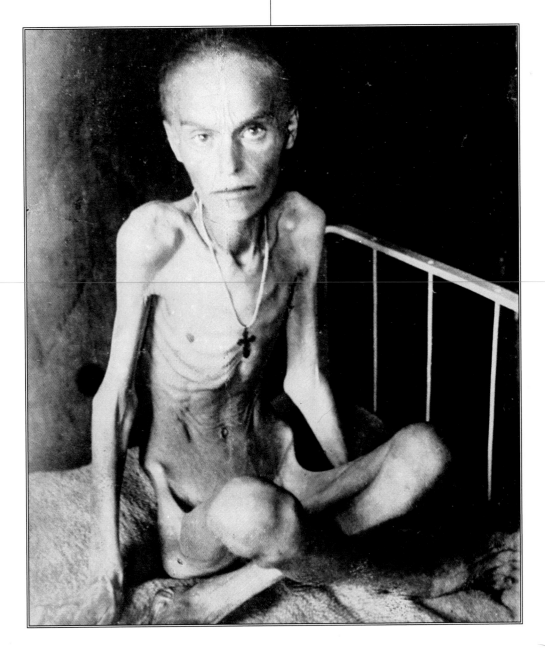

"Peace! Land! Bread!" was the slogan of the Bolsheviks, but starvation, disease, and government-sanctioned murder resulted in a death toll of more than five million between 1918 and 1922.

telephone to a slice of beef. Alcoholism was endemic. The war in Afghanistan was bleeding the country in the same way the Vietnam War tortured the United States a generation earlier.

Stagnation was the byword. "Generation to generation, the system was churning out obedient slaves," said Soviet journalist Vladimir Molchanov.

Yet, unlike their parents in Khrushchev's time, the Soviet people of 1985 were educated and better informed. Communism had brought universal secondary schooling to the masses – and therein planted one of the seeds of its own destruction. Educated people typically yearn for democracy.

Over three-quarters of a century, the Communist Party had insinuated its influence and control into every segment of society. What it did not control directly, it did through its control of other organizations such as the KGB, the Interior Ministry, the propaganda organs, the education system, and the military. The Party general secretary exercised absolute power, but his decisions had to be implemented by Party secretaries at a lower level. These local Party bureaucrats became the nobles in a vast modern feudal system.

In fact, this nobility had its own name — the *nomenklatura*, those important leaders whose jobs were listed in a secret book. This group of officials received its own privileges, depending on rank. They got free vacations, the best schools for their children, the right to buy cars or apartments, international travel, ability to shop in special stores, and even rations of caviar and sturgeon to celebrate holidays. At its height, this bureaucracy numbered 19 million members. In return for their privilege they promised the Party absolute loyalty. They themselves offered no criticism, and they brooked no criticism from others. They made sure that indoctrination in

A starving family in rural Russia in 1922. To provide bread for factory workers in the cities, Lenin's government confiscated grain from the peasants, leaving them nothing to eat or plant.

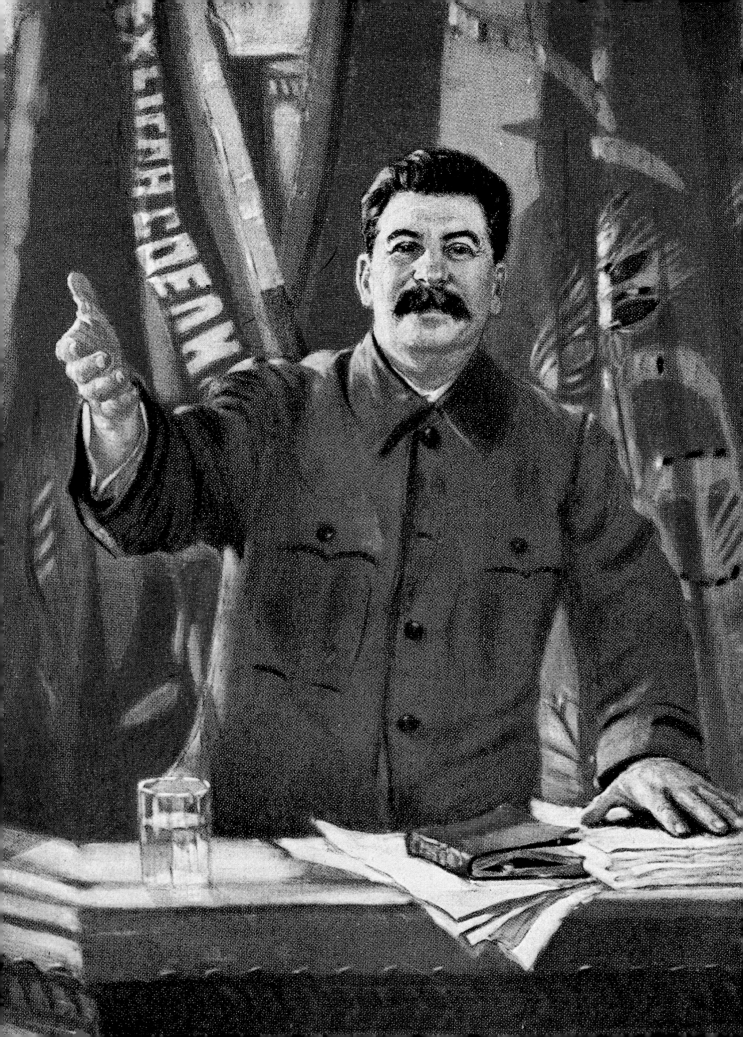

this loyalty started in kindergarten.

The Party described itself as "revolutionary," dating from its days as Lenin's vanguard but it had long since grown into the most conservative force in the Soviet society.

Gorbachev's reforms started slowly, and most observers believe he was trying to save communism and the totalitarian system. He began traveling the country, meeting ordinary Soviet citizens on street corners, listening to their complaints, talking up the need for a change in attitudes. The people were captivated with this change of style.

To back up his words, there were deeds. He halted the arrest of dissidents, and then slowly began to free political prisoners. In one dramatic gesture, he freed Andrei Sakharov, once the designer of the Soviet Union's hydrogen bomb and later human rights activist, from house arrest and exile in Gorky and allowed Sakharov to become active again in Moscow. The Western world was surprised and pleased.

Eduard Shevardnadze, who served as Gorbachev's foreign minister from 1985 to 1990, said they took a lonely walk together years before coming to power, and admitted to each other that "all is rotten" in the country and the Communist Party, and without radical changes, the Soviet Union was doomed, the Washington Post reported.

In May 1988, high-ranking Soviets began to leak news so stunning that Western editors doubted their correspondents' reports. Gorbachev, it was said, would be proposing real democratic reforms at the Communist Party conference in June, including elections, transfer of power from the Party to the government, and creation of a real legislature that would debate and pass laws. To the astonishment of the Soviet people, who watched excerpts of a Party leadership meeting on television for the first time, that is what happened.

In October, the pace of change began to accelerate. First came a new law allowing multi-candidate — but still not multi-party — elections. The law also called for a real, working parliament to replace the token legislature infamous for robot-like approval of Communist Party decrees.

The Baltic republics of Estonia, Latvia, and Lithuania quickly grabbed the opportunity provided by Gorbachev's reforms and entered into a chess game with the Kremlin to regain the independence they lost when forcibly annexed under Red Army occupation in 1940. The Estonians in particular were brilliant, calculating ten moves ahead while the Kremlin was still dealing with their first outrageous act of Parliament.

The Estonian declaration of sovereignty in November 1988 was absolutely unexpected, and perfectly executed. Knowing their best defense against a Kremlin crackdown was world attention, Estonians drew foreign correspondents to Tallinn — where the journalists were stunned to find the Estonian Parliament giving itself the right to overturn Soviet laws on Estonian territory.

It was the first direct challenge to Kremlin rule. Gorbachev said the declaration of sovereignty was illegal, but he took no decisive action against it. The Estonians cleverly made their first independent decisions on politically unopposable issues like environmental protection, and their decision stood.

Eventually, every one of the fifteen Soviet republics would follow Estonia's lead, shattering Kremlin control.

Gorbachev's reforms started a flood of discontent, as Soviets used the new freedom to bring up old problems. Ethnic strife flared in

OPPOSITE: Despite his fatherly, benevolent image, Joseph Stalin ruled the Soviet Union with an iron fist, crushing enemies and "suspected" enemies alike, in purges that killed hundreds of thousands of his own people. ABOVE: A Soviet propaganda poster portrays the glory of the revolution and workers united. OVERLEAF: Workers on a collective farm in the Panino District of the Soviet Union in August 1930.

OPPOSITE: In accordance with precepts of communism, all workers received the same wage, including this woman coal miner from the Don Basin in the Ukraine. LEFT: After years of denial, the Soviet government finally confronted the fact that up to fifty thousand people had been killed by Stalinist agents and buried in a mass grave near the village of Bykovnia in the Ukraine. BELOW: Molotov (left) and Hitler (right) sit with official interpreter, Schmidt, in negotiations for signing the Russo-German pact of 1939. OVERLEAF: Painting by Soviet artist K.F. Yuon depicts the November 7, 1941, parade in Red Square celebrating the anniversary of the Bolshevik Revolution.

Armenia, Azerbaijan, Uzbekistan, Georgia, and a host of other places where Stalin's deportations and arbitrary borders had uprooted people from homelands they still wanted back.

Hard-liners were dumbfounded as well when Gorbachev told the United Nations he planned to cut 500,000 troops unilaterally.

But even as he loosened controls, Gorbachev's problems drew him into an increasingly tighter bind. He elevated Boris Yeltsin to prominence as Moscow Communist Party chief and then dismissed him when the provincial from Siberia began complaining about high-level Party corruption. Ethnic strife flared in the Armenian enclave of Nagorno-Karabakh in Azerbaijan. On the "left," the Baltic governments continued to heckle the Gorbachev government, while the Communist Party establishment undermined him from the right. And then, as if he did not have enough trouble, an earthquake struck in Armenia, killing more than 25,000.

The earthquake dramatized the Soviet Union's need for help from

outside. Thousands of international relief workers arrived to the amazement of the Soviet people and the gratitude of Gorbachev.

The spring of 1989 brought the Soviet people the first free elections since the 1917 Revolution. The Communist Party was still the only political party, but for the first time, people could vote against it. And they did.

• In Lithuania, the Sajudis reform group won thirty-nine of forty-two seats running against local Communist Party bosses.

• Boris Yeltsin, a self-described "political corpse" after Gorbachev fired him from the Politburo, received a stunning 89 percent of

the vote running to represent Moscow.

• In Leningrad, voters turned down a member of the Kremlin inner sanctum, Communist Party Politburo member Yuri Solovyov, even though he was running unopposed. Voters crossed his name off the ballot and he failed to win the necessary 50 percent of the votes.

Voters learned quickly they could have an effect with real elections. Communists lost by even greater margins in the run-off rounds.

The new Congress of Peoples' Deputies opened on a gloriously sunny May day in the Kremlin, with lilacs and tulips in full bloom. The country stopped work, enthralled by the sight of their new legislators denouncing the state of the union and detailing problems on live nationwide television. Production dropped noticeably.

Still, the euphoria of watching that first Congress unleashed pent-up demands from the Iron Curtain to the Pacific. Coal miners literally sick from eighteenth-century working conditions staged the country's first nationwide strike. Long-hidden ethnic conflicts flared into fatal pogroms.

Expectations were high. But gradually, the people were disappointed, for although the Congress included radicals like Yeltsin, Sakharov, and the delegations from the Baltics, it was still 80 percent mainline Communist.

Over the next two years, the Congress and its working legislature, the Supreme Soviet, would approve landmark laws guaranteeing freedom of the press, travel, and religion. But on dozens of other critical issues, it did nothing. It went through at least fifteen separate economic reform plans, all coming close to the idea of a market economy, but none daring to use that unmentionable word, "capitalism."

The Lithuanian Communist Party took a hard look at its political future and opted

Engine drivers A. Alexandrov (left) and I. Karakin (right) were cited for "selflessly accomplishing their combat tasks" of getting munitions to the front during WWII. OVERLEAF: The moment of triumph. Russian soldiers unfurl the Soviet flag from the roof of the Reichstag in Berlin on May 1, 1945.

"Welcome to the leader of a neighboring country." Gorbachev was livid. Independence activists brought 300,000 people to a rally on a freezing January night to show Gorbachev that they were not just a small bunch of opportunists, as he insisted.

Still trying to leap ahead of the wave of change, Gorbachev promised a referendum on secession from the union — but said he was certain most Lithuanians would vote to remain in the Soviet Union. Lithuanians did not believe he was offering much, and they proved to be correct. Gorbachev's law on secession set conditions that made it virtually impossible to leave.

At his last stop in Lithuania, Gorbachev dropped the real bombshell. Taking a final question as he left a Lithuanian Communist Party meeting, he said nonchalantly, "I see no tragedy in a multi-party system. We should not be afraid of it, the way the devil is afraid of incense."

This time, even reporters on the scene could not believe it.

Within three weeks, Gorbachev had

to join the fight for independence. The Party divided, with a 20 percent, mostly Russian, minority remaining loyal to the Kremlin. The Lithuanian Parliament legalized non-Communist parties.

An alarmed Gorbachev decided it was time to visit Lithuania. But his concern came far too late. At his first stop, friendly demonstrators greeted him with signs reading,

ABOVE: Workers in a Moscow factory read "Pravda" on their lunch hour in this government photograph taken in March 1947. RIGHT: The bodies of Lenin and Stalin lie in state in Lenin-Stalin Mausoleum. Stalin's body was moved in 1961 to a nearby site out of public view.

pushed the revolutionary idea through the 249-member Communist Party Central Committee, after packing the meeting with 700 mostly progressive guests. "There will be a normal democracy," said one of the participants, a happy Dr. Svyatoslav Fyodorov, as he emerged from the Kremlin after the decision.

The next month, March 1990, was crucial.

Gorbachev scheduled a special session of the Congress to repeal formally the Communists' constitutional monopoly on power. But the session was also scheduled to give him new powers as President and to pass laws making it more difficult for republics to break away. Lithuania decided it dared not wait. Its newly elected republic Parliament declared independence the night before the Congress opened.

Gorbachev immediately launched a war of nerves, sending Soviet Army units on threatening troop maneuvers through the Lithuanian capital of Vilnius and imposing a ten-week blockade of fuel and many other products. Lithuanians ignored everything Gorbachev threw at them. Thousands of

paratroopers in armored vehicles and trucks headed straight for Parliament late one night, where legislators nervously cracked jokes about the Soviet invasion of Czechoslovakia in 1968. The column came within a few hundred yards of the building and then moved on.

When a Moscow official tried to take over the office of the Lithuanian-appointed prosecutor, he found himself facing a hostile room full of staff lawyers refusing to cooperate. The Kremlin sent troops into the building to keep the Lithuanian prosecutor out, but his staff reported to him in another building, ignoring the man from Moscow. It was the beginning of the end of Gorbachev's authority, and not just in Lithuania.

Other republics soon learned the lesson that Kremlin orders could be ignored. Across the Soviet Union, elections held that spring for republic parliaments brought to power far more radical reformers than had won in the elections for the national Congress a year earlier. The difference set the stage for paralysis, with the republics pushing for radical change

Soviet author Alexander Solzhenitzyn, whose work was banned in the USSR and who emigrated to the U.S., has now received a personal invitation from Gorbachev to return home.

Vice-President Richard Nixon meets Premier Nikita Khruschev for official talks in Moscow in July 1959.

and the central government hanging back.

The Soviet Union got its first non-Communist governments in the three Baltic states. The Russian Parliament turned out to be half traditional Communists and half reformers. It chose Boris Yeltsin as its leader by a handful of votes, and then joined the parade of republics declaring its own actions superior to those of the Soviet government.

Soon, Gorbachev found himself in a "war of laws" with republics passing radical economic and political reforms that conflicted with national laws. Local administrators did not know whom to obey; government was paralyzed.

Gorbachev's prime minister, Nikolai Ryzhkov, announced plans to raise the price of nearly everything and people panicked. Already sparsely supplied stores were stripped bare as the public tried to beat the price hikes. With nothing to buy, people lost the incentive to work, at least in the state-owned businesses that still constituted the vast majority of the economy. "Why bother? The factory only pays 150 roubles a month," said a young man in Tashkent who could

earn that much in a few days using his own car as an illegal taxi.

Hope flickered in September, when Gorbachev and Yeltsin agreed on a 500-day plan for economic reform, including the sell-off of government factories, apartments, and land, and a real switch to a market economy. But suddenly, Gorbachev reversed himself after the hard-liners rose up in anger.

They had a long list of grievances: the loss of Eastern Europe; the reunification of historical enemy Germany; the Baltic drive for independence; troop withdrawals from Afghanistan, Czechoslovakia, and Hungary; the dismantling of thousands of nuclear missiles under an arms-control treaty with the United States; the brain drain as hundreds of thousands emigrated; the loss of mind control as censorship faded and millions of Soviets traveled abroad; the crumbling economy; loss of Soviet prestige as a superpower; rejection of long-time ally Iraq and support for United Nations-backed intervention in the Persian Gulf war.

Gradually, through the autumn of 1990, Gorbachev began to reverse his own reforms.

Most shocking, he blocked his original policy of glasnost, or openness, by reimposing censorship on state television. He fired Vadim Bakatin as interior minister in charge of police and riot-control troops for being too soft.

He appointed three of the future coup conspirators to key positions: Boris Pugo, a former KGB general, to interior minister; Finance Minister Valentin Pavlov to prime minister; and Gennady Yanayev as vice-president.

When asked after the coup why he had appointed the conspirators to such positions of power, Gorbachev explained that it was an attempt to head off a return to dictatorship and bloodshed. "Last December, one heard, 'Down with the President' at the Congress, and there were calls to create a certain National Salvation Committee" that would dissolve all parliaments and political parties and restore dictatorship, Gorbachev said. He said he acted to preserve his reforms and prevent bloodshed.

"We must never forget what society we are reforming," he said. At an earlier point, a coup "would have succeeded."

"My task was to carry out reform as far as possible, and to bring society to the point where the reactionary forces had less chance of success," he told journalists. He sounded almost surprised that he had come so far.

The world watched with trepidation as Gorbachev backtracked on reform. But it was shocked when Shevardnadze resigned from his post as foreign minister to protest impending "dictatorship."

Less than three weeks later, Shevardnadze's warning proved accurate.

Soviet troops and tanks attacked unarmed demonstrators guarding the television tower, and sixteen people were killed. As the tanks approached, loudspeakers blared an announcement that a self-styled "National Salvation Committee" was taking over Lithuania from its elected government. A few days later, Soviet troops attacked the headquarters of Latvia's Interior Ministry.

Gorbachev failed to condemn the violence. Instead, he blamed the Lithuanian government, saying its insistence on independence caused the tension and the clash.

Finally, after nine days of outcry from around the world and from the staunchest Soviet supporters of his reforms, Gorbachev appeared before reporters to read a lukewarm statement rejecting unconstitutional actions. Still, he seemed convinced that the demon-

OPPOSITE: An East German worker puts another brick in the wall that would separate East and West Berlin for almost thirty years. LEFT: Khruschev, Castro, and Brezhnev (l to r), followed by conspirators Suslov and Kosygin, attend the 21st Party conference in 1964 shortly before the successful overthrow of Khruschev. BELOW: Leonid Brezhnev calls for unity in the "Socialist Commonwealth" and is enthusiastically applauded by the delegates of the 5th Congress of the Polish Workers' Party.

strators were to blame for the deaths, even though fifteen of the sixteen dead were civilians. The sixteenth was a KGB agent from the Alpha Group — later to play a key role in the August coup. Gorbachev's failure to take either side wound up alienating both hardliners and reformers. The President was losing support on all sides.

The men who would later lead the August coup — KGB chief Vladimir Kryuchkov, Communist Party official Oleg Shenin, and Gorbachev's chief of staff Valery Boldin — were all heavily involved in the violence in Lithuania. Interior Minister Boris Pugo gave a glimpse of the conspirators' faith that the world had not changed and that they could still get away with brazen lies about their actions. One incredible evening he told foreign journalists, "There were no tanks in Vilnius." Several correspondents stood and replied, "Yes, there were — they were shooting at me!" Journalists did not know whether to be more amazed at the lie or at Pugo's attempt to foist it on a room full of eyewitnesses.

Chief of staff Boldin also used his control over Gorbachev's appointments and Kremlin hiring and firing to push progressives out of the inner circle. Gorbachev became more isolated.

In March — according to Alexander Yakovlev, Gorbachev's close ally in reform — Kryuchkov persuaded Gorbachev that democratic demonstrators were planning to storm the Kremlin walls "with hooks and ladders." That prompted Gorbachev to order tens of thousands of troops into the capital to halt a pro-democracy demonstration. Tens of thousands of Muscovites defied the ban and marched up to the noses of the riot troops, but violence was averted.

Extreme hard-liners went public with suggestions that all power be transferred from Gorbachev and the Parliament to a National

Soviet soldiers seem almost "otherworldly" as they take part in an exercise designed to prepare them for chemical warfare.

ABOVE: Chernobyl-area workers check radiation levels in May 1991, five years after the worst nuclear disaster in history. BELOW and RIGHT: The Cold War thaws as disarmament treaties result in the destruction of Soviet warheads and the dismemberment of aircraft.

Salvation Committee, just like the one that tried to take power in Lithuania. A meeting with Kryuchkov gave the committee legitimacy. One member, Vladimir Zhirinovsky, ran for Russian president in June, promising to create a "State Emergency Committee" and to suspend political parties and parliaments. It was a blueprint for the August coup.

Gorbachev entrusted economic policies to Prime Minister Valentin Pavlov. These became so senseless that a progressive Gorbachev ex-aide charged after the coup that Pavlov deliberately sabotaged the economy to prepare the way for Gorbachev's ouster. Pavlov raised wholesale prices to lev-

els higher than retail. Thousands of factories stopped production rather than sell at a loss.

Oil production sank, and exports had to be cut in half. Soon, there was no money to import raw materials and parts, in a country utterly dependent on them. A lack of one chemical could keep a factory from producing glue, and that, in turn, idled shoe manufacturing. Shortages spiraled through the economy. The economy shrank 10 percent in the first three months of 1991.

The government had printed billions of roubles not backed by goods, services, or even government bonds. By 1991, Soviets were holding half a trillion roubles more in cash than they had goods and services to buy with that money. This wrecked the value of the rouble. The black market exchange rate plummeted, from three roubles to the dollar to thirty.

Pavlov then declared 100- and 50-rouble notes worthless in what he said was an attempt to sop up some of the excess money supply that he had created. Millions of honest citizens lost their savings. People were furious.

Then Pavlov doubled and tripled the various state-set prices. No one felt compensated enough, and anger grew. Old women said, "It was better in Stalin's day. At least we had meat in the stores." They forgot that the real price of that meat in Stalin's time was measured in human lives, not roubles.

In April and again in July, Gorbachev took his problems overseas in search of aid. He traveled to Japan but did not have enough authority to bargain away the Kurile Islands for help from the Japanese. In July he traveled to London where he won worldwide attention for the Soviet economic problems but little in terms of material aid at the annual economic summit of the G-7, the world's seven most important industrial nations. Increasingly isolated and ineffective at home,

Coal miners, literally sick from eighteenth-century working conditions, stage a strike in 1989.

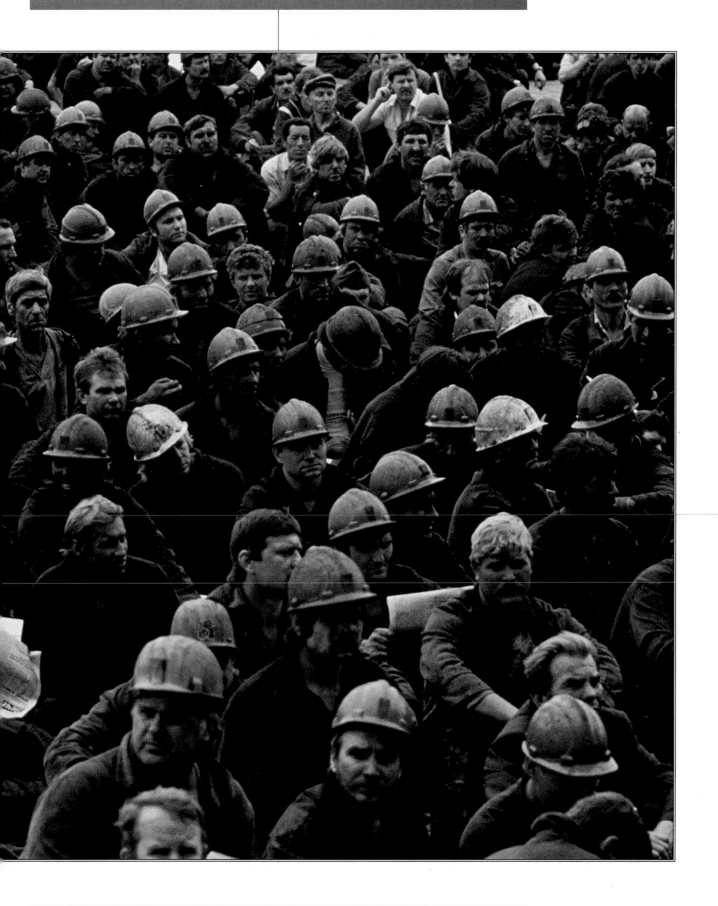

he still cut an important figure on the world stage.

At home, Gorbachev's alliance with the conservatives came to a dead end. He could not do enough to please them. They could not handle the country's problems. It was time for another sharp turn. He gave up his position of confrontation with the republics. He gave up his dream of a new treaty preserving the Soviet Union with all fifteen repub- lics. Instead, he began negotiations with a more realistic nine republics, leaving out Lithuania, Latvia, Estonia, Georgia, Moldavia, and Armenia — the six seeking independence.

In May and June, Gorbachev and the nine drafted a new treaty of unification, shifting most authority from the Kremlin central government to the republics. The USSR, left without even the power to levy its own taxes, would be little more than a shell of a state.

As the summer of 1991 approached, the Communist Party was staring into the abyss of extinction. Boris Yeltsin and many others had already publicly resigned. Gorbachev had transferred many functions previously reserved for the Party to the state. Now the Party *nomenklatura* saw his Union Treaty as an end to its power base in the massive central bureaucracy. They tried to stop it with a constitutional coup on June 20, when Prime Minister Pavlov asked the Supreme Soviet legislature to give him the same emergency powers to decree laws that it had already given Gorbachev. Reformers immediately saw that the unpopular prime minister had no need of such sweeping powers — unless his plans were radically different from Gorbachev's.

Three of the men who were to be co-conspirators in August — Pugo, Kryuchkov, and Yazov — supported the move in secret speeches to a closed session. Yazov com-

OPPOSITE: In January, Lithuanians occupy their own Parliament Building for several days and nights to prevents its takeover by Soviet soldiers. The troops were sent to Vilnius as part of Gorbachev's "war of nerves" after the Lithuanian Parliament declared the republic's independence. ABOVE: Example of the kind of posters hung outside the Supreme Council in Vilnius denouncing Gorbachev and communism.

plained that troops were understrength by 353,000 because independence-minded republics were not obeying the draft. Kryuchkov spoke of a CIA plot, dating back fourteen years, to install agents in high posts in the Soviet Union to wreck its economy. Another future coup conspirator, Vice-President Gennady Yanayev, claimed Gorbachev did not see the proposal as a polit-ical challenge; however, Pavlov admitted that the proposal was made without Gorbachev's knowledge.

Gorbachev's allies managed to hold up the proposal several days, long enough for the President to come and dismiss it. Gorbachev did not fire the group for its insurrection. He told Yakovlev later that Pavlov simply did not know what he was saying.

A month later, Gorbachev had yet another warning. A virulent appeal to the military and others to halt "disaster and humiliation" was published in *Sovetskaya Rossiya* newspaper on July 23. "The motherland…is perishing, breaking up, sinking into darkness and non-existence," the article said, and it clearly blamed Gorbachev. "Why have crafty and pompous masters…sneering at us…seized power? Why are they stealing our wealth, tak-ing from the people their homes, factories, and lands, cutting the country into

BELOW: Gorbachev takes his problems to London in July 1991 for the annual economic summit of the world's seven most important industrial nations, but comes away with little in the way of material aid. OPPOSITE: Soviet stores are cleaned out after the announcement of price increases.

pieces…dooming us to a miserable existence of vegetation in slavery and subordination to our all-powerful neighbors?"

The article was signed by three of the men later charged with planning the August coup: General Varennikov and Emergency Committee members Vasily Starodubtsev

and Alexander Tizyakov.

About this same time, Yakovlev sat down with Gorbachev for a three-hour, heart-to-heart talk. "I appeal to you. You have terrible people around you. Do something about this dirty circle," Yakovlev said he pleaded with the President.

"You exaggerate," Gorbachev scoffed, according to Yakovlev.

Frustrated, Yakovlev could only surmise that the President trusted people too much, or that Gorbachev thought he could out-maneuver those opposing him.

Gorbachev, his international "hero" status

reinforced by his G-7 debut in London and his summit meeting with President George Bush in Moscow, was on his Crimean vacation when Yakovlev tried one more time to send him a warning.

Two days before the coup, Yakovlev warned that a "Stalinist" core of Communist Party leaders were planning to oust the President. "The truth is that the Party leadership, in contradiction to its own declarations, is ridding itself of the democratic wing of the Party and is preparing for social revenge and for a Party and state coup," Yakovlev told the Interfax news agency.

He said later he had no concrete evidence. "For months, there had been a creeping coup," he said. "The smell was in the air."

But when the conspirators made their move, they grossly miscalculated the effect of Gorbachev's reforms. By this time, anti-Communist demonstrations were routinely drawing 100,000 people in many cities. Dozens of independent news media had cropped up — from the already reliable Interfax that used fax machines, to the Independent Newspaper and Radio Echo. Copy machines, once sharply restricted, had become accessible and became a "weapon" of democracy. His lieutenants thought that Gorbachev's sinking popularity meant public support for their move, but democratic passions and modern technology had brought profound change to the country. Fax machines and computers combined with a free press had made it much easier for people to unite and for protest to spread.

Most importantly the conspirators did not read properly the lesson of 40 million Russians who voted to elect Boris Yeltsin their president only two months earlier. For the plotters to succeed, they had to think most of those same 40 million would support them. History turns on such miscalculations.

In August 1991, farmers in the Ukraine seem virtually untouched by time and technology. Here, they gather the harvest much as their ancestors did for hundreds of years.

Russian Political Timeline

★ 1848: Karl Marx
publishes
"Communist
Manifesto" in
London

★ 1902: V. I. Lenin,
in exile, writes a
revolutionary pamphlet,
"What Is To Be Done?"

★ August 1914:
Beginning of
World War I.

★ March 3, 1918: Brest
Litovsk peace treaty
Germany.

★ July 1918: Bolshevik
defeat anti-Commun
opponents to become
single ruling party.

★ July 17, 1918: Nichol
and family are execut

★ 1918: Lenin nationali
the economy, private
trade is barred, collec
farming is instituted.

...1848............1861............1902............1905............1914............1917............191

★ March 3,1861: The
beginning of the
"Era of Great
Reforms," in which
all serfs were freed
from bondage.

★ 1905: After a popular
uprising in St. Peters-
burg, Czar Nicholas II
establishes the Duma
(Parliament).

★ March 2, 1917:
Abdication of Nicholas II.

★ November 7, 1917:
Bolsheviks sieze power.

★ December 7, 1917:
Creation of the Cheka,
later known as the KGB.

★ August 23, 1939: Non-aggression pact between Germany and the USSR signed.

★ September 1, 1939: German invasion of Poland. Beginning of World War II.

★ September 17, 1939: Red Army enters eastern Poland.

★ November 1939: USSR annexes the western Ukraine and western Byelorussia.

★ November 30, 1939: Soviet-Finnish war.

★ 1930s: Stalin orders the death or imprisonment of untold millions of Soviets during the Great Purge.

★ January 21, 1924: Death of Lenin.

1922	1924	1929	1930	1933	1939	1940

April 1922: Stalin elected general secretary of the Central Committee of the Russian Communist Party.

December 1922: Founding of the USSR.

★ January 1929: Stalin's rival Leon Trotsky is expelled from the USSR.

★ April 1929: Sixteenth Party Congress approves the First Five-Year Plan.

★ November 16, 1933: Diplomatic relations established between the USSR and the United States.

★ June-August 1940: Annexation of Northern Bukovina, Lithuania, Latvia, and Estonia

★ August 20, 1940: Assassination of Trotsky in Mexico.

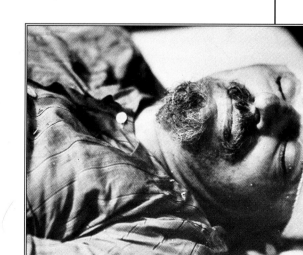

Russian Political Timeline

★ June 22, 1941: Germany invades USSR. Beginning of the German-Soviet war.

★ December 1941: German offensive stalls outside of Moscow.

★ November 28, 1943: Teheran Conference (Roosevelt, Stalin, and Churchill).

★ March 5, 1946: Winston Churchill makes his famous "Iron Curtain" speech.

★ 1946: The Cold War begins.

★ April 4, 1949: Signing of the North Atlantic Treaty (NAT

....1941.............1942.............1943.............1945.............1946.............1948.............194

★ May 1942: Treaty between the USSR and Great Britain agreeing to a military alliance against Germany and its European allies.

★ January 1945: Soviet offensive through Poland.

★ February 1945: Yalta Conference (Roosevelt, Stalin, Churchill).

★ April 25, 1945: U.S. and Soviet forces meet at the Elbe River in Germany. Germany surrenders on May 2.

★ July 1945: Potsdam peace talks divide Germany, Berlin, and most of Europe into Western and Communist blocs.

★ October 10, 1948: Launching of the first Soviet guided ballistic missile.

★ August 8, 1945: USSR declares war on Japan.

★ September 3, 1945: Japan signs surrender, ending World War II.

★ October 1962:
Khrushchev's
decision to place
nuclear weapons in
Cuba touches off the
Cuban missile crisis.

★ October 4, 1957:
USSR launches
Sputnik, the
earth's first
artificial satellite.

★ May 14, 1955:
Warsaw Pact
is signed.

953 . . . . 1955 . . . . 1956 . . . . 1957 . . . . 1961 . . . . 1962 . . . . 1964 . . .

★ March 5, 1953:
Stalin dies.

★ September 1953:
Nikita Khrushchev
succeeds Stalin as
first secretary of the
Central Committee.

★ February 1956:
Khrushchev
criticizes Stalin's
rule of terror.

★ October 1956:
Soviet forces quell
Hungarian uprising.

★ April 12, 1961:
Vostok, the first
manned space
vessel, is launched
with Cosmonaut
Yuri Gagarin.

★ July 1961: Talks
between President
Kennedy and
Khrushchev in
Vienna.

★ August 1961: Berlin
Wall is erected.

★ October 14, 1964:
Khruschev is ousted
by Communist Party
leadership. Leonid
Brezhnev assumes
power.

Russian Political Timeline

★ August 1968: "Prague
Spring" movement in
Czechoslovakia is
stopped by Soviet forces.

★ 1975: Soviet-Cuban
intervention in Angola.

★ December 1981:
Declaration of martial
law in Poland.

★ February 9, 1984:
Andropov dies.

★ February 13, 198
Konstantin Chern
assumes leadersh

1968..........**1971**..........**1975**..........**1979**..........**1981**..........**1982**..........**1984**

★ May 1971: President Nixon
visits Moscow. Signing of
the first Soviet-American
agreement on strategic nuclear
arms limitation. (SALT I).

★ September 11, 1971: Death
of Nikita Khrushchev.

★ December 1979:
Soviet troops invade
Afghanistan.

★ November 10, 1982:
Brezhnev dies.

★ November 12, 1982;
Yuri Andropov
becomes head of
USSR.

★ 1988: Gorbachev creates a full-time parliament and multi-candidate elections.

★ 1990: Lithuania, Estonia, and Latvia declare independence.

★ 1986: Gorbachev calls for *glasnost* (political openness) and *perestroika* (rebuilding of economy).

★ October 1988: Gorbachev is named USSR President.

★ July 1990: Yeltsin and other reformers leave the party.

★ 1986: Boris Yeltsin becomes a Politburo member.

★ 1988: 250,000 Soviet troops begin to withdraw from Eastern Europe.

★ December 1990: Eduard Shevardnadze resigns as foreign minister.

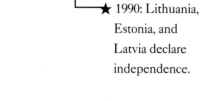

985.............1986.............1987.............1988.............1989.............1990.............1991.

March 10, 1985: Chernyenko dies.

March 11, 1985: Mikhail Gorbachev becomes the Party general secretary.

★ December 1987: Gorbachev and Reagan sign a treaty cutting intermediate-range nuclear arms in Europe.

★ April 1989: Gorbachev purges Central Committee of hard-liners.

★ May 26, 1989: Yeltsin wins Moscow seat in election for the new Congress of Peoples' Deputies.

★ June 12, 1991: Yeltsin becomes president in Russia's first popular election.

★ July 1991: Warsaw Pact is disbanded.

★ Fall 1989: Popular revolutions oust Communist regimes in Eastern Europe.

★ November 1989: The Berlin Wall falls.

★ August 1991: Vice-President Gennady Yanayev and other hard-liners try to oust Gorbachev. Failure of the coup leads to the disintegration of the USSR.

★ 1989: Soviet troops are withdrawn from Afghanistan.

CNN Reports

From U.S. President George Bush's vacation White House in Kennebunkport, Maine, to President Boris Yeltsin's Russian White House in Moscow, CNN brought live August coup coverage to viewers in 123 countries. In this section seven CNN correspondents go behind the news to capture the hopes, fears, aspirations, opportunities, and dangers of the Second Russian Revolution. They report from inside the corridors of power and from the grass roots, describing their own emotions as history's witnesses.

Finally Nicholas Daniloff, a professor of journalism at Northeastern University in Boston and long-time Moscow correspondent, examines the importance of the mass media in defeating the August coup.

A Rural Village: Sour Apples & Sukharay

BY RICHARD BLYSTONE

"Give this gentleman an apple," Katerina Adyoshena tells her granddaughter, and the little one hands it over.

It is small, green, hard, knotty, sour as a lemon, and covered with spots.

"There's nothing but hardship to our life here," she says. "We envy you in America. We've been deceived, told that your only goal was to attack us, but it was just the other way around...

"I'm on my way to the shop. The neighbors tell me there's supposed to be *sukharay* today. Let's go."

The awesome authority of the *babushka* on her own turf. Today you may laugh in the commissar's face, thumb your nose at the KGB, but the old lady in the kerchief had better get her way.

She swallows the granddaughter's small hand in her own and we stump up the middle of the one paved street of Rosha.

Hard, spotty, green apples weigh down the branches in the cottage gardens behind the fences.

They seem to come from different worlds: Grandma solid, in denim coat, head bound in a flowered peasant kerchief, black rubber boots to the knee. Granddaughter, blonde and petite in a pink dress, nibbling the core of an apple; she looks like a girl from the world of Golden Delicious. So, no doubt, did Grandma, a lot of sour apples ago.

If we'd been caught in this village last spring when the apple trees were in bloom, we would have been arrested and returned to Moscow, three bumpy hours' drive away. A lot can happen in one apple season.

"See, kid, your grandma's going to be on American TV. They'll come and grab me afterwards. Take me away."

She laughs, and covers her mouth with a hand, a little bit shocked at what she's said.

Laughter looks good on Katerina Adyoshena. It gives the Asian lines of her eyes something to do.

But it's one of those Russian faces that are also good at suspicion and hostility, as seen in food lines, in shops, behind hotel desks, topping off police uniforms. The masks of caged wolves. The faces of people whose mission has been to watch, report, restrict, restrain, obstruct, detain, stop.

It is a week after the collapse of the coup, and not even *we* are sure it's legal for us to be here. No diplomat has been free to walk this road, no journalist, no tourist. For decades, only the occasional student or businessman or scholar would have had the chance to slip out and meet Russia's country people without a watcher from the government close at hand.

To each other, we and the people of the village ought to seem exotic creatures. But a couple of crates of oranges arriving at Rosha's *produkti* shop would have caused more of a stir than we have.

Katerina Adyoshena plows right through the need for an interpreter. If you speak Russian clearly enough, anyone can understand. She is almost right.

"It's about time they got rid of the Communist Party," she declares. "I wish there'd never been one. From them we've had nothing but promises.

"We have 190 households here: collective farmers, industrial workers, intellectuals. All kinds of people. The district Party committees told us we're not their business, because our people are employed all over. We have electricity, but we don't have running water or gas. We have to buy coal and firewood at three or four times the normal price…

"We're nobody's people."

Nobody's people are busy shifting for themselves: men wheel cans of water from the well up the road; women split firewood and dig vegetables from the gardens. And you can tell why.

A chill, gray drizzle is washing away the end of August. The mist and the smoke from the cottage chimneys turn Rosha into

a somber watercolor, in grays, greens, and pastel blues and earth tones. Carved white wooden doilies frame the windows and the eaves. Over the hill, old red tractors crawl the dark earth of a collective farm.

This is the sickle part of the Hammer and Sickle, about as far as you can get from the ten-lane boulevards and the frigid twenty-story cellblocks where Muscovites live. But there is no risk of thinking you've made a wrong turn and wound up in Switzerland. The asphalt crumbles into the roadside mud. Weary electricity poles lean on their crutches. Grass and bushes grow as they will, just like the mud puddles.

The cottage gardens are what remains for the children and grandchildren of peasants who were ripped from the lands they owned, or were made to exchange one serfdom for another — in the name of what seemed, to a few men with clean fingernails, an idea worth forcing on people.

Here the stereotype of grim, grumpy, grudging brutes with no use for outsiders collides with the Marxist vision of happy peasants reaping the bounty of selfless toil for the people – and with the reality: patient souls and a life of sour, green apples.

"Things are quiet here. We're concerned with daily life," says Katerina Adyoshena. "We hope things will get better now. Yeltsin has promised improvements, but I don't know…Nothing ever really changes here."

The *produkti* is locked. Lena the shop girl has gone off to the depot to collect the *sukharay*. A half-dozen women are sheltering in the entryway, bulky women with broad faces and broad ankles. "What are you telling them things like that for?" one woman rebukes Katerina Adyoshena.

"You go see what her house is like inside," the woman says to us, "and she keeps complaining."

Civic pride rises like a blush to the defense of Rosha:

"Things are okay. The situation's difficult right now, but we'll pull through. Everything will be just fine here."

"You should have been here ten years ago. We had everything, stacks of things, bags and boxes. We had oceans of wine and vodka. Cookies and biscuits. You name it. The stores were crammed. Then there was a period when you couldn't buy anything in the stores, but food was rotting in the warehouses. Now the food is coming back.

"We can get sausage, candy. Sometimes we even get booze."

A gust of rakish laughter from the old girls.

They're afraid we're going to portray them as poor — which they are. But today they're just able to think we might also show them as ordinary nice people — which they also are.

"It makes no difference what happens in Moscow as long as we have food in the stores."

It should be no surprise to hear that from a country housewife in a time of shortage.

But at this moment the Parliament in Moscow is debating the very bones of the country's future. And the bescarved matriarchy of Rosha is waiting for *sukharay* and worrying about being patronized.

They don't see democracy as naturally *right*. It's just another imposed system, and they can only hope the new batch of leaders is better than the old.

"They should be doing something about the harvest instead of talking," says Lena. She has come back and unlocked the shop. But no *sukharay*. She'll try again later.

The *produkti* begins where the kitchen garden stops. It is the size of the potato-chip section of a Western supermarket and has a big abacus instead of a cash register. It is stocked like the bitter end of a clearance sale. A couple of dozen jars of preserves here and there, bags of sugar, a few overcoats.

Amid her customers Lena looks trendy in black, with a pink smock that matches her apple cheeks.

"Nothing changes here," she says. "We hope there'll be more order and less black-marketeering. At least the new [Russian] government is trying to do something about it. But nothing ever changes here."

But manifestly some things have changed here. The monastery that marks the town with ten turrets has been given back to the church and is being restored. There's the paved road and the new telephone line. *We're* here, for Heaven's sake, and they're telling us what they think.

"Myself, I'm ashamed to say I was a Communist Party member for twenty-three years," says Vera Sergeevna, whose big gold tooth predates her conversion to capitalism. "Our hopes are in our kitchen gardens. We only hope there'll be no war; we can cope with everything else."

The past seems to lie like some optimism-inhibiting lesion in their brains so that they see history as an eternal cycle of a little better, a little worse. And what does it take to change that?

There *is* one person in Rosha who's "politically aware," who has been listening to the debate in Parliament and wants to get back to it: Nadezhda Nicolayeva, decorated World War II veteran, retired tractor mechanic, Party member for 40 years…And still proud of it.

She invites us home for tea. Home, a legacy from her mother, is a large white cottage with light blue trim and walls a foot-and-a-half thick. Nadezhda Nicolayeva and her husband share it with two relatives.

As we wipe our boots, some member of Parliament, through the red-and-white plastic radio, is summing up the national question: "Where are we going, and how?" Nadezhda knows only where she's been.

Her name means Hope. In the era when English-speakers were naming their baby daughters Wendy, Russian girls were getting names like Hope and Energy. The Party was trying to fan enthusiasm for the task of "Building Socialism." For Nadezhda the Party meant something, and its departure has left a hole.

"As a Communist I feel very sad," she says. "I've worked honestly and conscientiously all my life. I don't know about the Party leaders, but in the rank and file we thought we should work harder than other people and set an example. I'm not giving up my membership."

On the wardrobe in the parlor, a black-and-white photo of a

couple in World War II uniforms sits incongruously beside a bright blue plastic toy dinosaur.

"Maybe there'll be another party, under a different name, like the Russian Democratic Party. I'd be happy to join that."

A shot-put natural with her hair in a bun, you can imagine her as an elevator watcher or some Party "obstructocrat." And it's hard to reconcile that with her insistence that you take some more homemade jam.

She splashes hot water into the cups and saucers to warm them. "My mother used to do it with holy water," she says.

Her husband comes in and has a good laugh. "They told me in the street that my house was full of Americans, and I thought they were putting me on."

On his coat Ivan Sefanovich wears a postcard-sized bank of World War II ribbons, including the prized Order of Lenin. He never joined the Party. And it becomes apparent that political debate has been enlivening this couple's tea table for thirty years. But never before in front of strangers.

Ivan: They used to force people to join the Party.

Nadezhda: That's not so.

Ivan: It's not a parliament. It's a bazaar.

Nadezhda: You're wrong.

Ivan: No other parliament has such poor discipline. They keep elbowing each other away from the microphone. They won't let the chairman speak. The U.S. has just one president, and we have so many.

Nadezhda: They're not asking you about that; they're talking about something else. I think that when they take the correct decisions they'll help improve our life a lot.

Ivan: It's very hard to improve the economic situation. Nobody cares about the rouble anymore. There could be a one-rouble note lying on the floor of a bus and nobody would bother to pick it up. Contacts between producers have been cut. There are no raw materials. It's very difficult to put the house in order. If anyone can do it, it's not going to be Gorbachev.

(Now here is something Nadezhda and Ivan can agree on: Gorbachev, the "Joe College" who took over the Party and thought he was so smart.)

Nadezhda: It's all Gorbachev's fault. He shouldn't have hung on to two posts at one time [President and Party general secretary]. It was under him that the Party went the wrong way.

Ivan: The people have quit believing the Communist Party. We believed all of our lives that we'd have socialism and after-

ward communism. That we'd have our own apartments, one for each family, by the year 2000. That there would be plenty of food. We always voted "in favor." Nobody ever asked any questions.

Nadezhda Nicolayeva is looking like she'd like to send a certain person to Siberia. But Ivan Sefanovich isn't finished.

"The terrible thing is that we were taught contempt for you," he tells us, gesticulating across the language fence. "Believe me, we've been told that you Americans exploit people, that you will collapse as a system soon. The people swallowed all they were told. And all the time we should have been learning from you.

"We're friends. We fought World War II together. We hugged each other then, but later we were told all that stuff. We should learn how to live from you."

Nadezhda Nicolayeva admits there's something in that.

"I've invited you to my house and I'm not afraid of anyone. That's to Gorbachev's credit. I can go to church freely and no one is going to reproach me. In the past I would be reminded that I was a Party member. There was no way I could bake an Easter cake or paint eggs. I used to do it in secret. In my family we are all believers. I've always been a believer myself deep in my heart."

And she believes something else: "The U.S., Japan, and others are willing to help us. First, we'll get some support from our friends. After our economy gets more stable, we won't need any help. We'll be helping other countries once again."

Nadezhda-Hope would find the bright side in a coal pit. After hot tea in her heatless, running-waterless house, our Christian-Communist hostess stops outside at the rain barrel and splashes her face.

"That's usually the first thing I do when I come home," she says. "It feels so good. There's no fun in washing up from a tap."

She goes to her kitchen garden and comes back laden with presents. Not green apples. Great big Commie-red tomatoes.

Oh, yes…

Lena finally came back with the *sukharay*.

The dames of Rosha had waited five hours for slices of thick, sweetened toast to eat with tea.

It tastes a bit stale. They say it's supposed to. You can get used to it.

CNN Reports

City Streets:
Babushka at the Barricades BY EILEEN O'CONNOR

What's he saying? What's he saying?" the frail Russian voice asked right behind me. We were both standing at the foot of a tank, but upon this tank was Boris Yeltsin, standing tall against gray sky and gleaming white Russian Parliament Building.

"He's reading a Russian government statement… He says the Emergency Committee is anticonstitutional and to spread the word," I told Marina, the thin *babushka* straining to hear her hero's message.

Tears welled in her eyes, already clouded with age and the tough memories of a Soviet past. Marina was two when the Communists overthrew the failing democratic government that had barely replaced the czars. For Marina, history was repeating itself.

"I heard them on the radio this morning," she said with resignation. "Where's Gorbachev? Why are they playing that music… is he dead?"

The man next to her shouted the same to Yeltsin, "Where's Mikhail Sergeyevich?" The cry spread through the crowd.

"My friends, I don't know," said Yeltsin helplessly. "I don't know."

No political rivalry or personal opinion could diminish the human concern you could see in these faces. Even Boris Yeltsin paused, pained at the obvious. They knew all too well that Gorbachev's life was in jeopardy.

There were fewer than a hundred people there, milling about the Russian White House, when it all began. Women, in drab housecoats on their way to shop, stopped to listen. The most hardened Moscow taxi drivers veered off the road, abandoning their dilapidated cabs to catch the "real" news. Even a top Soviet scientist and a few Peoples' Deputies, looking somewhat out of place in their best gray suits, were drawn to the one building in Moscow that had come to represent real democracy.

Glancing up the hill toward Kutuzovsky Prospect, they could see the government tanks rolling over the bridge even as Yeltsin spoke of defiance. The din of the tanks could not drown out his booming voice, but the entire city seemed to rumble as the tanks moved in from every direction, like a drum roll to a final act. The tanks were setting up roadblocks, trying to cut the people off from each other and the outside world. Yet the people continued to stream down the hill toward the White House. The word was already spreading. Yeltsin and the people would stand up to the coup leaders.

"We are the constitutionally elected government of Russia," said Yeltsin. "We must get the word out; this Emergency Committee is unconstitutional. We are calling for a general strike until the power is restored to the constitutional authorities, namely Gorbachev." A Russian flag appeared out of nowhere atop a tank and the people began to chant, "Yeltsin, Yeltsin," as he rushed back into the Parliament Building, confident that at least these people had heard the truth. But would they listen?

As Yeltsin disappeared inside, the lawns and steps outside the White House became a fertile field, from which sprang posters and placards, poems pasted on walls, but mainly people. Within hours they were hauling concrete blocks, rusty wire, steel rods, crates, coiled chicken wire…anything they could drag to the foot of this tabernacle. They had to protect the covenants it housed: freedom and self-determination. The Russian people knew for once they had it in them to say "No," to the authorities, to say, "We will not be told our destiny."

I have been told often by friends who also went to the barricades those days and by contacts who gave me information that, at first, they had been scared, that they had thought, "I will close the shutters and stay inside." But as one friend put it, "I realized I had to make a choice. I knew that you would be working, getting information. I knew I could help and I thought to myself, 'Now you must decide. Are you really with these people all the time or only when things are pleasant? If you mean what you say, you must act.'"

Men with new-found strength of purpose dragged a heavy concrete cylinder from the nearby metro station. Stooped over short straw brooms, women swept the remnants of food and paper strewn about in the haste to fortify. Along the bridge, people ran up to the soldiers in

A tank from the Taman Division stands ready to defend the White House.

the tanks, talking to them, handing them leaflets with the latest Yeltsin statement, and throwing them flowers.

As one earnest young woman in sneakers and jeans drew a crowd of soldiers with her impassioned plea, the group commander came rushing up. "Get back to your tanks," he shouted. "Where is your discipline?" Instead of retreating to their posts, the soldiers stayed to hear the young woman berate the commander, neat in his khakis and salt-and-pepper crew cut. "Why can't we talk?" she asked. "Are you afraid of the truth?"

"No one knows the truth," he smirked.

Each soldier had a different reason for being in Moscow. "We were told it was an exercise," said one. "Gorbachev's sick and needs to rest so we came in just to keep order," said another, slightly better informed of the "official" version. "As I understand, this is what everyone wants," said another. The more they talked, the more confused they got, but still they said they had to obey orders, a Soviet tradition and excuse.

But the people told them, "That's not good enough anymore." As one middle-aged woman walked away from a tank, she said, "How can they not listen to me? I'm a mother. He'd listen to his mother," she said, gesturing to a young soldier on a tank, looking straight ahead, bewildered, caught between what he was told was his "duty to the Motherland" and what appeared to be the voice of the Motherland itself.

As I walked away from the row of tanks surrounding the White House, passing the very tank from which Yeltsin had made his own impassioned plea, I saw that Marina, that frail *babushka*, had not strayed far. As I watched, I saw her tug on the sleeve of a younger woman bustling by, "Did you hear?" she asked, "Yeltsin was here and said we must fight."

CNN Reports

Outside the "White House"   STEVEN R. HURST

You could almost bump your head on the scudding clouds. Heavy, intermittent rain. The camera was live to the world. Counting tanks, armored personnel carriers. Twenty-four, twenty-five, they disappeared over the hump of the Kutuzovsky Prospect Bridge. Finally, there were too many to count.

Muscovites in their cars trying to get to work wove amongst the armor. For twelve years the possibility of a coup had fretted my subconscious. Loud bangs in the night, most often just unexpected flashes of fireworks to celebrate the myriad of Soviet holidays, always sent me running for a look outdoors.

I had seen these tanks churn through Red Square on many a Revolution Day…noisy, puffing exhaust into the already grimy Moscow air. I had seen them arriving in Afghanistan in 1980 and then climbing the long mountain road out of Kabul toward the Salang Pass when they left in 1989. I had seen them arranged strategically in Yerevan to quell unrest, in Baku, in Vilnius. A symbol both of Communist strength and weakness.

Now they were spreading out at midmorning through Moscow. A bemused populace watched. So did I. So did our camera from atop the building where CNN has its bureau.

My spiritual gloom matched the weather. I had always felt an objective observer of the Soviet scene, but watching those tanks finally stall in a column on the Kutuzovsky Bridge made me realize my psyche had actually been a cheerleader for Soviet change. I had become a fan of perestroika. Those tanks were crushing the team I was rooting for. But this was no game, and the outcome of this putsch would stand the world on its head.

By late morning, Monday, August 19, six-and-one-half years of change seemed a bonfire after an all-night rain — some embers still glowed pointlessly, waiting to die out. No way the charred remains would ever burst back into flame.

Boris Yeltsin played the hero. Clambered aboard a tank. Bellowed about unconstitutionality. Demanded Mikhail Gorbachev's return from house arrest. The few hundred assembled, cheered. Tank drivers, heads wrapped in leather caps, popped out of armored hatches, bewildered.

The camera atop our building was still live to the world. The vigil began.

Yeltsin stood tall. A crowd massed. But the Russian leader seemed destined for the KGB lockup, the crowd for flight before the burly tanks, the Cold War for Lazarus-like resurrection.

But questions kept cropping up. Why weren't those tanks in place before sunrise? Why was

Yeltsin, the obvious opposition lightning rod, still free? Why were international telephone circuits still up, telexes still operating? Why weren't people ordered indoors? Why had no shots been fired?

Why was our camera—bouncing its damning images off a Soviet satellite—still live from its immodest vantage point, glaring at this stand-off between Communist armor and a rag-tag assemblage of the unarmed and the mainly curious?

This Army had turned back Hitler's Third Reich. The Communist Party that was still issuing orders had not hesitated to kill millions of Soviet citizens with merely a movement of Josef Stalin's bushy brows. What was going on here?

The stand-off continued. Mothers, *babushkas*, gray clerks, Moscow River barge captains, all yelled at the confused tank crews.

Moscow traffic became a snarl of armored roadblocks. Commerce, or what passes for it in the Soviet capital, became a 45-rpm record played at 33. Paving stones, pried out of the ground, joined children's jungle gyms dragged from nearby parks in feeble barricades around the Russian Parliament.

Trolley-bus drivers parked. People pushed the behemoths, their rods disconnected from overhead electricity wires and waving in the air like grasshopper antennae, end-to-end across broad thoroughfares.

Supporters of Boris Yeltsin relax during their overnight vigil at the White House, August 20-21.

The champions of democracy began to assemble in Yeltsin's White House. Before the coup collapsed Yeltsin was surrounded by a virtual who's who: Eduard Shevardnadze, the former foreign minister who had predicted the coup; Alexander Yakovlev, the architect of glasnost; Gavril Popov, the reformist mayor of Moscow, a slouching, hawk-faced man with a bush of white hair who left his office downtown to join the group; the strident widow of Andrei Sakharov, Yelena

Bonner, who knew vigils well; Yevgeny Yevtushenko, poet for all seasons and all reasons.

The crowd grew through the day, so did hope. No answers to all those "why" questions. But I tell all visitors to leave their "why" questions at home. There are no answers to them in the Soviet Union. Should there be answers now, of all times?

Darkness came. No attack. The night was quiet after the coup plotters held their scoundrels' news conference. The rain continued to fall. Nobody went home.

Day two. Fatigue joined depression. The rain fell in earnest. And, amazingly, none of the men running the putsch had yet got around to shutting us down. The camera on the roof, its images fitful because the rain was so strong, electrical connections disturbed, showed the crowd expanding at Yeltsin's headquarters.

A giant balloon in the shape of a rocket was tethered at the Russian Parliament. It had been floating above an exhibition center down the river. In the night it was brought to the White House. Somehow it reminded me of the papier-maché goddess of democracy the Chinese students had erected during their vigil on Tiananmen Square.

Ten tanks of the Taman Division had turned coat in the night and arrayed themselves in defense of the White House. Tens of thousands of Muscovites were partying around the Parliament. President Bush was sounding tougher. Western European leaders were refusing to acknowledge the coup plotters' legitimacy.

The sun poked through the nasty clouds toward evening. The attack didn't come. Some tanks on the outskirts of town had moved ominously toward the center. Still the attack — first rumored for 6 p.m — didn't come. It didn't come at 8 p.m. either, as forecast by the Yeltsin crowd. Nor did it happen at 11 p.m., when a curfew was to take effect.

Defenders had ordered women and children to leave the vicinity. Gas masks and bulletproof vests were passed out. Someone started a rumor that the White House had been mined against an attack. I got frightened. My wife, Claire Shipman, was in that building, refusing to leave. She was watching when violence finally broke out, and reporting live for CNN as defenders attacked a tank with Molotov cocktails. Shots rang out at about 1 a.m., our live camera on the roof relaying to the world the sound of crackling AK-47s.

The White House had gone pitch black from where I stood a quarter of a mile away. Only a giant spotlight from a threatening military lit up the corner. I heard periodic crackling from automatic rifles. Three people were killed, jousting with the armor as it tried to break through the barricades of trolley buses on the Garden Ring Road.

The attack never came. But I was too frightened and too tired to understand what now is clear. The military did not have the stomach to move on the defenders of the White House. There would be no Tiananmen Square massacre at Boris Yeltsin's giant white bunker.

And finally day three dawned. The coup-that-couldn't was fast unraveling, we later learned.

The conspirators talked to Yeltsin. How would he like to fly to the Crimea to meet Gorbachev? Boris, no fool, said he would send representatives.

Then the coup plotters reportedly were fleeing. Speeding in Volga sedans for Vnukovo Airport. Rumors flew that they were escaping to central Asia, maybe China. In fact, they were going to see Gorbachev themselves, apparently to beg for mercy. There wasn't any.

The depression and fatigue of three days vanished in an instant. Almost biblically, the weather changed. The hide-and-seek sunshine of the past twenty-four hours glowed full, as it ought to in late summer in these latitudes.

The Yeltsin delegation saw Gorbachev; they met for hours. And then, not long before dawn of the fourth day, the Soviet President was back. Little did he know then what he had come back to.

The Soviet landscape has been ripped apart. Gorbachev is a stranger in a strange land, still wandering and looking for his niche. So is Yeltsin. So are we all, struggling to understand where this country is taking itself, taking all of us. It's as if the first seventy-four years of Soviet history were that first part of a roller-coaster ride, to the top, and now we are on the dizzying, stomach-wrenching drop, hoping the little cars hold to the rails.

Inside the "White House"

BY CLAIRE SHIPMAN

Late afternoon.

An hour-long stand-off with the guards at the door. Inexplicably someone relents, and we're inside the embattled Russian White House. It's like a tomb.

Militia men and their shadows huddle in every corner of the cavernous lobby-turned-command-post, their murmuring bouncing off the walls. Others clank across the marble floors, loaded down with guns, ammunition, and bulletproof vests. No nonsense here. We stay out of their way.

We try to be invisible so we won't be thrown out. Up the grand central staircase, we run into our friend Andrei Fyoderov, the deputy foreign minister of Russia. He tries to throw us out. We get a temporary stay. He tells us an attack is expected.

We set off in search of a view, of access to the vast balcony ringing the building. No easy task. The building is a maze; navigating is treacherous — and spooky. Empty halls, locked doors, a public-address system spewing out warnings, instructions, and Boris Yeltsin's rebellious words, over and over.

We walk for what seems like miles, probably in circles. At last a light — an open office — already temporary home to a militia squad and two armed, brawny, unidentified men glued to phones. We're welcomed, sort of, with raised eyebrows and almost imperceptible nods.

The militia team uses the window to crawl out onto the balcony, so we do too. Still enough light to see for half a mile around the building. Rain is imminent, but no sign of the predicted onslaught of tanks.

From this vantage point, the mesh, metal, and sticks below appear a formidable fortress, or at least a hurricane effort. Defenders have locked arms, barricading the building themselves. The monotone voice on the intercom informs that the attack is now expected in two hours.

Armed with Kalashnikovs, the militia patrol roams the roof, waiting. One of them, Anatoly, is tall, shy, and looks overwhelmed. But his words are confident:

"I don't think an attack will come — our country has changed too much in the last few years. We've experienced freedom. The Army won't turn on its own people."

His wife and two young children are away on holiday; he hasn't talked to them. Which is good, he figures — they'd worry if they knew exactly what he was doing.

Almost dark. Back through the window, the office is empty, the phones are ringing.

"Krasnodar calling. What's the situation? Give us details."

One of the burly men returns, takes the phone. It turns out they represent the Russian miners. They've been sent here to keep their finger on the pulse for the rest of the republic.

We commandeer one phone — it becomes our lifeline to CNN in Atlanta. The voice on the public-address system asks all nonessential personnel to evacuate.

Four floors down, and endless corridors away, Yeltsin's headquarters are dim and hushed, but bustling. Armed men guard every nook and cranny. Top aides come and go. Army General Konstantin Kobets, chief of the Russian armed forces becomes a well-known face in the inner sanctum.

Pavel Voshanov, Yeltsin's mild-mannered and retiring press

secretary, carries a gun on his hip. The Russian leader is holed-up, but members of his inner circle stride the hallways.

"Yazov is out."

"Bush called Yeltsin."

"Yeltsin talked to Yanayev."

The doors to the corridor leading to Yeltsin's office burst open. The Russian leader is surrounded by a circle of men, guns ready. Yeltsin towers above the group, looking tired and grim. They don't stop moving, propelled down the hall by the man in the center. Doors close behind them.

Volunteers, armed with AK-47s and pistols, stayed in the White House three days and nights on guard.

Ten minutes later, they return to Yeltsin's office. Former British Prime Minister Margaret Thatcher had called.

The evening becomes a series of trips between the Yeltsin information center and our camera and phone line on the balcony. Back and forth and back again.

Our militia friends have laid out a sausage-and-cheese picnic and invite us to join them. We get a care package from our bureau: food, bulletproof vests, other gear. We share.

One of the beefy miners, still armed, and much tougher looking than the militia men, insists, somewhat threateningly, that we give back his phone. We beg for more time.

A militia man calls home to tell his wife what's happening, which isn't easy. Nothing is clear. The public-address system announces that the coup leaders have ordered a curfew — the crowd roars. The attack is still expected, but later.

Atlanta says a rumor is flying around that the first floor of the building is mined. We marvel at the chance that they would know this and we would not. The militia chief says there aren't any mines, but wonders if we have extra bulletproof vests — they don't have enough.

Outside, we see the crowd has thinned, but thousands remain despite the curfew, and the rain. Candles flicker in the hands of solemn onlookers as a Russian Orthodox priest holds an extemporaneous service. The public-address system bellows in the background. A young man in fatigues wielding a stick of wood demonstrates fighting techniques to a group of volunteers.

Small groups huddle around fires, trying to keep warm. Makeshift tents are erected to fight the drizzle. First-aid centers are marked with red crosses. It suddenly seems impossible that the coup will succeed. These people are here to stay, but it's also eerily reminiscent of Tiananmen Square.

Inside, more details. Deputy Foreign Minister Andre Federov confirms that Yeltsin talked to coup plotter and Vice-President Gennady Yanayev and that Yanayev denied ordering an attack on the building.

Yeltsin and his entourage emerge again, heading toward what we figure is the telecommunications room. His guards still carry guns, but they've taken off the ski masks.

He speaks by phone to the president of the Ukraine, who promises support. The crowd chants approval when they hear the news a few minutes later.

Anatoly, the militia man, is taking a break in the office on the eighth floor. Was he really trained for this kind of work? We ask. He laughs. "We have good training, but it's funny because it's well known that being a militia man is supposed to be the least rigorous job of all the forces."

Something is happening outside: gunfire. We crawl through the window. Anatoly leaves his vest because it's too heavy. The public-address system is ordering all lights out. A rush to the corner of the roof. The militia men drop into place, cock their rifles. The people below are massing on the corner of the Kutuzovsky Prospect Bridge. A bright light is coming from somewhere beyond the crowd. There's intermittent gunfire.

"Our job is to defend the Parliament Building. Do not provoke the attacker," the disembodied voice on the intercom emphasizes. It's the same monotonous tone, but suddenly it inspires alarm. "Friends who have chosen to defend the White House, you are truly among the brave."

It seems the siege has begun.

We wait. We shiver from the cold and from fright. It's impossible to tell what is happening below. Reports come that people have been killed — two or three. Is there a battle out there, out of our view? Even Anatoly, whose words of courage had been somewhat reassuring, finally looks scared.

But there is no more gunfire. The crowd eventually starts to flow back toward the building. More waiting. After a time it appears that an attack is not on the way.

A Russian television reporter bolts out of the darkness, rushing madly across the roof. "Mikhail Sergeyevich is back," he shouts, his voice exploding with joy and relief. "Mikhail Sergeyevich is back!"

What? The people downstairs are cheering, thronging around someone. But how? Word drifts up that it's not Gorbachev, but his friend Eduard Shevardnadze. This noise dies down. People are saying an attack is no longer expected.

Rumors are becoming less frequent. One final bit of gossip sweeps around that Yeltsin has left the building.

"Are you kidding?" says the guard at his door. "Where else would he be as safe? He's here."

Everyone has finally closed up shop for what's left of the night. The building is pitch black and silent — except of course, for the ever-present loudspeaker. The voice no longer mentions an impending strike, just rattles out what are supposed to be inspiring messages. But as fatigue sets in, it's not inspiring, just annoying.

Anatoly, the militia man, is still on roof duty. Did he ever have any doubt about which side to serve?

"No. This is my job, to defend the Parliament Building. From early in the morning on the nineteenth, when we were told what had happened, I knew where I would be."

The light is coming. Megaphones near the river are making an announcement. It's hard to hear from up here. A few tired cheers filter up. It must be time to go.

Outside, as the threat is fading, the Committee for Defense of the White House hits peak efficiency. Wire racks brimming with freshly baked bread bounce hand over hand up to the food-distribution team. Big cars speed up the ramp with more milk and sausage in their trunks than ever appear in any Soviet store. "The mafia," someone shrugs. Near the outer ring of the barricades a garrulous and disheveled old man from Gorky talks to anyone who will listen. "I know a lot of the young men who built the barricades. I was too weak to help them, but I was never afraid — I myself forced some soldiers to turn off their tanks. It happened like this...." With the night, the danger indeed seems to have slipped away. In its place sits the dawn, and a heady sound...the construction of legends.

CNN Reports

Media Coverage
BY NICHOLAS DANILOFF

R ule Number One in plotting a coup is to seize the press, shut down the opposing media, and pump out an "authorized version" of events over radio and television. Coup leader Gennady Yanayev and the August plotters knew that well enough: they declared a state of emergency, banned unreliable newspapers, introduced censorship.

Yet their operation was so sloppy that word of their attempted takeover leaked almost immediately, allowing their most important enemy, Russian Republic President Boris Yeltsin, to rally the opposition successfully.

And despite the junta's efforts, scores of journalists, emboldened by the freedoms of glasnost, refused to be suppressed or to fall into line. They went right on collecting the news — much of it unfavorable to the junta — and discovered novel ways to get the word out.

True, the official news agency, TASS, obediently trumpeted the junta's declarations. In Washington, these were made public through the usual press releases of the Soviet embassy.

But cracks in the media facade began appearing very quickly, even in the media supposedly loyal to the conspirators. Moscow television announcers, for example, communicated fear and surprise by their nervous manner and unkempt appearance. One TV editor prided herself in getting on air a dramatic glimpse of Yanayev's trembling hands at the conspirators' first and only press conference.

The independent and reformist newspapers, although prohibited from publishing, proved even more daring. Their determination to undermine the junta grew with every hour.

"I first heard of the coup," said Alex Korgun, a junior editor at *Komsomolskaya Pravda*, "from Radio Liberty early Monday morning, August 19. I rushed to the office, getting there about 7 a.m.

"Immediately, we began organizing an emergency news service. We compiled a running chronology, drawing on reports from our own correspondents and supplemented by well-wishing citizens who called in on their own."

The minute-by-minute chronology, documenting tank movements, reactions throughout the country, and statements by leading figures, was posted in the newspaper's corridors for all to read and repeat to friends.

When a top editor announced that the newspaper was among those banned and would not be coming out, one of the younger reporters shot back: "No! We've already published! Look at the corridors!"

Additionally, *Komsomolskaya Pravda* faxed its chronology to thirty-five Soviet and international newspapers including the New York Post. Even more ambitious chronologies were compiled by two independent news agencies, Interfax and Postfactum. Drawing on hundreds of correspondents across the Soviet Union, these two services, which had been established only in the last several years, reported on provincial reactions.

At first, faraway leaders were cautious, seeking to find out which way the wind was blowing in Moscow. But slowly, the mood showed signs of changing. Some miners responded to Yeltsin's call to strike; some local leaders in other places denounced the plotters.

These reports encouraged resisters around the nation. Meanwhile, the conspirators were actually deceiving themselves about events. Their news-gathering capabilities, dependent in good part on Army personnel, were slow and inaccurate. The conspirators believed the nation was calm and supportive even as independent journalists reported growing resistance.

A rude surprise for the junta came when eleven newspapers — *Argumenty i Fakty*, *Kommersant*, *Kuranty*, *Megapolis Express*, *Moskovskiye Novosti*, *Moskovskii Komsomolets*, *Hezavisimaya Gazeta*, *Rossiskaya Gazeta*, *Rossiskaya Vesti*, *Stolitsa*, and *Komsomolskaya Pravda* — banded together to create a crisis sheet called *Obshchaya Gazeta*, or The Common Newspaper. From the start this novel enterprise denounced the coup as an unconstitutional mutiny.

The Common Newspaper, published only in the form of a broadsheet, was officially established on Monday, the second day of the coup, but not under the Soviet press law. Rather, the editors registered the newspaper under the press law of the Russian Republic.

It had a brief but glorious life. It was printed on the private presses of *Kommersant* (The Wall Street Journal of the Soviet Union) and reproduced as well by photocopier and mimeograph. The daily edition came out in 500,000 copies which were plastered by volunteers in the subways and street corners of Moscow and Leningrad.

The coup makers not only misgauged the potential for resistance, but from the start stumbled badly in springing their surprise. The creation of a State Committee for the State of Emergency was announced first in the Pacific part of the nation at 4 a.m. Moscow time. Word spread instantly to the capital, alerting Boris Yeltsin. By midday, when he delivered his dramatic call for resistance standing on a tank, Yeltsin's team had set up a primitive but effective press operation.

They photocopied Yeltsin's speech and a handful of presidential decrees, stressing that both Yeltsin and Gorbachev were legally elected leaders, whereas the Emergency Committee members were unconstitutional usurpers. Tossed out the windows like paper airplanes, the leaflets floated into the hands of demonstrators below. Young men and women, grandmothers and children, scooped them up and used them to persuade tank crews not to fire.

These flying press releases quickly hit Moscow's international press corps, estimated to be at least one thousand strong. Many of these journalists, reacting to word of the putsch, rushed to the Russian Parliament to see what was going on.

"I was walking around the Moscow White House," said Jerry Nadler, bureau chief of United Press International, "when I came upon a woman who had picked up a sheet off the sidewalk. It was the text of a statement by Deputy Mayor Sergei Stankevich describing the blocking of Gorbachev's planes in the Crimea."

"I convinced her to part with the paper. I rushed back to the UPI office and put out a terrific story, which nobody else had."

Reports like Nadler's were picked up by foreign broadcasting stations, including the Voice of America, Radio Liberty, the BBC, Deutsche Welle, and Kol Israel, and broadcast back into the Soviet Union.

Soviet citizens, no longer trusting their television, tuned into international broadcasts on short-wave. Even Gorbachev and his family, under house arrest in the Crimea, snared the BBC and Radio Liberty with a makeshift radio. The irony was exquisite: for decades, Soviet leaders denounced Radio Liberty as a subversive station. Radio Liberty became one of the heroes of the liberation of Moscow.

A secret network of free-lance Russian correspondents emerged from the woodwork. Andrei Babitskii, Mikhail Sokolov, Dmitry Volkov, made their way to the Parliament Building and regularly telephoned reports to radio headquarters in Munich, Germany. When the coup finally collapsed, Yeltsin announced that "Svoboda," as Radio Liberty is known in Russia, would be officially accredited in Moscow.

Another example of the plotters' incomprehensible negligence in controlling electronic communications was the fact that Artyom Borovik, managing editor of the independent newspaper *Sovershenno Sekretno*, or Top Secret, was able to broadcast regularly from the Parliament to CBS News in New York. Nor could the junta prevent Diane Sawyer of ABC News from interviewing Yeltsin inside the building.

A small, independent radio station blossomed into a serious competitor for Radio Liberty. This was *Ekho Moskvy*, or Echoes of Moscow, sponsored by the Moscow City Council and the Moscow University Department of Journalism. *Ekho Moskvy* stayed on the air throughout the coup, broadcasting about troop movements and other developments on a low power signal heard locally. Orders went out to shut down the station, but the radio journalists evaded suppression by constantly changing the transmitter's location.

"We listened to *Ekho Moskvy* all the time. It was terrific," said one Muscovite. "It was at least two to three hours ahead of Radio Liberty."

Another source of over-the-air information was Cable News Network. CNN has been available in Moscow in government offices and hotels over the last eighteen months. A 100-watt transmitter has been beaming a signal as a test prior to introducing pay cable service. Because the signal can be captured with a simple antenna, many Moscow citizens already had access to the "unofficial" CNN report.

Muscovites grab for copies of "Obshchaya Gazeta" or The Common Paper. From the start, this paper denounced the coup.

In mid-August American television bureaus in Moscow had no special resources for covering a coup. CNN had only two television crews on hand; ABC, four. All bureaus, however, immediately called for reinforcements as soon as they realized what was happening. Additional American crews from Eastern and Western Europe, as well as from the United States, began to arrive on Monday, August 19. Some tried entry without visas and were turned away at Moscow airport. Still others were admitted in the confusion.

"I was enormously impressed by the courage and energy of your American correspondents," said Alexander Khlopyanov of the Soviet Foreign Ministry. "They went to work instantly, never worrying about their own personal safety."

Why did the Moscow junta prove so incompetent in managing the media during their unsuccessful coup? Although fuller explanations will develop as more information becomes available, this much is clear already:

•In the two most recent precedents — the failed "anti-Party group" attempt against Nikita Khrushchev in 1957 and his successful ouster in 1964 — the press did as it was told by the winners. Khrushchev, after all, never allowed press independence as did Gorbachev. The junta apparently thought it would be sufficient in 1991 to announce the takeover in a loud voice, and then both the media and the nation would follow.

•The junta members were operating under a tight deadline, namely the departure of Gorbachev on vacation to the Crimea in early August and the expected signing of the Union Treaty on August 20. They did not have much time to prepare or to provide for precise management of the complex media situation.

•Yanayev and his cohorts probably could not have pulled all the plugs to blank out the press. Direct-dial telephones, telex, fax, and satellite links provide numerous channels of communication. Even if these channels had been blocked, the State Department would have authorized American correspondents to file pool reports over the U.S. embassy's secure lines. There was no way the junta's actions could have been hidden from the world.

•Finally, the usurpers' real aims were instantly transparent. Their public relations failure was horrendous. They tried and failed to present their coup as a constitutional transfer of power occasioned by an alleged Gorbachev illness and a deepening national crisis. If the transfer really was legal, why suppress part of the media? Why deploy tanks? Why tremble before the television camera?

Glasnost revealed the ugly side of Soviet life and prompted the usurpers to seize power in a vain effort to restore their kind of order. But glasnost also created major resistance to tyranny. That resistance, in the end, saved reform as well as Gorbachev's life.

CNN Reports

Meanwhile, In Washington... BY CANDY ALT CROWLEY

Washington in August, unbearably hot and oppressively humid, is generally recognized as no place to be. President Bush was vacationing at his summer home in Kennebunkport, Maine. Secretary of State James Baker was getting in some R&R on his ranch in Wyoming. Defense Secretary Richard Cheney had gone fishing in British Columbia. Congress was in recess, its members scattered around the world.

MONDAY, AUGUST 18,1991

The President of the United States was awakened shortly before midnight, Sunday, and told of the Soviet coup. The messenger was Brent Scowcroft, head of the National Security Council, one of the few top Bush aides on hand at the summer retreat. Scowcroft had seen the news on television.

Throughout the early hours of Monday morning, the U.S. White House "situation room" sought to stay on top of the evolving crisis, but there was little information beyond public knowledge to tell the President when he checked in around 6 a.m. The first official reaction was only an acknowledgement. In a written statement issued in Kennebunkport, Deputy Press Secretary Roman Popaduk told reporters, "We are aware of the press reports concerning President Gorbachev. We have no details at this time… .We are continuing to seek details."

George Bush sought to fill the information gap by working the phones. Before 8 a.m., he had spoken with British Prime Minister John Major, French President François Mitterand and German Chancellor Helmut Kohl, U.S. Secretary of State James Baker, and the U.S. deputy chief of mission in Moscow, Jim Collins. Collins, according to the President, had information probably "as sketchy as the rest of the world's."

Unsure who was in charge or who he would sit across the table from at the next U.S.-Soviet summit ("We didn't know who was alive and who was dead,"said one Bush aide.), the President hedged his bets in his first reaction to the coup. Meeting with the press corps at 7:50 a.m., Bush called the coup a "disturbing development" and probably "extra-constitutional," but there was no strong condemnation of those who had seized power.

Neither was there much in the way of support for Russian President Boris Yeltsin:

Q: "Mr. Yeltsin seems to have called for a general strike and protest. Do you support that?

The President: "Well we'll just see what happens on that."

Q: "Mr. Yeltsin has said that the Russian Federation will not abide by the new decrees. Do you support that, sir?"

The President: "Well, I support what I've outlined here as our principles, and certainly I can understand where an elected leader like Mr. Yeltsin is coming from.….I think what he is doing is simply expressing the will of the people there to have these reforms and have democracy, the steps already taken to democracy, strengthened. I hope that people heed his call."

The President's initial hesitancy was based on uncertainty about where Yeltsin stood. It reflected a deep-seated suspicion of Yeltsin within the White House, particularly on the part of Brent Scowcroft. The national security adviser's doubts dovetailed with the President's distaste for what he saw as Yeltsin's disloyalty to Gorbachev in the early days of glasnost. Still, by the end of the day, the President's tone was to change markedly.

Having dispatched an Air Force plane to pick up his vacationing secretaries of state and defense and Robert Strauss, the U.S. Ambassador-designate to the Soviet Union, the President decided to return to Washington. Convinced he needed his own envoy in Moscow, he wanted to swear in Strauss as soon as possible.

While the President was aloft, Deputy Secretary of State Lawrence Eagleburger was meeting with Viktor Komplektov, the Soviet ambassador to the U.S. This first official U.S.-Soviet contact since the coup was later described as "icy." Eagleburger all but scoffed at Komplektov's explanation of Gorbachev's "illness." When Komplektov tried to convey the coup leaders' pleasure at the President's "moderate" tone at his morning news conference, Eagleburger responded that the entire administration was outraged at the course of events. After handing over a letter pledging continued Soviet commitment to international agreements, the Soviet ambassador was gone in fifteen minutes.

Back at the White House, President Bush met with his

President Bush talks with Gorbachev for the first time since his house arrest. The twenty-minute conversation was described as "very emotional and effusive" according to a Bush aide.

Soviet Ambassador Komplektov leaves his embassy to meet with U.S. officials on August 19. The brief meeting was described as "icy."

national security advisers and was told there was little new to report from the scene. But a major change in the U.S. response to the coup was in the making.

Early Monday evening, in a written statement, the President placed the U.S. firmly in the Yeltsin camp. Condemning the Soviet takeover as a "misguided and illegitimate effort," he added, "we support President Yeltsin's call for restoration of the legally elected organs of power and the reaffirmation of the post of USSR President M. S. Gorbachev."

Senior administration officials trace the turnaround to a call placed shortly after Bush's first news conference. From inside the Russian White House, Yeltsin phoned the chargé d'affaires at the U.S. embassy in Moscow. Yeltsin's message: "We need your help." In particular, Yeltsin said, a call from Bush would be

helpful. That plea, and the pictures of the Russian president shouting his defiance of coup leaders from atop a Soviet tank made believers out of the Bush administration. Said one official, "We did not know until Monday afternoon and the Yeltsin call, and when Yeltsin stood on the tank, that there was anyone to support." Another added, "Whatever doubts we had about Yeltsin were mitigated by his sheer physical courage. The President was impressed."

TUESDAY, AUGUST 20,1991

When presidential spokesman Marlin Fitzwater entered the Oval Office on Tuesday at 7:15 a.m., he found the President at work at his computer in the study. On the screen was a "to-do" list, a mixture of mundane administrative chores and the outlines of an agenda the President would use for the National Security Council meeting later in the morning:

1. Make an assessment. How can we influence? arms control/economic aid? [The President had already said there would be no business as usual with the Soviets, but options actually to influence events were limited. One State Department official described U.S. programs, with the exception of grain sales, as "chicken feed."]

2. Get Marlin back to Kennebunkport. [Long-time presidential spokesman Fitzwater had been among the vacationing staffers when the coup began.]

3. Contact the South American Leaders. [Always a firm believer in the power of the global voice, the President wanted as many world leaders as possible on board condemning the coup plotters.]

4. Make sure the U.S. message is constant and steady. [Circumspect with his initial "soft" response, the President wanted to make sure the new leadership in the Soviet Union had gotten the message.]

5. Stay in touch with Yeltsin.

6. No politics. [Expecting a rash of complaints from Democratic opponents, the President did not want to be drawn into a political battle. In fact, other than some initial dissatisfaction with the President's first remarks, there was virtually no criticism of the President's handling of the crisis.]

7. Get our information out to our people.

8. Change work schedule. Meetings in Kennebunkport with Soviet experts. [Having envisioned a four-week vacation with minimal work, the President was anxious to return to Kennebunkport, but knew it could not be "vacation as usual" amidst so much uncertainty.]

Outgoing CIA Director William Webster opened the NSC meeting with a ten-minute agency report on the status quo. It was becoming increasingly clear that the coup was not a professional job. The airport remained open. Some opposition news media were operating. Perhaps most significantly, there had been no move to take Yeltsin into custody. A news conference by the Emergency Committee was generally seen in the U.S. as "amateur hour." Bush officials were also encouraged by the size and fervor of street opposition throughout the Soviet Union. Nevertheless, the tanks rolled.

Robert Gates, nominated to take Webster's place, followed the presentation with a lengthy list of various economic and other sanctions that could be considered as options. The President immediately ruled out two areas: arms control and grain sales. The former he saw as too important to use as leverage; the latter, he told aides, should be avoided in order not to get into a "Carter situation" where, "it hurt us more than it hurt them." Meeting with the press corps after the swearing-in of Ambassador Strauss, the President revealed that he had spoken with Boris Yeltsin. Aides say the phone call served to calm whatever anxieties remained about Yeltsin's intentions, at least in the short run. During the conversation Yeltsin emphasized that he was the Russian president, while Gorbachev was the Soviet president. Bush's support for both Yeltsin and Gorbachev was unequivocal during the Rose Garden news conference.

With Strauss headed for Moscow, and Secretary of State Baker on the way to Brussels for an emergency meeting of NATO foreign ministers, the President returned to Kennebunkport. "Basically, all we could do was stay in touch and watch it all unfold," said one administration official. "The framework of our policy was in place. There was not a lot more we could do."

WEDNESDAY, AUGUST 21, 1991

The effects of Hurricane Bob had brought rain to Kennebunkport Wednesday morning, dousing the President's plans for an early morning golf game. A briefing from Scowcroft made clear that the climate was changing in the Soviet Union as well.

Overnight, the unraveling of the coup had accelerated. Morning broadcast reports said a delegation of Russian officials, sympathetic to Mikhail Gorbachev, were on the way to the ousted President's dacha. Other reports told of a second plane, with some members of the Emergency Committee of Eight, also headed to the Crimea, while Boris Yeltsin was quoted as saying that leaders of the coup were trying to flee Moscow.

Thousands of Yeltsin supporters had spent the night around the Russian Parliament Building, a gutsy grassroots line of defense against attack. There were numerous reports that large sections of the Soviet military were abandoning the coup effort. Much of the news was confirmed, or repeated, by Yeltsin in a lengthy telephone call to President Bush at 8:30 a.m., U.S. time.

A short time later, the President spoke with Ambassador Robert Strauss, now in place at the U.S. embassy in Moscow.

Strauss had mostly second-hand reports, but nothing to contradict Yeltsin's assessment. British Prime Minister John Major, a frequent Bush contact during the crisis, added bits and pieces to the story about planes heading toward the Crimea.

By midmorning, the prevailing feeling was that the beginning of the end was at hand. The coup, it seemed, was disintegrating rapidly. But, when he appeared at 10:30 a.m., the President hedged.

"Overall," he told reporters, "while the situation remains highly fluid and uncertain, I think it is safe to say that the situation appears somewhat more positive than in the earliest hours of this coup...But I guess I would say to the American people these developments are positive."

In response to a question, Bush also reminded reporters of his Monday statement that "coups can fail." The original statement was based on nothing more than a bit of history and the President's wishful thinking. Forty-eight hours later, the words looked prophetic.

Weeks after the coup was over and Gorbachev restored, a top Bush official reflected on the President's restraint Wednesday morning. "It was more than the usual 'prudence thing.' The President was truly troubled about the fate of Gorbachev," said the official. "It was clear the coup was falling apart. What we did not know was what or who we would find when the dust settled."

The President touched on the uncertainties when asked during the crisis to speculate on Gorbachev's post-coup standing. "Well, who knows?" he responded, "I mean, we can't even get in touch with Mr. Gorbachev. But Yeltsin is strongly supporting him, and so are we." When the President left the news conference Wednesday morning, he told reporters he would keep trying to contact Gorbachev.

After taking a brief phone call from Secretary Baker in Brussels, Bush returned to his Kennebunkport home and planned a fishing trip. Headed back to the compound with reports, Fitzwater underscored the doubts now plaguing the administration. Asked about reports that some of the conspirators were headed for Gorbachev's summer home, Fitzwater

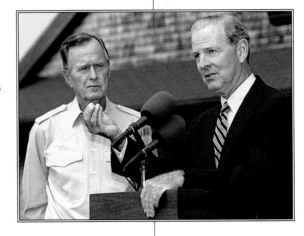

At a news conference on August 22, a relieved Baker (right) and Bush talk about U.S. post-coup policies.

said, "We don't really know where they're going. We don't know what they're going to say. Are they going to make a deal? Are they going to say 'join us'? Going to say 'we're sorry'? Are they going to take him under arrest? Take him out of there? Shoot him? We don't have any idea."

Forty-five minutes later, the answers came. Bush and his buddies had not even had time to get their fishing lines wet when military aide Wayne Justice, back on shore, relayed a message over the short-wave radio that a "head of state" was on the phone. Because such transmissions can be monitored, Justice did not identify the caller more specifically. Turning his boat around, the President and his party returned to Walker's Point. When President Bush picked up the phone, Mikhail Gorbachev was on the line.

The twenty-minute call, Gorbachev's second (after a talk with Boris Yeltsin) included little time for details. It was, according to a Bush aide "very emotional and effusive." Gorbachev thanked the President and the American people. "Their personal relationship came through," said the aide.

In front of the news media for the second time in three hours, the President was fuzzy on details of Gorbachev's confinement or immediate plans, but he was very clear that the climate over Moscow and Washington had turned sunny.

"It's a very fine day. It's been an emotional day in a sense... being right in the middle of this history. And I think people know of my respect for Gorbachev, indeed, the way I feel about him. And I was just delighted to hear that he was fine, delighted that he appeared to be well."

Wednesday evening, George Bush's vision of a new world order, shaken by the political earthquake in the Soviet Union, began to settle back into a semblance of calm, though aftershocks would continue to register. "Everything went back into place," said a top Bush official, "and nothing will be the same again."

CNN Reports

Soviet Nuclear Security: The Pentagon View

BY WOLF BLITZER

When the first TASS report announcing Gorbachev's unspecified illness reached Washington around 11:30 p.m., Sunday evening, Pentagon officials as well as analysts at the Central Intelligence Agency and the National Security Agency rushed back to their monitoring stations. They were under pressure to find out what was going on. Like everyone else in the world, they were surprised by the timing of the coup, although for months they had been predicting something along these lines.

"I can't say anybody anticipated the coup right at the moment," National Security Adviser Brent Scowcroft would say the next day. Sen. Sam Nunn (D-Ga.), chairman of the Armed Services Committee, would go further. "There were a lot of experts who have been pointing out some of these dangers — one danger, of course, has been a military coup. But I don't know of anyone who predicted precisely what was going to happen."

By 12:30 a.m. (7:30 a.m., Monday, in Moscow), a top CIA Sovietologist had already concluded that a coup had taken place. That assessment, conveyed to the White House four hours later, was based largely on two factors: the language used in the communiqué issued by the Emergency Committee and the fact that communications — scrambled as well as unscrambled — going in and out of Gorbachev's summer dacha in the Crimea, had come to a dead halt. The U.S. had stepped up listening — and heard nothing.

Of immediate concern, of course, was the security of the Soviet nuclear arsenal. Observation by satellites and other intelligence-gathering equipment was intensified. All major air bases and strategic rocket installations were monitored. There was no high-level direct contact between U.S. and Soviet officials. A decision was made in Washington to do nothing that might enhance the authority of the coup plotters.

What followed during those three tense days was a delicate and almost silent minuet that could only have been played out by the superpowers. During the four decades of the Cold War, they had honed their skills in learning just how to read each other's intentions.

After the crisis, Pentagon spokesman Pete Williams and other U.S. officials discounted the danger publicly. "We don't believe there was any increase in the risk of the use of nuclear weapons during the coup," Williams said. "We don't believe there's any increase in the risk since the coup." Bush made the same point in public: "We see no reason to be concerned about that. Our people are taking a hard look at that all the time."

Privately, Pentagon officials were very nervous as they watched and waited. And word came from the White House not to do anything that might alarm the Soviets. "This isn't the time to threaten militarily or to move forces around just to show machoism," Bush said on Tuesday. "That's not what's called for here."

The Pentagon as a result did not scramble any aircraft or move any aircraft carriers. And there was no change in the U.S. military's state of alert — the so-called DefCon, or defense condition, status. The last thing the U.S. wanted to do was to escalate the crisis and reinforce Soviet military anxieties. U.S. officials knew that Soviet satellite intelligence would immediately pick up any changes in the U.S. strategic posture.

Early during the coup, therefore, U.S. officials sought to reassure the Soviets. Officials told reporters at the Pentagon that while long-term U.S. and NATO interests might be deeply affected by the political situation in Moscow, they did not see any immediate strategic threat. And they added that the acting Soviet leadership appointed by the Emergency Committee was showing no inclination to trigger a serious military confrontation with the West.

Soviet generals, including the commanders of the Air Force, the Navy, and the Strategic Rocket Forces, were also nervous as they discovered that Defense Minister Dmitry Yazov was a member of the Emergency Committee. Yet despite Yazov's involvement, they had deep doubts about what was happening. Knowing that Washington would be watching very closely, they decided to take an extraordinary set of measures, unnoticed by the outside world, designed clearly to reassure the United States.

During those critical three days, the Soviets began to move their mobile strategic nuclear missiles back to their garrisons, knowing U.S. spy satellites were watching. By exposing these missiles to more vulnerable locations, U.S. officials say, the Soviet military high command was signaling its desire to avoid any accidental nuclear confrontation. The message was heard — loud and clear. "There were no actions that were picked up by anybody that sent any signals of concern on that in terms of movement or things you would associate with any concern for a nuclear threat of any kind," Bush said.

And those Soviet commanders opposed to the coup did

more. U.S. electronic intelligence picked up considerable Soviet communications traffic during the coup, but it was largely one-way: messages going out from the Defense Ministry in Moscow with few replies coming in from bases around the country. Many base commanders, officials say, simply did not answer their phones.

The U.S. has a good idea how the Soviet nuclear command-and-control system works. At the time, officials did not know that the coup plotters had taken the nuclear codes from Gorbachev. "There was a different leadership," Scowcroft later confirmed. "Actual control for a time did shift some."

But even if they had known, officials insist that they would not have been overly alarmed. They say the Soviet nuclear stockpile is perhaps even more secure than that of the United States. "The Soviets have given every evidence of recognizing they've got a special responsibility as a nuclear power to make certain they maintain control of those systems," Defense Secretary Dick Cheney said.

"It appears that there are two separate sets of Soviet codes," said Matthew Bunn, an arms-control expert in Washington, "one coming from the civilian leadership and one coming from the military leadership and that both of these codes are necessary in order to launch a Soviet land-based missile at the United States."

Even before the coup, the Soviets knew that the security of their nuclear weapons was a source of great concern in Washington. On August 8, the chief of the General Staff, General Mikhail Moiseyev, had written to the U.S. chairman of the Joint Chiefs of Staff, General Colin Powell, proposing talks on nuclear weapons security. "The Soviets have been at pains to reassure us that their nuclear forces would remain under central control, despite the crisis they've faced in some of the republics," said a senior Pentagon official.

Gorbachev, despite the decline of his political power since the coup, remains in overall control of Soviet nuclear weapons. But now he shares that responsibility with Defense

Minister Yevgeny Shaposhnikov, the former commander of the Air Force who sided with Russian Federation President Boris Yeltsin during the coup. "At present," says Shaposhnikov, "there are no grounds for concern, and the international community should rest assured that everything is fine."

But the disintegration of the Soviet Union raises new questions about Soviet nuclear power. Immediately after the coup, for example, Yeltsin welcomed word that Kazakhstan did not want nuclear weapons on its soil. He said Kazakhstan had declared itself a nuclear-free republic and that all strategic weapons on its soil would be moved to Russia. But two weeks later, Kazakhstan's influential president, Nursultan Nazarbayev, said he was "absolutely" opposed to having all of the Soviet Union's nuclear weapons stockpiled only "in one republic, irrespective of how large that republic is."

Western analysts say these apparently conflicting statements underline their worst-case nightmare scenario: smaller republics declaring themselves nuclear powers and refusing to give up their tactical nuclear weapons. Soviet Foreign Ministry spokesman Vitaly Churkin says there's no reason for concern. "We have a very clear understanding among everyone involved that we're going to have a united army and a central command of the nuclear weapons," he says.

But like so much else in today's Soviet Union, that assertion is being seriously questioned by both Soviet and Western experts. "Who knows what will happen in half a year or in a year?" asks Soviet military expert Alexei Arbatov. "Some extremist forces might come [to power] in some of the republics, and they might claim the right to have control over the nuclear weapons."

In describing why the coup failed, this Soviet officer explained, "It does no harm to want to do something, but you need the muscle to do it." The Army would not provide the muscle.

But Soviet military leaders express reassuring thoughts. The new chief of the General Staff, General Vladimir Lobov, says the Soviet Union no longer regards the U.S. as a military threat. He says it's "absurd" for the U.S. to see the Soviet Union as a threat. "It is my belief that the threat on the part of the U.S. is gone — a thing of the past."

Indeed, Lobov says the U.S. and the Soviet Union should expand military contacts, including exchange programs that will enable Soviet officers to attend U.S. military academies and vice-versa. He says more than 90 percent of the Soviet people favor closer ties with the U.S.

Like Shaposhnikov, Lobov says that all nuclear weapons in the Soviet Union remain "in reliable hands." Still, he wants talks with the U.S. and also with NATO to eliminate all short-range tactical weapons because, he says, these weapons are more prone to various accidents. Experts in Washington believe that the U.S. and other Western nations should continue to push for even greater control of Soviet nuclear forces. "It's something we have a very strong interest in knowing and we should work with them in trying to avert any sort of accidental launches," says Gabriel Schoenfeld of the Center for Strategic and International Studies.

Shaposhnikov says he is ready to begin such talks. "I believe that the time will come when we will reach the frontiers of understanding and we will hold such negotiations. I'm not opposed to them."

Another reassuring factor, says Shaposhnikov—only 49 years old—is that those military leaders who supported the coup were from a different generation. They were men born in the 1920s, who could not grasp the degree of popular support for perestroika and democracy. Shaposhnikov says his generation of younger men now in control of the military have no such problem. Lobov adds: "The people here have changed. The nation has changed. We are all aware of democracy. We have had a taste of democracy — of free life."

SEVEN DAYS THAT SHOOK THE WORLD

A Shaken World

AFTERWORD BY STUART H. LOORY

As with any revolution, the aftermath of the August 1991 Kremlin coup promised instability not only for the Soviet Union but for the entire world far into the future. On November 7, 1991, the USSR was just one year short of its diamond jubilee. Instead the famous Red Square celebration, when the nation traditionally paraded its military might, was cancelled. This superpower, shaken to its foundations, has fallen so far that it is a country without a name.

The symbols of power had disappeared: Moscow was capital of a country without a flag, without a national anthem, and without a national day. For weeks after the coup attempt, the leadership all but paralyzed itself into inactivity.

Boris Yeltsin, that tower of strength atop a tank, fell ill and then hied himself off to the Crimea for a two-week vacation, reportedly to write a book. Mikhail Gorbachev struggled to regain some semblance of power. He also wrote a book and candidly admitted he ignored warnings before August 18 from George Bush, among others, that a coup was in the making. The leaders of the other republics all sought safe political boats from which to navigate the shifting currents of history in the making. Helmsmanship was easier in a time of totalitarianism.

The question of what comes next perplexes observers. One hesitates to accept the clear evidence pointing to continued disintegration of the nation, to political chaos, ethnic conflict, and economic deprivation. Among Soviet friends who were skeptical and pessimistic about the future of their country in the pre-coup days, there is now a strained optimism as if they cannot bear to confront the real picture.

CNN REPORTS
244

A Shaky Future

The plotters of the coup accurately diagnosed both the scope and the breadth of the nation's problems. The inhabitants of the former Soviet empire confront a crisis with many facets.

There is the *political* crisis of how to reorganize the empire. How many republics will emerge? What will be their relationship to each other? Which ones will have their own armed forces, their own currencies, their own international relationships?

There is the *economic* crisis. How do they take an economy driven into breakdown and rebuild it so that the inhabitants of the newly independent republics can again feed, clothe, and house themselves in a manner to which they should be accustomed in such resource-rich lands. There is the *internal security* crisis. In an economy of scarcity, a criminal element has arisen that renders citizens of the former Soviet Union unsafe on the streets and in their homes. Goods that were always fair game for the criminally unscrupulous are now even more prone to theft. There is the crisis of a *deteriorating infrastructure*. Streets, sewers, water supplies, transportation facilities, and buildings are going to ruin. In cities like Moscow and St. Petersburg, buildings dating back to the eighteenth century, which have withstood more than two centuries of war and other hardships, have been allowed to decay in the past five years, perhaps irreparably. Whole sections of downtown Moscow look as bad as the worst slums in Western cities.

There is a crisis of *population migration*. Too many of the best intellects in the country, instead of trying to solve the common problems, are looking for ways to emigrate. Once emigration is completely freed, the danger of a brain drain lurks in the background.

There is a crisis of worsening *racial, ethnic, national, and religious conflict*. The Soviet Union has been revealed as a flawed melting pot. Once Communist oppression disappeared, various groups again turned on each other. Their conflicts have been intensified by competition for scarce goods and services.

There is a crisis of *truth in history*. "Ordinary people" took part in the oppression and terrorism. There were, for example, millions of informers, to say nothing of the secret police, tyrannic bureaucrats, and other kinds of opportunists. It is often said that no one in the country was from a family untouched by Stalin's terror. Similarly, few in the country were from families that did not, in some way, take part in the oppression. How will they face facts and recognize their contribution to state terror?

Finally, there is a crisis of *perspective*. Too many citizens expect instant economic results from the shift away from socialism without the necessary personal exertion. Too many others expect democracy to be imposed without creating winners and losers in a system where free choice will prevail. And still others object that they will have to make decisions previously made for them. In short, too many do not understand it takes effort and good will to operate a democracy.

How do Mikhail Gorbachev or Boris Yeltsin, Anatoly Sobchak or Gavril Popov (mayors of St. Petersburg and Moscow, respectively) or republic leaders like Zviad Gamsakhurdia (Georgia), Vytautas Landsbergis (Lithuania), or Leonid Kravchuk (Ukraine) begin solving their nations' problems?

All of the politicians know that difficult decisions involving great hardships for the people are necessary. Few have been willing to take the steps necessary to set solutions in motion. Their own positions would be jeopardized. In a market economy those steps would raise prices to the point where goods and services were beyond the ability of many to pay. Unemployment would be brought into the open. Inequities in the allocations of housing and other goods, though they long existed, would have to be admitted.

The hundreds of thousands of troops coming home from bases in Eastern Europe are an example. There is no housing for them and there are no jobs. Yet the government cannot afford to keep them in uniform. That is the kind of problem that has brought military coups to other countries in the past.

Another example involves Soviet central television, with 90,000 workers throughout the country. But its operations have been drastically scaled back as independent republics and cities such as Moscow and St. Petersburg have taken over their own broadcasting functions. The central TV workforce must be cut to 25,000 — perhaps in six months. Thousands of middle-class, white-collar workers will be thrown out onto the streets.

Failure to heed the warning signs could lead to tragedy. The reasonable solution to the nation's problems would appear to start with formation of a common economic market in which each of the republics has political independence but all band together for mutually beneficial economic relations. History, geography, economic infrastructure, and population distribution mandate that solution.

The Ukraine, for example, is the second largest republic in the country after Russia. Though it has never known real independence, now the Ukraine is talking about raising its own army and printing its own money, ultimate acts of independence. Such talk actually creates a danger of armed conflict with Russia. The issue would be the Donets Basin, a mineral-rich area in the eastern Ukraine where the population is more Russian than Ukrainian. Russia would not give up that territory easily.

Professor Yuri Medvedkov of Ohio State University, is a world-renowned economic geographer who emigrated from the Soviet Union in 1986. In his view, the surviving republics "will be forced to cooperate. They are still linked by the impossibility of competing with the Western nations. They will develop as a common market with difficulty, with hardship, with inconsistency."

It will take great forbearance, however, on the part of jealous leaders. Yeltsin, for example, returned from vacation to a government that had lost its prime minister while he was away. After two weeks of drift, he asked the Russian Federation's Parliament to name him prime minister as well as president and revealed he would, by fiat, declare necessary reforms into being. Those included freeing of long-controlled prices, privatization of many businesses, and severe cutbacks into the payments that would be made to Gorbachev's central government. Yeltsin called on other republics to follow his lead but said Russia would go it alone if necessary. Gorbachev's popularity began to fall when he made similar statements more than a year before the attempted coup.

Most observers expect that instability will dominate the political picture for many years. Politicians like Eduard Shevardnadze and Alexander Yakovlev see the continued danger of a right-wing coup. Organizations like Pamyat, the right-wing, nationalistic, anti-Semitic Russian political association have a great deal of support in the country.

If the optimists see only instability, the pessimists see chaos. They foresee the danger of civil war or another right-wing coup attempt. They point to the manner in which bureaucrats of the discredited Communist Party are burrowing into the new political organizations, even Yeltsin's. Instead of inspiring change, these officials are using their new positions to settle old scores. "There used to be rules for the way the game was played. Now it is the same game, but there are no longer any rules," said a central television correspondent.

Or, in the ironic words of Leonid Kravchenko, the fired head of Soviet television, speaking on behalf of former Communist Party officials, "We may have to call on the Western press to protect our civil rights."

It is a world turned upside down, a world in which only one thing is certain: Change will go on.

Conventional wisdom these days says that the information explosion which helped open

A celebrant holds a portrait of Czar Nicholas II at ceremonies returning Leningrad to its former name, St. Petersburg.

the Soviet Union to the outside world will prevail, further accelerating the drive toward liberalization. That is a reasonable and hopeful outlook. It ignores, however, the demonic forces that have provided so much anguish in the twentieth century. Despotism has a way of dealing with technology and information by bending their benefits into chains of bondage.

The entire world has a stake in the outcome of the anguish in the Soviet Union. For example, there is the problem of keeping the Soviet nuclear arsenal under control. As the old empire breaks up, controlling the 30,000 nuclear weapons it created becomes more and more difficult. In the world's largest country, the prospect of a many-sided civil war involving nuclear weapons has dangerous implications far beyond the borders of the former USSR. Similarly starvation or other instability could cause problems that would reverberate dangerously throughout the entire world, as those in Yugoslavia are now shaking Europe.

After Nikita Khrushchev's fall in October 1964 the clock of progress was turned back, and it was not until more than a generation later that it again started to tick forward.

When Gorbachev convinced the leaders of the seven most important capitalist nations in the world to give his country associate membership in their group, it confirmed the idea that the well-being of the new Soviet Union is important to the rest of the world.

The task for Gorbachev, Yeltsin, and other leaders inside the country is to convince the people that voluntary sharing of sacrifice is necessary to bring lasting progress. Most world leaders have shown they are ready to respond generously to initiatives for political democracy and economic freedom in the old Soviet Union.

COUP RESISTORS

VADIM V. BAKATIN

Bakatin, 53, was fired as Soviet interior minister in December 1990 under pressure from Kremlin hard-liners who distrusted his reformist views. During the coup, Bakatin rallied to the side of Russian leader Boris Yeltsin to help organize resistance. Soviet President Mikhail Gorbachev later rewarded Bakatin by making him KGB chief to replace Vladimir Kryuchkov, a key member of the junta.

An ethnic Russian, Bakatin was born into a well-off family in the Siberian coal-mining town of Kiselevsk. He joined the Communist Party in 1964 and rose steadily through the ranks until his appointment as interior minister in 1988.

Condemning the old KGB as a tool of state terror, Bakatin vowed upon taking over to reduce drastically the agency's size and activities. He pledged to eliminate all domestic spying and to give citizens access to their KGB files and, to avoid even the appearance of a conflict of interest, fired his own son who was a KGB agent.

NURSULTAN NAZARBAYEV

Nazarbayev, 51, denounced the putsch on its second day and resigned from the Communist Party. He revealed that in the coup's earliest hours, Central Committee members in Moscow secretly had urged local Party organizations to obey the junta. He also made a key phone call on the second day, extracting a promise from junta member Yanayev not to carry out an expected attack on Russia's Parliament Building, the anti-coup stronghold.

Nazarbayev became one of the most powerful men in the Soviet Union soon after his appointment as Kazakhstan's leader in 1989. Resource-rich Kazakhstan is the second largest Soviet republic after Russia. In recent years, he boosted his stature by becoming the chief spokesman for the mostly Muslim central Asian republics

An ethnic Kazakh, Nazarbayev joined the Communist Party in 1962. Rising quickly through Party ranks, Nazarbayev was appointed prime minister of the republic in 1984. He was elected president of Kazakhstan in 1990, the first such election in the republic's history.

ALEXANDER V. RUTSKOI

Rutskoi, 44, was elected vice-president of Russia in June 1991. Two months later, the charismatic Afghan War hero acted as Yeltsin's ablest lieutenant in defeating the coup. Yeltsin put Rutskoi in charge of defending the Russian Parliament Building. But nothing epitomized Rutskoi's pivotal role more than his flight to the Crimea to liberate Gorbachev and arrest members of the junta.

Before entering politics, Rutskoi had achieved fame by surviving a plane crash and imprisonment by enemy guerrillas in Afghanistan. His reputation as a survivor gave him influence as a Russian Parliament deputy.

A long-time member of the Communist Party, Rutskoi nonetheless broke ranks with Party hard-liners when they tried to unseat Yeltsin as Parliament leader. Rutskoi led the defection of about 100 reform-minded Communists to Yeltsin's side, assuring him of victory. As a leader of the new group and a war hero, Rutskoi was the perfect running mate to help Yeltsin appeal to moderate Communists, military, police, and KGB.

YEVGENY I. SHAPOSHNIKOV

Shaposhnikov, 49, commanded the Soviet Air Force, and his refusal to obey the junta helped to bring about the coup's collapse. The colonel general, a former fighter pilot, was ordered to lead an assault on the Russian Parliament Building. He declined, lobbying Yazov to withdraw the troops and threatening to use the Air Force against any attackers.

A grateful Gorbachev later appointed the liberal-minded Shaposhnikov to be the nation's new defense minister, making him the youngest head of the Soviet armed forces since Leon Trotsky.

One of Shaposhnikov's first acts in his new post was to resign from the Communist Party. He has said he favors creating an all-volunteer military with at least 500,000 fewer troops. But Shaposhnikov is no dove. After the Gulf War, he urged that Soviet Air Force technology be upgraded to match that of the United States. He also has said a pullout of Soviet troops from the newly independent Baltic nations must wait until 1994, when the withdrawal from Eastern Europe is completed. He has vowed that all Soviet nuclear weapons will remain under one, central command.

EDUARD A. SHEVARDNADZE

Shevardnadze, 62, acted as the prophet of the coup drama, foretelling it in December 1990 when he resigned as Soviet foreign minister. Shevardnadze had warned that a hard-line dictatorship was coming, but his words went unheeded by Gorbachev. When the coup began, he condemned it and rallied to the side of Yeltsin to help the resistance.

After three Muscovites were killed during the coup, Shevardnadze suggested in a speech that they should be honored by being buried in the Kremlin wall. To make room, he added, "heroes" there now could be moved.

Shevardnadze's stunning resignation was taken as a betrayal by Gorbachev, who had known his friend since they were teen-agers. Together they had concluded sweeping arms-control treaties with the United States, pulled Soviet forces out of Afghanistan, and made possible the collapse of Communist regimes in Eastern Europe. After resigning, Shevardnadze founded a coalition called the Democratic Reform Movement, which seems poised after the coup to become a major political force.

ANATOLY A. SOBCHAK

Sobchak, 53, had already achieved fame before the coup as the reformist mayor of Leningrad and a star democrat in the Soviet Parliament. On August 19, he prevented a bloodbath and foiled the junta's plan to take control of the Soviet Union's second largest city. Flying back to Leningrad after meeting in Moscow with Yeltsin, Sobchak convinced the local military commander, General Samsonov, to disobey orders to send tanks into the city. Next, Sobchak condemned the putsch in a televised speech and called on the city to resist it.

Sobchak moved to Leningrad in the 1970s to teach law. After years of declining to join the Communist Party, Sobchak changed his mind in 1988 and became a member, then resigned in 1990.

The charismatic Sobchak has long been touted as a possible Kremlin leader. As a trusted advisor to both Yeltsin and Gorbachev, Sobchak acts as a go-between, yet remains independent from both. But he faces formidable challenges as mayor of a city (now, again, St. Petersburg) badly in need of new industry and investment.

ALEXANDER N. YAKOVLEV

Yakovlev, 67, quit the Communist Party on August 16, 1991, warning that a clique of Stalinists threatened to turn back the clock on reforms. Two days later, Yakovlev's fear became reality. After the coup collapsed, he urged his long-time friend Mikhail Gorbachev to resign as leader of the Communist Party. One day later, he did.

The outspoken Yakovlev is often referred to as the architect of glasnost, because his ideas provided much of the intellectual framework for Gorbachev's reforms. The two men met in 1971, when Yakovlev held a powerful post as the Communist Party Central Committee's chief of propaganda. But in 1973 Yakovlev was "banished" to Canada as ambassador for writing an attack on Russian nationalism that did not sit well with Soviet leader Brezhnev.

When Gorbachev became Soviet leader he recruited Yakovlev for his inner circle. But the two men had a falling out in 1991 over Yakovlev's growing conviction that communism was a lost cause and could not be reformed. In July of 1991, Yakovlev joined Shevardnadze in founding the Democratic Reform Movement.

BORIS N. YELTSIN

Yeltsin, 60, emerged on August 21 as the victorious hero over the coup plotters and the most powerful man in the Soviet Union. It was more than a little ironic that four years after Gorbachev drummed Yeltsin out of the top ranks of the Communist Party, Gorbachev needed the democratically elected president of Russia to save him from political, if not actual, death.

Yeltsin had risen to become secretary of the Central Committee for Construction and boss of the Moscow Communist Party when he was tapped in 1987 to join the Party's ruling Politburo. But in October of that year, Yeltsin broke with Gorbachev, sharply criticizing the slow pace of reform. Gorbachev forced him to resign from his Party posts. From then on, the populist Yeltsin began appealing directly to the masses. The strategy worked.

In May of 1990, he was elected leader of the Russian Republic by its Parliament. Next, he called for the creation of a Russian presidency. On June 12, 1991, Yeltsin was elected president in the first popular election of Russia's 1,000-year history.

COUP PLOTTERS

OLEG D. BAKLANOV

Baklanov, 59, joined the junta and signed the decrees by which the group maintained its brief grip on power. He brought influence to the group as deputy chief of the State Defense Council. The hard-line Baklanov, whose career in the Soviet military-industrial complex had won him a Lenin Prize, was arrested after the coup and charged with treason.

A weapons expert, Baklanov had shown hard-line leanings more than a year before the coup when he helped convince Gorbachev to drop a radical plan to save the economy. In June 1991, while Gorbachev was out of Moscow, Baklanov supported an unsuccessful bid by Soviet Prime Minister Pavlov to seize emergency economic powers.

Born in Kharkov, in the Ukraine, Baklanov systematically worked his way up the ladder of Soviet industry. Along the way, he joined the Communist Party and rose to become Central Committee secretary in charge of the military-industrial complex. Gorbachev named him deputy chairman of the State Defense Council in 1991.

VALERY I. BOLDIN

Boldin, 56, had been Soviet President Gorbachev's chief of staff since 1985. But when coup leaders went to the Crimean dacha where they ordered Gorbachev to be confined and insisted that he give up power, Boldin was among them. After years of keeping Gorbachev's appointments and protecting him from unwanted visitors, Boldin betrayed his boss.

An ethnic Russian, Boldin owed his rise through the ranks of the Kremlin staff entirely to Gorbachev. Boldin was never a public figure. He was a career aide, known to be conservative, and his distaste for Gorbachev's reforms eventually overcame any loyalty to the man.

He joined the Communist Party in 1960 and took a job as an assistant to the editors of the official government newspaper *Pravda*. His rise in the Party started in 1961, when he worked part-time for the staff of its Central Committee. In 1981, Gorbachev helped Boldin obtain a post as assistant to a Central Committee secretary, and in 1985 tapped Boldin to be his personal aide.

VLADIMIR A. KRYUCHKOV

Kryuchkov, 67, the KGB chief and a mastermind of the coup, remained unrepentant after its collapse. During questioning after his arrest, Kryuchkov said: "I regret nothing I've done. If I could do it again from the beginning, I would do it more energetically, deprive Russia of her leadership sooner."

Kryuchkov was still a defense factory worker in Stalingrad when he joined the Communist Party at age 20. After receiving a law degree from the All-Union Jurisprudence Institute in nearby Saratov, he worked briefly as a prosecutor before applying to the Higher Diplomacy School of the Soviet Ministry of Foreign Affairs in Moscow. After graduating, he was appointed third secretary in the Soviet embassy in Hungary.

During four years in Budapest, Kryuchkov became a protegé of Soviet Ambassador Yuri V. Andropov, the future KGB chief and Kremlin leader. In 1956, both men took part in the crushing of the Hungarian revolution by Soviet forces. In 1988, after becoming a member of the Party's ruling Politburo, Kryuchkov was named KGB chairman by Gorbachev.

ANATOLY I. LUKIANOV

Lukianov, 61, protested his innocence after the coup, but few believed him. A friend and law school classmate of Gorbachev, Lukianov did nothing to oppose the putsch, and some believe he helped plan it. Gorbachev said he believed the junta intentionally kept Lukianov "behind the scenes, to give a touch of legality to the situation."

Lukianov, Speaker of the Supreme Soviet, admitted after the coup that plotters had told him of their plans beforehand, but denied ever backing the coup. He insisted that he had privately appealed to the junta to pull troops out of Moscow and rescind its decrees. Lawmakers voted overwhelmingly to strip him of parliamentary immunity so he could face trial.

Lukianov joined the Communist Party in 1955. He worked as legal advisor to the Supreme Soviet in the 1960s, becoming an expert on the nation's constitution, and in the 1970s held a series of administrative posts. Lukianov was appointed deputy chairman of the Supreme Soviet Presidium in 1988 and elected in 1990 to be the body's speaker.

VALENTIN S. PAVLOV

Pavlov, 54, the Soviet prime minister, was one of the junta members who mysteriously came down with "coup flu" on August 20, just as they started to face stiffer resistance. Some reports said Pavlov suffered a stroke; others said he took large doses of drugs and checked into a hospital complaining of hypertension.

Pavlov studied at Moscow's Finance and Economics Institute and later worked as a tax inspector and state price-setter before Gorbachev appointed him Soviet finance minister in 1989. After becoming the nation's prime minister in December of 1990, Pavlov took the drastic and unpopular step of seizing all 50- and 100-rouble banknotes from the people in order to curb inflation. In April of 1991, he doubled or tripled state prices on bread, meat, milk, fish, and other items in another highly criticized action.

Pavlov made headlines abroad when he accused Western banks of plotting to overthrow Gorbachev by flooding the Soviet Union with smuggled banknotes to create hyperinflation. A few months later, his involvement with the hard-line coup plotters resulted in his arrest.

YURI S. PLEKHANOV

Plekhanov, 51, was a key figure in the betrayal of Gorbachev. As the KGB officer in charge of presidential security — similar to the U.S. Secret Service — Plekhanov was supposed to protect Gorbachev. Instead, he helped the junta keep Gorbachev in a Crimean dacha under house arrest. One day after the putsch failed, Gorbachev fired Plekhanov from the KGB and stripped him of his military rank as a lieutenant general.

In 1951, Plekhanov became a leader of the Komsomol Communist Party youth organization in Moscow. He graduated from the Moscow State Pedagogical Institute, completing courses in the school's correspondence division, and moved over to a Party post in the Bauman District of the city, where he worked until 1964.

In 1967 he began his career in the KGB, becoming first an officer and later, in 1970, head of an entire department. He remained in this position until 1983, when he was appointed head of the KGB's 9th Directorate, including the presidential security service.

BORIS K. PUGO

Pugo, 54, the Soviet interior minister, was a key instigator of the coup. As the nation's police chief, Pugo controlled most of the Soviet security apparatus. His first move on becoming minister in December 1990 was to send joint army-police patrols into the streets of major cities. In June 1991, he called for a state of emergency to deal with what he said was nationwide disorder during Russia's presidential election. Nobody listened. Two months later, on August 19, Pugo emerged as the most hard-line member of the eight-man State Committee on the State of Emergency.

Pugo became the head of Latvia's KGB in 1980. In 1984, he was appointed Communist Party boss of the republic. Pugo was summoned to Moscow in 1988 to run the Party's Control Commission, requiring him to check up on Party members and discipline or expel disloyal ones.

When the coup failed, Pugo and his wife used a pistol in what appears to have been an attempted double suicide. Pugo died from a shot through the mouth. His wife survived.

ALEXANDER I. TIZYAKOV

Tizyakov, 65, was the least-known figure of the *vosmyorka*, the eight-man junta which tried to seize power. Tizyakov's role was similar to that of junta member Oleg Baklanov, deputy chief of the State Defense Council. Together, the two men could claim to speak for the Soviet military-industrial complex, which was clearly unhappy with the direction of Gorbachev's reforms. Tizyakov aspired to be Soviet prime minister under the post-coup government. Instead, he was arrested for treason.

Born near the Russian city of Sverdlovsk, Tizyakov fought in World War II and was decorated as a military hero. Later he rose to become a Party organizer and received an appointment as chief engineer of a Sverdlovsk production association.

In 1990, Tizyakov was named president of the Association of Soviet State Enterprises and Industrial, Construction, Transport, and Communications Facilities. He often claimed that the organization spoke for all Soviet industries, but in reality its membership consisted mostly of defense-related enterprises.

GENNADY I. YANAYEV

Yanayev, 53, the Soviet vice-president who assumed power as titular leader during the putsch, was a pliable front man for the rest of the junta. At the news conference on the first day of the coup, reporters laughed out loud at Yanayev's shaking hands and unconvincing lies about the alleged ill health of the ousted Soviet President.

Yanayev owed his post entirely to Gorbachev, who browbeat the Supreme Soviet into approving Yanayev as vice-president. Yanayev became Gorbachev's yes-man, saying all the right things about the need for reform.

Trained as an engineer, Yanayev also earned a master's degree in history and a law degree. He rose through the ranks of the Communist Party, eventually becoming chairman of the All-Union Central Council of Trade Unions. In 1990 he was appointed a secretary of the Party's Central Committee. He voted against democratic reform proposals and opposed granting sovereignty to the republics.

After the coup, Gorbachev said: "I see that the Congress was right when it did not accept the vice-president in the first round."

DMITRY T. YAZOV

Yazov, 67, was perhaps the most pivotal member of the junta. No coup could possibly have succeeded without the backing of the burly Soviet defense minister. Yazov, who had received the rank of marshal in April of 1990 from Gorbachev, did not approve of the Soviet President's Cold War-ending foreign policies. They had diminished the military's power in Eastern Europe, Afghanistan, and at home. In June of 1991, Yazov took the first step in a plan to reassert this power, when he ordered several senior officers to take their vacations in August. Already, he was eliminating potential resistance to the putsch.

An ethnic Russian and lifelong soldier, Yazov was born in 1923 near Omsk in Siberia. He graduated from Frunze Military Academy and the Military Academy of the Soviet Armed Forces General Staff. He was appointed defense minister in 1987. His predecessor, Marshal Sergei Sokolov, was sacked after the young West German pilot Mathias Rust evaded Soviet air defenses and landed a light plane on Moscow's Red Square.

ALEXANDER A. BESSMERTNYKH

57, was fired as Soviet foreign minister after Gorbachev accused him of "passivity" during the coup. Later it was revealed that he had cabled Soviet embassies around the world and told them to put a "good face" on the putsch.

DMITRY A. KOMAR

23, was the first Muscovite to die in clashes with Soviet troops on the second night of the coup. Komar died of a head injury after falling from an armored personnel carrier.

LEONID P. KRAVCHENKO

53, director-general of the Soviet State Television and Radio Network, enabled the junta to control the official media throughout the coup. Gorbachev fired Kravchenko and replaced him with Yegor V. Yakovlev, editor of the Moscow News.

ILYA KRICHEVSKY

28, became the third Muscovite killed in the coup in the wee hours of August 21. Krichevsky, an architect, was shot during a clash between crowds and troops on the Garden Ring Road.

MIKHAIL A. MOISEYEV

52, the former Soviet armed forces chief of staff, may or may not have helped plan the coup. After the coup failed, Gorbachev named Moiseyev acting defense minister, but Yeltsin and others objected. One day later, Gorbachev replaced Moiseyev with Yevgeny Shaposhnikov.

BORIS T. PANKIN

60, as Soviet ambassador to Czechoslovakia, publicly denounced the coup in its earliest hours, one of the first Soviet diplomats to do so. Gorbachev later rewarded Pankin's loyalty by making him Soviet foreign minister.

GAVRIL K. POPOV

55, Moscow's mayor and an unlikely hero to face down a military coup, was a key member of the resistance. After the junta sent tanks into the capital to enforce its will, he made speeches and issued written decrees defying the hard-liners.

IVAN S. SILAYEV

60, acted as Boris Yeltsin's main negotiator with coup leaders. As the top official in Yeltsin's government, Silayev backed a plan for radical reform, including proposals to allow private ownership of land and industries.

VLADIMIR A. USOV

37, was the second Muscovite killed on the Garden Ring Road. Usov was killed when a soldier inside an APC shot Usov point blank in the head. Then the vehicle started backing up again, and Usov's body was crushed.

Photography Credits

Great care has been taken to credit all photography sources accurately. Individual
credits [top (t), bottom (b), top left (tl), bottom left (bl), top right (tr), bottom right (br),
center right (cr), center left (cl)]
4, © TASS
9, © 1991 Cable News Network, Inc.
12-13, © Schwartz/Stern/Black Star
15, © Pinkhassov/Magnum
16, © UPI/Bettmann
17, © TASS
18-19, © Archive Photos
20-21, © TASS
22, © East News/SIPA Press
24-25, © Rondou/San Jose Mercury
News/SIPA Press
26-27, © TASS
28, (t) © Novosti/ SIPA Press
29, © Cable News Network, Inc.
30-31, © Laski/SIPA Press
32, © TASS
34-35, © Horvat/SABA
36-37, © Reisinger/Black Star
38-41, © TASS
43, © Rondou/San Jose Mercury
News/SIPA Press
44-45, © Stevens/SIPA Press
49, © Sherbell/SABA
50, © Sherbell/SABA
51, © TASS
53, © Nogues/Sygma
54-55, © D. Turnley/Detroit Free
Press/Black Star
57, © P. Turnley/Black Star
58-59, © TASS
60-61, © Sergei Chistyakov
65, © Laski/East News/SIPA Press
66, © Novosti/SIPA Press
69, © Sichov/SIPA Press
71, © Sherbell/SABA
73, © Reisinger/Black Star
74-75, © TASS
77, © Sherbell/SABA
79, © Novosti/SIPA Press
80-81, © Reisinger/Black Star
84, © East News/ SIPA Press
85, © Pcholkin/Black Star
86-87, © Reisinger/Black Star
88-89, © TASS
90-91, © Reisinger/Black Star
92, © East News/SIPA Press
94, © TASS
95, © East News/SIPA Press
96-97, © Reisinger/Black Star
99, © Reisinger/Black Star
103, © Chesnot/SIPA Press
105, © Pinkhassov/Magnum
107-111, © TASS
112-113, © Pinkhassov/Magnum
114-116, © TASS
117, © Pinkhassov/Magnum
118-119, © TASS
120, © Pinkhassov/Magnum
121, (t) © Pinkhassov/Magnum
121, (b) © Delay/AFP
124, © TASS
125, (t) © East News/SIPA Press
125, (b) © Kessler/SIPA Press
126-128, © TASS
130, © Pinkhassov/Magnum
131-133, © TASS
135, (t) © Sherbell/SABA
135, (b) © TASS
137, © Horvat/SABA
138, (t) © Sherbell/SABA
138, (b) © Pcholkin/Black Star
139, © Sherbell/SABA
140-141, © Horvat/SABA
142-148, © TASS
149, © Sichov/SABA
150-153, © TASS
155, © Hernandez/SIPA Press
157, © East News/SIPA Press
158-159, © Pcholkin/Black Star
160, (t) © TASS
160, (b) © De Keerle/Grochowiak/Sygma
161, © TASS
162, © EPIX/Sygma

163, © TASS
164, © Laski/SIPA Press
165, © Laski/SIPA Press
166, (t) © Chesnot/SIPA Press
166, (b) © Segretain/Sygma
167, (t) © TASS
167, (b) © Pcholkin/Black Star
168, © Pcholkin/Black Star
169, © TASS
170, © P. Turnley/Black Star
171, © East News/SIPA Press
172, (t) © East News/SIPA Press
172, (b) © East News/SIPA Press
173, © East News/SIPA Press
175, © Archive Photos
176, © Archive Photos
177, © Archive Photos
178-179, © Culver Pictures, Inc.
180, © Culver Pictures, Inc.
181, © TASS
182, (t) © Archive Photos
182, (b) © TASS
183-185, © TASS
186, © Culver Pictures, Inc.
187, © Culver Pictures, Inc.
188-189, © UPI/Bettmann
190, © UPI/Bettmann
191, (t) © Tonsing/White Tiger
191, (b) © Archive Photos
192-193, © Photri/Stock Market
194-195, © Culver Pictures, Inc.
196-197, © Archive Photos
198, (t) © Archive Photos
198-199, (b) © Archive Photos
199, (t) © Archive Photos
200-201, © Archive Photos
202, © UPI/Bettmann
203, (t) © TASS
203, (b) © Archive Photos/Camera Press
204-205, © Burkhard/Bilderberg/SABA
206, (t) © Ivleva/Magnum
206, (b) © Novosti/SIPA Press
207, © TASS/SIPA Press
208-209, © Laski/SIPA Press
210-211, © Pinkhassov/Magnum
211, © Abbas/Magnum
212, © Reardon/Katz/SABA
212-213, © Sherbell/SABA
214-215, © P. Turnley/Black Star
216, (tl) © Brown Brothers
216, (tr) © Archive Photos
216, (bl) © Culver Pictures
216, (br) © TASS
217, (tl) © UPI/Bettmann
217, (tr) © Archive Photos
217, (c) © TASS
217, (bl) © TASS
217, (br) © Archive Photos
218, (tl) © Archive Photos
218, (tr) © TASS
218, (bl) © Archive Photos
218, (br) © Archive Photos
219, (tl) © UPI/Bettmann
219, (tr) © Archive Photos
219, (c) © Archive Photos
219, (bl) © Archive Photos
219, (br) © UPI/Bettmann
220, (tl) © UPI/Bettmann
220, (tr) © UPI/Bettmann
220, (m) © UPI/Bettmann
220, (bl) © UPI/Bettmann
220, (br) © Sherbell/SABA
221, (tl) © Novosti/SIPA Press
221, (tr) © Tonsing/White Tiger
221, (cr) © Dak/Sygma
221, (cl) © Cable News Network, Inc.
221, (bl) © Kabul/Bettmann
221, (br) © Laski/SIPA Press
223, © 1991 Cable News Network, Inc.
224, © 1991 Cable News Network, Inc.
227-235, © TASS
237, © Susan Biddle/White House
238, © Washington Post
240, © Rodgers/Sygma
212, © Cable News Network, Inc.
243, © Cable News Network, Inc.
247, © Novosti/SIPA Press
248-252, © TASS

Source List

The following newspapers, magazines, and
television news organizations and programs
were used as sources in compiling the
account in this book. Wherever possible
sources were carefully double checked.

Argumenti I Fakti, Associated Press,
Baltiyskaya Gazeta, Business Week, CNN,
Der Spiegel, Financial Times, Interfax,
International Herald Tribune, Izvestia,
Kommersant, Komsomolskaya Pravda,
Krasnaya Zvezda, Kuranty, Literaturnaya
Gazeta, Los Angeles Times, Moscow

Guardian, Moskovsky Komsomolets,
Moscow News, Newsweek, Hezavisimaya
Gazeta, Nightline, Obshchaya Gazeta,
Ogonyok, Pravda, Postfactum News
Agency, Reuter, Russian Information
Agency, Rossiskaya Gazeta, Smena,
Sobesednik, Sovietskaya Molodyozh,
Sovietskaya Rossiya, Sovietsky Sport,
Soyuz, TASS, The Observer, The
Guardian, The Wall Street Journal,
The Washington Post, Time, Trud,
U.S. News and World Report, Vesti,
Vremya, and Vzglyad

Interview List

The following were interviewed either by
the authors of this book or by CNN correspondents during and after the coup and
provided insights and information for *Seven
Days That Shook The World*.

Ales Adamovich, Supreme Soviet deputy;
Alexei Adzhubei, free-lance journalist; Yuri
Afanasiyev, Supreme Soviet deputy; Iskar
Akayev, president of Kirgizia; Anatoly
Alexeyev, member of Russian Federation
legislature; Capt. 1st Class Victor Afereyev,
Black Sea border guard marine
Commander; Viktor Alksnis, Supreme
Soviet deputy; Vadim Bakatin, advisor to
President Gorbachev, post-coup KGB chief;
Sergei Belozerdtsev, Supreme Soviet
Deputy; Alexander Bessmertnykh, foreign
minister, USSR, before coup, dismissed;
Yuri Boyars, Supreme Soviet deputy;
Fyodor Burlatsky, Supreme Soviet deputy;
Dzemma Skulme, Supreme Soviet deputy;
Roman Chervotsev, Moscow city council-
man; Robert Conquest, historian, Stanford
University; Alexander Dzasokhov,
Communist Party Politburo member;
Valentina Fokina, Russian Federation assis-
tant prosecutor; Dr. Svyatoslav Fyoderov,
Supreme Soviet deputy; Mikhail Gashpar,
Supreme Soviet deputy; Mikhail
Gorbachev, president; Alexander Gournov,
television journalist; Sergei Grigoriev, for-
mer deputy press secretary to President
Gorbachev; Lt. Dmitry Guroshko, border
guard at Gorbachev dacha; Lt. Col. Victor
Humatov, border guard leader at Gorbachev
dacha; Vitaly Ignatenko, press secretary to
President Gorbachev; Maj. Gen. Oleg
Kalugin, retired KGB official and democratic member of the Russian Federation
Legislature; Maj. Gen. Alexander
Karbainov, KGB Press Department chief;
Col. Pyotr Kharlamov, Crimean border
guard commander; Alexander Kondrashov,
defender, Russian White House; Leonid
Kravchenko, Soviet television chief, dismissed after coup; Vytautas Landsbergis,
president of Lithuania; Olga Lanina, personal secretary to President Gorbachev;
Valentin Lazutkin, Soviet television first
deputy chairman; Gen. Alexander Lebed,
deputy chief of the Soviet paratroopers;

Endel Lippmaa, minister without portfolio,
Estonia; Col. Vladimir Lopatin, Russian
Defense Committee; Anatoly Lukianov,
chairman of the Soviet Parliament, arrested;
Tatania Makayeva, free-lance photogra-
pher; Alexander Merkushev, editor-in-chief,
TASS English Language Service; Arkady
Murashov, Supreme Soviet deputy;
Nursultan Nazarbayev, president of
Kazakhstan; Vyacheslav Nikonov, aide to
KGB chief Vadim Bakatin; Boris Pankin,
foreign minister; Nikolai Petrakov, former
economics advisor to President Gorbachev;
Mikhail Poltaranin, Russian Federation
minister of information; Gavril Popov,
mayor of Moscow; Yevgeny Primakov, aide
to President Gorbachev; Oleg Rumyanski,
Russian Federation Supreme Soviet
deputy; Alexander Rutskoi, Russian
Federation vice-president; Eduard
Sagaleyevy, first deputy chairman, Soviet
Television; Col. Viktor Samoilov, Russian
Federation Defense Committee; Valentin
Sergeyev, Russian Federation minister
without portfolio; Georgi Shakhnazarov,
aide to President Gorbachev; Gen. Yevgeny
Shaposhnikov, Air Force chief, post-coup
defense minister; Yuri Shcherbak, Supreme
Soviet deputy; Ivan Silayev, Russian
Federation prime minister; Anatoly
Sobchak, mayor of St. Petersburg; Sergei
Stankevich, deputy mayor of Moscow;
Valentin Stepankov, Russian Federation
chief prosecutor; Col. Nikolai Stolyarov,
Russian White House defender, post-coup
aide to KGB chief Bakatin; Vasily Tso,
Supreme Soviet deputy; Sergei
Tsypalyayev, Supreme Soviet deputy; Dr.
Anatoly Virgansky, President Gorbachev's
son-in-law; Alexander Vladislavlev,
Supreme Soviet deputy; Gen. Dmitry
Volkogonov, Moscow historian; Alexander
Yakovlev, aide to President Gorbachev;
Yegor Yakovlev, Moscow News editor-in-
chief, post-coup head of Soviet television;
Veniamin Yarin, aide to President
Gorbachev; Boris Yeltsin, Russian
Federation president; Yevgeny
Yevtushenko, poet

INDEX

CNN and the authors wish to acknowledge with appreciation and thanks the help of the following officials, profession-als, and workers in various fields and many places who contributed to the success of this book. The authors, of course, remain responsible for any errors that have found their way into this text.

Gennady Cherkashkin, St. Petersburg journalist; Alexander Drubinin, Tass English service editor; Andrei Golovanov, foreign relations department; Gosteleradio; Andrei Grachev, press secretary to President Gorbachev; Maj. Gen. Alexander Karbainov, chief of KGB press department; Alexander Kitsenko, TASS protocol department chief; Pavel Kuznetsov, Gosteleradio journalist; Nele Laanejarv, Estonian television producer and correspondent; Igor Malashenko, deputy press secretary to President Gorbachev; Robert Markaryan, aide to Yevgeny Primakov, advisor to President Gorbachev; Alexander Merkushev, editor-in-chief, TASS English Language Service; Col. Vladimir Nikonorov, Ministry of Defense Press Department; Col. Vladimir Nikanorov, Ministry of Interior press office; Vyacheslav Nikonov, aide to Vadim Bakatin, KGB chief; Alexander Petrov, general director, CNN Moscow Pay TV Channel; Anna Popova, aide to Kazakh President Nazarbayev; Boris Rud, Yalta driver; Boris Semyonov, Soviet deputy chief of foreign relations; Lisa Shtaiger, journalist; Col. Ivan Skrylnik, Ministry of Defense press office; Valentin Yegorov, Soviet television foreign rela-tions department; and Leonid Zolotarevsky, Soviet television chief of foreign relations.

This book is the result of the efforts of many loyal, dedicated, and diligent full-time and contract employees of CNN and Turner Publishing, Inc. Without their help, the completion of this book on such a tight deadline could not have been accomplished. We have tried as hard as possible to recognize everyone who contributed. If we missed anyone we apologize. With gratitude we recognize:

Katherine Bird, Laura Heald, Vivian Lawand, Lori Jones, Rhonda Myers, Marcia Dworetz, Lisa E. Oliver, Stephen Finch, Rebecca Aqua, Cheryl Corrigan, Diane Joy, Anthony Wilkins, Chris Harris.

TASS PHOTOGRAPHY STAFF
Sergei Mamontov, Tatania Makayeva, Boris Kippel.

RESEARCHERS AND TRANSLATORS:
Louise Dechovitz, Researcher
Denis Mikhailov, Translator
Yuri Somen, Translator

CNN MOSCOW BUREAU:
Yelena Berezovskaya, Office Manager
Bruce Conover, Producer
Sergei Gerasimov, Driver
Yuri Ilyin, Driver
Yuri Ivanov, Driver
Igor Krotov, Producer
Lisa MacHale, Consultant
Vladimir Olkhovsky, Producer
Helga Pender, Consultant
Vladimir Tkachev, Driver

Anna Williams, Consultant
Boris Zagoruiko, Correspondent

CNN INTERNATIONAL STAFF
Eason Jordan, International Managing Editor
Peter Humi, Paris Bureau Chief
Jim Clancy, Correspondent
Tom Fenton, Assignment Editor
Alessio Vinci, Assignment Editor
Siobhan Darrow, Producer
Kira Grishkoff, Producer
Gigi Shamsi, Producer
Andrew Key, London Bureau Engineer
Malcolm Robinson, London Bureau Engineer

CNN ATLANTA
Tom Mintier, Correspondent
Miriam Pena, Assistant to Stuart Loory

CNN SPECIAL EVENTS
Alec Miran, Producer
John Towriss, Producer

CNN WASHINGTON BUREAU
Peggy Soucy, Deputy Bureau Chief
Sara Mulrooney, Secretary

GRAPHICS INTERNATIONAL, INC.
David Allen, Lisa Davis, Tim Potts, Staci Weinstein.

R.R. DONNELLEY & SONS
Steve Neely, Debby Turoff and staff.

TURNER ADVERTISING & MARKETING